The
Biblical Theology of
SAINT IRENAEUS

The Biblical Theology
of
SAINT IRENAEUS

By
JOHN LAWSON
M.A., B.D.(Cantab.), B.Sc.(Agric.) Lond.

Wipf & Stock
PUBLISHERS
Eugene, Oregon

Wipf and Stock Publishers
199 W 8th Ave, Suite 3
Eugene, OR 97401

The Biblical Theology of Saint Irenaeus
By Lawson, John
Copyright©1948 Clockie, Rachel Helen Faith and Lawson, Stephen Alexander
ISBN: 1-59752-580-4
Publication date 2/21/2006
Previously published by The Epworth Press, 1948

To
My Dear Wife

PREFACE

THE IMPARTATION of an idea may take as many seconds as fulfilment does years, yet he who imparts the idea has the chief place of honour among helpers, for the major part of any task is the original inspiration to begin it. That place of honour belongs to my former Tutor, my very good friend the Reverend R. Newton Flew, M.A., D.D., Principal of Wesley House, Cambridge. One like the present writer, who gave most of his early attention to the study of Science, and not very academic Science at that, would hardly have been so bold as to set his hand to a work like this had he fully considered the matter beforehand. However, Dr. Flew suggested that I should compete for the Hulsean Prize, 1937. From that modest beginning my interest in the fascinating study of the theology of S. Irenaeus grew by insensible degrees, and very grateful I now am for that initial impetus. My present hope is that the discriminating reader will cast an indulgent eye upon any deficiency in classical learning which he may detect herein. Throughout the years Dr. Flew has been a friend indeed, particularly in the greatest of all services that can be rendered to one studying far from the customary haunts of scholars, namely, by giving advice from his wide knowledge as to what there is to be read upon a given subject. To this I would join my heartfelt tribute to the whole Staff and my fellow-students at Wesley House. Their society it was that taught me to love sound learning, and which opened my eyes to the spaciousness of the life and the profundity of the creed of the Church Catholic.

I wish also to take this opportunity of expressing my sincere thanks to the Ely Professor of Divinity, the Reverend W. Telfer, M.A., D.D., for valued advice, and for gracious encouragement in season. Likewise would I speak of one who since College days has been my firm friend, the Reverend Rupert E. Davies, M.A., B.D. His mature appreciation for the Classics and the humanities has helped me more than I can say in giving balance to my results. His acute critical faculty has been the means of removing many minor blemishes. I wish also to thank Canon H. Goodrich, M.A., Vicar of Corby and Rector of Irnham, for his help and fellowship. Gratitude is also due to the Referees appointed to read this Dissertation when submitted at Cambridge for the B.D. Finally I acknowledge the good offices of the Epworth Press, by which this work goes to Press even amidst the present manifold difficulties in the publishing business.

The bulk of this Dissertation has been written while I was engaged in the care of village churches centred around Colsterworth, Lincs. I wish to testify to the help that has come to me through fellowship with my people, and from the privilege of quiet rural residence during almost the whole of the late war. There is a strong contrast between the application of the mind to the problems of distant antiquity and of eternal truth, and the endeavour to declare the riches of the Faith in a manner acceptable to those among whom there are many who are the salt of the earth, but few who have much inclination to abstract thought or interest in the academic. In this contrast there is mental health and stimulation. He who administers small affairs of passing interest in the Church stands in need of constant reminder that this apparent routine is actually the embodiment of a momentous divine purpose 'to sum up all things in Christ'. Intellectual contact with one of the great souls brings refreshment to the sense of divine calling. Conversely, he who is honoured by God with a calling to serious study stands in need of reminder that the Christian Faith is not a way of thought only. It is a way of life, and a way to which God calls the plain man. May none of those who minister in holy things shirk either part of this salutary discipline.

As one composed earlier chapters 'the terror that flieth by night' could be heard moaning his way inland, solitary and in long succession, throughout the protracted hours of darkness. One grieved for one's fellow-citizens. As one proceeded with later revisions one could see multiplied and frightful retribution going out, at first by summer twilight, at length in broad day. Both occasions brought the solemn realization that it was upon others that the ruin was visited. He who has, through no desert of his own, been allowed to continue in his quiet way while millions of his fellows have faced terror, or death, or transportation far from the amenities of life, feels that he is not his own. He has been bought with a price. He must devote himself anew to the building up of the Body of Christ, and the healing of the wounds of humanity. In this high task the study of far-off Irenaeus perhaps has a very modest place, inasmuch as Irenaeus spoke to the Church regarding Authority and Catholicity. In some countries respect for Parson and Bible has with multitudes counted for less and less as recent years have gone by. In some less happy lands the most august organs of ecclesiastical authority that Christendom has known now face the possibility of unparalleled temporal calamity. In this situation is to be found alike the necessity and the incentive for making the unity of Christ's Church more apparent in outward form and in practical action, in the eyes of the world and of believers everywhere. Only so can the authentic Word of God again be declared with authority, and the wrath of man subdued to reverence. The study of such figures as S. Irenaeus of Lugdunum gives contact with the culture of nations alienated upon the field of battle. Above all, it carries one back behind many painful breaches in the Church Visible. May the present study contribute some small thing to the advancement of that day for which we pray when we show forth the Lord's death, the day in which 'all they that do confess Thy holy Name may agree in the truth of Thy holy Word, and live in unity and godly love'.

LINCOLN   JOHN LAWSON
May Day 1946

CONTENTS

Table explanatory to References in Foot-notes

Harvey, ii.50   represents Volume II, page 50 of W. W. Harvey's edition of the Greek, Latin, Syriac, and Armenian texts of *Adversus Haereses* (Cambridge, 1857).

II.**30**.6, i.235   represents *Adversus Haereses*, Book II, chapter 30, paragraph 6, trans. by Roberts and Rambaut: being found on page 235 of Volume I of the translation of S. Irenaeus in the *Ante-Nicene Christian Library* (T. & T. Clark, Edinburgh, 1868). N.B. *This translation follows the chapter divisions of Massuet and Migne*, to which the references given consequently correspond.

Dem. 54   represents *The Demonstration of the Apostolic Preaching*, Chapter 54, as translated from the Armenian and edited by Dr. J. Armitage Robinson, 'Translations of Christian Literature' (S.P.C.K., London, 1920).

II. WORKS CITED

Anthropologie d.H.I.   *Die Anthropologie des Hl. Irenaeus*, Ernst Klebba (in *Kirchengeschichtliche Studien*; Knöpfler, Schrörs, Sdralek) (Münster, 1894).

Christus Victor   *Den kristna försoningstanken*, Gustav Aulén (Stockholm, 1930), trans. under the title *Christus Victor* by A. G. Hebert (S.P.C.K., 1931).

Corps Mystique   *Le Corps Mystique du Christ*, Émile Mersch, Second Edition (Paris, 1936).

De 'ΑΝΑΚΕΦΑΛ-ΑΙΩΣΕΩΣ	De 'ΑΝΑΚΕΦΑΛΑΙΩΣΕΩΣ in Irenaei Theologia Potestate, Gustav Molwitz (Dresden, 1874).
Der Mittler	Der Mittler, Emil Brunner, Second Edition (Tübingen, 1930).
Dictionnaire	Article 'Saint Irénée', by F. Vernet, in Dictionnaire de Théologie Catholique, Volume VII (Vacant, Mangenot, Amann) (Paris, 1923).
DG.	Lehrbuch der Dogmengeschichte, Reinhold Seeberg, Volume I, Second Edition (Leipzig, 1908).
Entstehung d.a.K.	Die Entstehung der altkatholischen Kirche, Albrecht Ritschl, Second Edition (Bonn, 1857).
Essai	Essai sur la Théologie d'Irénée, Paul Beuzart (Paris, 1908).
H.D. II	History of Dogma, A. von Harnack; translation of Third Edition by Neil Buchanan, Volume II (1896).
Idea of Faith	The Idea of Faith in Christian Literature, W. H. P. Hatch (Strasbourg, 1925).
Irenaeus	Irenaeus of Lugdunum, F. R. Montgomery Hitchcock (Cambridge, 1914).
Irenäus Christologie	Des heiligen Irenäus Christologie in Zusammenhange mit dessen theologischen und anthropologischen Grundlehren, Ludwig Duncker (Göttingen, 1843).
Jesus and His Church	R. Newton Flew (London, 1938).
Jesus and His Sacrifice	Vincent Taylor (London, 1937).
Kirche b.I.	Die Kirche bei Irenäus, Wolfgang Schmidt (Helsinki, 1934).

Kyr.Ch.	*Kyrios Christos,* Bousset (Göttingen, 1921).
L'Église	*L'Église Naissante et le Catholicism,* Pierre Battifol, Fifth Edition (Paris, 1911).
Logosidee	*Geschichte der Logosidee in der Christlichen Litteratur,* Anathon Aall (Leipzig, 1899).
Marcellus	*Marcellus von Ancyra,* Theodor Zahn (Gotha, 1867).
m.Vollkommenheit	*Die Christliche Lehre von der menschlichen Vollkommenheit,* H. H. Wendt (Göttingen, 1882).
Paulinismus	*Der Paulinismus des Irenaeus,* Johannes Werner (in *Texte und Untersuchungen,* Gebhardt & Harnack, Volume VI) (Leipzig, 1889).
Reich-Gottes	*Die Geschichte des Reich-Gottes-Gedankens in der alten Kirche bis zu Origenes und Augustin,* Robert Frick (Giessen, 1928).
Romans	*Moffatt New Testament Commentary,* C. H. Dodd (London, 1932).
St. Paul	*Christianity According to St. Paul,* C. A. A. Scott, Second Edition (Cambridge, 1932).
Studium DG.	*Leitfaden zum Studium der Dogmengeschichte,* Friedrich Loofs, Fourth Edition (Halle, 1906).
Theologie d.I.	*Die Theologie des Irenaeus,* G. Nathaniel Bonwetsch (Gütersloh, 1925).
Theophilus	*Theophilus von Antiochen adversus Marcionem und die anderen theologischen Quellen bei Irenaeus,* F. Loofs (in *Texte und Untersuchungen,* Harnack & Schmidt, fourth series, Volume I) (Leipzig, 1930).
Other works	References given *in loco.*

The

Biblical Theology of

SAINT IRENAEUS

Irenaeus ist Biblicist und er ist der erste grosse Vertreter des Biblicismus.—REINHOLD SEEBERG

Irenaeus ist Schrifttheologe, ein wirklich tiefgehendes Schriftverständniss gibt ihm die Kraft, anders als die Apologeten an die Botschaft Jesu anzuknüpfen.—ROBERT FRICK

Chapter One

INTRODUCTION

T HE HISTORICAL background of the present subject may first be established by observing that S. Irenaeus of Lugdunum was born, more probably of Greek than of Semitic parentage, at some place in Asia Minor about the year A.D. 130. The evidence for this date is that he was old enough to have gained a distinct recollection of the aged S. Polycarp, who was martyred *c.* A.D. 155. The letter of S. Irenaeus to Florinus, so fortunately preserved in Eusebius, may be quoted both as the most important portion of the extremely scanty knowledge of a biographical and human interest that has come down to us regarding Irenaeus, and also as illustrating the antiquity of the tradition for which he speaks. 'I remember the events of that time more clearly than those of recent years. For what boys learn, growing with their mind, becomes joined with it; so that I am able to describe the very place in which the blessed Polycarp sat as he discoursed, and his goings out and his comings in, and the manner of his life, and his physical appearance, and his discourses to the people, and the accounts which he gave of his intercourse with John and with the others who had seen the Lord. . . . These things being told me by the mercy of God, I listened to them attentively, noting them down, not on paper, but in my heart. And continually, through God's grace, I recall them faithfully.' [1]

In those days the south of France appears to have been the overseas missions field for the strong and flourishing Church of Asia Minor. This link would be natural, in view of the kinship in race and speech of the Gauls to the Galatians. This doubtless accounts for the circumstance that we next hear of S. Irenaeus in A.D. 177 as a priest at Lugdunum,

[1] Eus. *H.E.*, V.xx.4-7.

3

now Lyons. He had presumably come to Gaul as a young man, for by this year he was already a figure of trust and repute. We also know that he wrote as though he had long dwelt among non-Greek-speaking people. 'Thou wilt not expect from me, who am resident among the Keltae, and am accustomed for the most part to use a barbarous dialect, any display of rhetoric, which I have never learned, or any excellence of composition, which I have never practised, or any beauty and persuasiveness of style, to which I make no pretensions.'[1] Irenaeus here gives a too modest view of his accomplishments. He has great powers of persuasiveness, can one but perform the considerable feat of carrying oneself back into the mental background of his writings. There is, indeed, little rhetoric in his work, and he lacks the epigrams of Tertullian, but he can rise to real beauty of expression when he moves from polemic argument to piety. In the year 177 he was sent to Rome on an important mission, namely, to bear to Bishop Eleutherus the letter of the Gallic Confessors interceding for the peace of the Church in face of the Montanist issue.[2] On his return to Lugdunum he was elected Bishop, apparently in succession to the martyred Pothinus.[3] S. Irenaeus seems to have continued Bishop until his death at the turn of the century. His greater surviving work, the five books entitled Ἔλεγχος καὶ ἀνατροπὴ τῆς ψευδωνύμου γνώσεως, commonly known as *Adversus Haereses*, appears to have been written over a fair period of time during the early years of his episcopate. This is a controversial work, aimed principally at Gnostic heresy. Another work, mentioned by Eusebius [4] under its title, Εἰς ἐπίδειξιν τοῦ ἀποστολικοῦ κηρύγματος, *The Demonstration of the Apostolic Preaching*, was, like the remainder of the writings of Irenaeus, regarded as lost until an Armenian translation was found in 1904. *The Demonstration* was written after *Adversus Haereses*, i.e. *c.* A.D. 190, and is a simple handbook of Christian Evidences, non-controversial in tone.

[1] I.Pref.3.
[2] Eus. *H.E.* V.iii.4; iv.1, 2.
[3] ibid. V.i.29–31.
[4] ibid. V.xxvi.

Practically all the remaining certain historical information we possess regarding S. Irenaeus concerns the letter of protest he sent to Victor of Rome, *c.* 190. A widespread consensus of opinion had rejected the Quartodeciman observance of Easter,[1] but the Church of Asia Minor refused to conform.[2] Victor attempted to enforce the decision by excommunication,[3] though other bishops did not approve this drastic course.[4] Particularly mentioned by Eusebius as among these is Irenaeus,[5] who, though himself disapproving of the Quartodeciman rite despite his Asiatic origin,[6] made a strong and cogent plea for toleration,[7] citing in particular the happy precedent of the mutual respect shown over this very matter by Polycarp and Anicetus. The conclusion to be drawn from this action is that the authoritarian unity of the Catholic Church, for which S. Irenaeus was so ardent an advocate, was conceived of by him more as theological than as administrative or ritual. Rome guarantees orthodoxy, but does not rule the Church; a result in keeping with the general interest of Irenaeus. In his account of this affair Eusebius makes S. Irenaeus almost Primate of Gaul, though this is probably a case of reading back later conditions into the second century. Thus he writes of Irenaeus 'sending letters in the name of the brethren in Gaul over whom he presided' ($\dot{\eta}\gamma\epsilon\tilde{\iota}\tau o$),[8] and of 'the Churches in Gaul that Irenaeus managed' ($\dot{\epsilon}\pi\epsilon\sigma\kappa\dot{o}\pi\epsilon\iota$).[9]

This almost exhausts our established historical knowledge of one of the greatest figures of the first ages of the Church. However, the writings of S. Irenaeus, though almost devoid of autobiographical touches, display the mind of the man, and what is seen is complementary to the known facts. This circumstance serves to some extent to fill in the outlines of the portrait. S. Irenaeus was born in the East and worked in the West. His work shows him to have been of a compre-hensive genius, no extremist, and one who combines ele-

---

[1] Eus. *H. E.* V. xxiii.
[2] ibid. xxiv.1–8.
[3] ibid. xxiv.9.
[4] ibid. xxiv.10.
[5] ibid. xxiv.11.
[6] ibid. xxiv.11; xxiii.2.
[7] ibid. xxiv.14–17.
[8] ibid. xxiv.11.
[9] ibid. xxiii.3.

ments that have become characteristic of the Western Church with others that are associated with the Eastern. He was, in short, a true Catholic. Furthermore, Irenaeus lived the life of a busy missionary bishop, not of a retired scholar. To match this his work is practical in intention, not academic. The aim of *Adversus Haereses* is the simple one of discrediting and exposing those who would seduce believers from the Church. Profound thought is there, and the raw materials for a comprehensive theological system, but the rambling style of the composition, as well as the not infrequent formal inconsistencies of statement, make it patent that the author was not moved by the speculative and systematizing interest. His work is the work of a pastor rather than that of a theologian in the proper sense, yet that of a pastor who finds that theological controversy is necessary if the sheep are not to stray from the fold. This is an interest which blends naturally with the strongly Biblical cast of the mind of S. Irenaeus, for the Hebraic mind was fundamentally concrete and unspeculative. That one so truly Catholic and Scriptural should be cast in this mould reminds us that the essence of Christianity is not an intellectual system, but the Gospel of a real Divine redemption, and of a visible Church in which the redeemed are to live and act. Christian theology and philosophy are needful to display and account for the facts of religion, but these systems of thought are much less than the religion itself.

Inasmuch as the present study does not cover the whole of the theology of S. Irenaeus the succeeding chapters will perhaps be rendered more intelligible if a brief comprehensive survey be first made of the field. This may be done by giving a summary of a selection of the extensive literature existing upon this subject. Of the two works calling for particular notice at this point the first is: *Des heiligen Irenäus Christologie in Zusammenhange mit dessen theologischen und anthropologischen Grundlehren*, by Ludwig Duncker, published at Göttingen in 1843. This may perhaps be regarded as the beginning of modern scientific work upon

S. Irenaeus. Despite its age the work is still of value, for many of the problems raised by the theology of Irenaeus are correctly appreciated by Duncker, and much of his constructive work still stands.

Duncker observes that Irenaeus attacks Gnosticism by the affirmation that the Creator of the universe is God (pp. 9, 13). He starts from Christian experience, not from independent speculation (13, 14, 74). The world reveals God, who is in Himself not for man to know (15). The will of God is the absolute and all-sufficient and immediate cause of Creation (18, 19). The creative Hands of God, the Son, and the Spirit, are not distinct from God as intermediary organs (22). God is the transcendent Lord of the Universe (23, 30). The Creation is a work of divine love, and is the self-revelation of the ineffable God (32–3, 76). S. Irenaeus founds the doctrine of the Trinity upon the antithesis between God unknown as regards His power, and known as regards His love (34). The distinction of λόγος ἐνδιάθετος and λόγος προφορικός is to be rejected as an exposition of the Trinitarian relationship (37), for man must not inquire how the Divine Son was begotten (39). There is, however, no opposition to the Christian Logos-doctrine as such, for that which is unknown as pure speculation is known through the experience of revelation (40). The Father is the hidden God, who has made Himself known in the Son (41–42). Here is the foundation for a non-speculative Logos-doctrine, which is yet hardly behind the brilliant work of Alexandria in theological and scientific worth (44).

The Logos is divine and eternal (46, 48). There is a real and essential distinction of Persons (50, 52–3), though the manner of expression found for this is sometimes imperfect (56, 66). While many expressions suggest a subordination of the Son, this is definitely excluded by the clear distinction made between the Son and all created things (57). Furthermore, as was natural at that period, Irenaeus was less clear on the doctrine of the Holy Spirit (58). The fact that God is Father and Son makes conceivable the revelation of an

ineffable God, but this revelation is not actually effected
unless the creature be given power to perceive. This is done
by the agency of the Spirit (59, 60). In regard to the unity
of the Spirit with the Father, and the distinction of the
Persons, the position is analogous to that of the doctrine of
the Logos. The eternity of the Spirit shows that the distinction is real and essential, and no mere human thought-form
(62–3, 65). The Logos and the Spirit are the Two Hands of
God (67). This doctrine is intended as the antithesis to
emanationism (68), i.e. God has within Himself the agency
of Creation, and needs no mediator (69). The 'subordinationism' of the doctrine is an imperfection of expression
only (68). Thus the Trinity is clearly formulated in simple
Biblical language (70), though S. Irenaeus goes beyond this
to illuminate the nature of God who by the Son and Spirit
lifts man up to Himself (71–2). The aim of the whole course
of created nature is the self-revelation of the love of God, to
the end of the education of man (76, 78). At this point we
pass from theology to anthropology.

Man is a creature separated from Nature by an endowment of reason and free-will (81–7). By nature he is of a body
and a soul, which latter receives the Divine Spirit (90–3),
though the πνεῦμα can also be spoken of by Irenaeus as a
part of human nature (94). He distinguishes between the
Image of God (εἰκών) in man, and the Likeness of God
(ὁμοίωσις): the former being a part of man's nature, before
he receives the gift of the Spirit; the latter a gift to which man
has to attain (100). The two words can also be used in the
wide sense, without a distinction between them (99), while
one passage speaks of man as originally created in the
Image and Likeness of God (101). The contradiction may
be solved by observing that man is destined to rise above the
creaturely to communion with God: the conception of 'The
Image of God' represents this destiny. The destiny of
attainment through later growth to the Likeness of God was
given originally, and hence it can also be said that man was
created after the Likeness of God (102–3). This doctrine is

not speculative, but experimental and Biblical (106). S. Irenaeus does not perfectly succeed in his aim of uniting anthropology to theology. His doctrine of man's freedom and reason is based on God's loving revelation, his doctrine of the Image of God on man's position in the world (107–8).

Sin is not original to the Creation, but is the consequence of moral freedom (113). The Fall and its consequences are described in Biblical language (116–20). Sin is man's fault (122), but God showed mercy, and also exacted punishment (123–5). Irenaeus describes the damage done by sin as death, bodily and spiritual (128–30). Man has failed his destiny, i.e. the Likeness of God is lost, the Image of God darkened (131–2). Man is now a debtor to God, and a slave to Satan (133–5), while Irenaeus foreshadows the later doctrine of Original Sin, inasmuch as he teaches that the consequences of the first transgression were universal sin, and the moral and physical ruin of the race (137–40). He likewise foreshadows S. Augustine in seeing a causal connexion between Adam's sin and the sin of all men (140–2). Adam was the true representative of the race, the universal man, whose act is the act of the race (146–7). Each man shares Adam's guilt, for Adam's sin is the sin of each (144). Against the Gnostics, Irenaeus is anxious to show that sin did not arise in any principle independent of God (149). The Fall, indeed, has actually realized the will of God (150), for fallen man, knowing that his salvation is by grace, is confirmed thereby in his love for God (151–2). So Irenaeus attempts to hold alike the freedom of man and the sovereignty of God, but sin is not seen as a necessary part of man's development (155).

The Christology of S. Irenaeus has a double aspect (158). Based upon the experience of man's moral struggle is the anthropological aspect; upon God-consciousness, the theological. The latter has precedence (159), showing Irenaeus to be in an intermediate position between the Eastern and Western Churches. The foundation of his thought is undoubtedly the Pauline distinction of a double train of

human development, from the Fall, and from Christ the
Second Adam (160). To Irenaeus Christ is the turning-
point of history, His work having a double character, the
vanquishing of sin and death, and the establishment of a
new life for man. Both these aspects are comprised in the
Pauline term ἀνακεφαλαιοῦν (161–2). This word is often used
in the sense of 'to repeat in summary form' (164), but when
used of Christ as the Recapitulation of man the sense is
chiefly that of restoration (165). Finally, Christ the Head
unites the multiplicity of things (166). Christ the Recapitu-
lator is related to the whole natural development of the race,
as its End. He made a new start for the race, uniting all men
in an act which is the act of all; and He became the Head of
a new community of the righteous (168–71). In the conception of ἀνακεφαλαίωσις we have a rational doctrine of salvation,
the Christology being connected with the anthropology, yet
without deserting experience and launching into speculation
(176).

The world is the means by which God reveals Himself,
while man, as destined for God, is the central point of
Creation. The Incarnation is thus the goal of Creation, for
in the Son Incarnate God is perfectly manifested, and man
completely united to God. Inasmuch as man had sinned,
Christ is also the Redeemer (178–80). However, Duncker
does not judge that S. Irenaeus would have made the
Incarnation conditional upon the Fall (181). Neither
Adam nor any man could redeem the race, for all were
in bondage, but at the same time the Redeemer must be
in organic connexion with the race (186–90). Only the
Divine Logos could bring man to his destined goal (193–4).
The relation of the two natures in the incarnate Christ was
intimate and indissoluble (194–5), and the union was
possible because man was the work of God (197). Despite
some phrases, Irenaeus does not describe the humanity of
Jesus as a body only. The term 'Incarnation', 'the taking of
flesh', answers to 'flesh' as a designation for man in his
natural condition (206–10). In contending against the

Gnostic division of Christ Irenaeus at times seems to deny the distinction of natures in Christ, but other passages make the distinction clear (215–16).

To perform the two-fold act of Recapitulation, namely, the release of man from bondage to Satan, and from enmity to God, Christ shared every experience of man (222–7). Through resistance to temptation the Redeemer conquered Satan (227–34). There is no notion that the devil had any rights over man (236–40). Christ is indeed spoken of as a Ransom, but this is not intended as an equivalent price paid to Satan (241–2). The whole obedient life of Christ was one saving activity, but the death upon the Cross is emphasized as the climax of atonement (243–4). For S. Irenaeus the death of Christ is the climax of His coming to us, and of His becoming like us. It is hence the means by which we are wholly united to Him, so that we partake of all that He is (245–8). Christ gave Himself for us, but there is no idea of an equivalent price offered, or of His sufferings as the satisfaction of the divine Righteousness (251–2). The breaking of man's fetters is succeeded by the leading of man into freedom, but this completion of the work of Christ is treated of less explicitly (253–4). The hidden Father progressively makes Himself known from eternity by the Logos through Creation, the Law, and the Prophets, and the whole teaching activity of the incarnate Christ (256–9). With this the race is perfected by the progressive inflowing of the Spirit. To the preparatory work of the Logos in the Prophets corresponds that of the Holy Spirit who enlightened them (260), while with the coming of Christ the Spirit became accustomed to dwell in man (261). The Lord pours out the Spirit on His followers, and makes them living members of His Body (262).

We are first bound to observe how significant it is that so substantial a body of Christian theology, and of theology which has been approved by later thought and experience, should stand to the credit of one so early in the history of the Church as S. Irenaeus. He certainly represents a great

advance on anything that had gone before. The following
propositions from Duncker's work may be regarded as of
permanent value. (i) S. Irenaeus is not a speculative writer.
(ii) The creative Hands of God are not emanations. The
Supreme God needs no intermediaries between Himself and
the created universe. (iii) Christ the Word (λόγος) of God is
not an emanation of the reason (λόγος) of God. (iv) S.
Irenaeus expounds the doctrine of the Image and Likeness
of God in man, though he does not always allow of a distinction between the Image and the Likeness. This subject is the
occasion of obscurity (which Duncker is a little too self-
confident in resolving). (v) The exposition of the work of
Christ as a Recapitulation is Pauline (though Duncker does
not sufficiently view this saving work as a real victory of
Christ over the satanic powers). (vi) There is no substitutionary or satisfactory Atonement in S. Irenaeus. The main
adverse criticism that one would make of Duncker is that
he makes S. Irenaeus a little too subtle and systematic. He
almost writes as though one were to imagine Irenaeus himself as aware that his various theological propositions can
be analysed, and connected one with another. This can
indeed be done, but it is important to bear in mind that the
actual work of S. Irenaeus contains only the raw materials
for a profound theological system. The systematization is
something that has to be brought to him.

As a complement to Duncker we may take the valuable
Essai sur la Théologie d'Irénée of Paul Beuzart (Paris, 1908).
Beuzart greets S. Irenaeus as a safe rather than a great man,
who writes practically and polemically, not speculatively
(pp. 1, 5, 6). The Church of his time was becoming learned
as well as popular, growing in organization and decreasing
in intensity. Irenaeus is the leading voice of conservative
ecclesiastical authority answering Gnosticism.

It is then observed that the master-idea of Irenaeus, to be
used against the Gnostics, is the formula 'One Creator-God
revealed in Christ' (31). This rests upon the proof, supremely
of Scripture, and of reason (or the unreason of dualism).

[margin handwritten note: Helpful analysis of Duncker's work; word of caution at the end of the [??] regarding too much systematizing]

The Gnostic error is a form of anthropomorphism. Creation is the sovereign act of a good God, who employed the Logos as His instrument, save in the special case of the creation of man, where He used His Two Hands, the Word and the Spirit (42f.). Irenaeus does not seek to discover why God created by means of an intermediary. There is equality of Person between God and the Logos. God was revealed in the Old Dispensation as well as the New, the difference between the two being quantitative, not qualitative, even to the obscuring of the Pauline antithesis of Law and Grace (48). S. Irenaeus does not investigate the mystery of the relation of the Divine Logos to God. The importance of his work is rather that he transformed the Logos-doctrine into a part of ecclesiastical Christology. The Logos is eternal, and not an emanation. Son and Logos are interchangeable terms (50). The Spirit is so completely 'the action of God in man' that it is not always easy to say whether Irenaeus is speaking of the Holy Spirit, or of the divine principle in man (51). He has not the doctrine of the Trinity, but has the basic affirmations upon which it rests, particularly in his doctrine of The Two Hands of God. The Three Persons are more than stages by which one arrives at God. Had S. Irenaeus attempted to produce a precise formula he would probably have arrived at an economic Trinity (55).

In antithesis to Gnostic theories Irenaeus asserts that man was created by God Himself. Man's destiny is to develop, for his imperfection does not arise from the impotence of the Creator, but from the circumstance that man is a created being. Adam was not adult in knowledge. The natural man is constituted of two elements, body and soul, but the perfect receive the Spirit (62f.). The thinking of S. Irenaeus on this point is somewhat loose, but he shows real psychological insight (64). In order to show that all men alike are connected with God, and yet all fallen, in opposition to the Gnostic doctrine separating humanity into classes, Irenaeus embarks upon the distinction of the Image and Likeness of God in man (66–7). The Likeness of God in man is free moral

choice. Irenaeus deals little with the ultimate questions
relating to sin, and confines himself to the Genesis Fall-
story. The solidarity of the race means that Adam's sin has
consequences for all humanity. As against Gnosticism, he
teaches that man remains free to choose between good and
evil, a position which hardly seems to agree with what he has
said regarding the loss of the Likeness of God (69–70). It
appears that man's freedom is impaired by the Fall, but not
destroyed in principle (71). Sin is apparently not regarded as
hereditary, yet death, the fruit of sin, is. This displays
another obscurity in the theology of S. Irenaeus. The
problem 'Whence is evil?' is not resolved. He observes that
a moral life presupposes the possibility of sin. At times he
inclines to say that sin itself is part of God's plan, at times to
deny this (72). His thought bears the imprint of a somewhat
superficial moralism (73).

Regarding the destiny of man, S. Irenaeus teaches that
the departed await the General Resurrection in a state of
consciousness (75). Christ died also to redeem the just of
ancient times. Irenaeus holds firmly to the expectation of
the General Resurrection as an essential part of the Faith,
and strongly argues against the Gnostics for the resurrection
of the body.

With the doctrine of Christ we pass to the most important,
as well as the only really new part of the system of S. Irenaeus
(83f.). Of the Incarnation he uses the word σάρχωσις (translated *incarnatio*) rather than the richer term ἐνανθρωπήσις.
The Incarnation is necessary in order that man's enemy
should be conquered by Man, and that man should be
deified (92). Others have centred around the Cross the
interests of religious adoration, and of pardon and holiness.
Irenaeus, by contrast, looks to the Incarnation (93). Following
tradition, Irenaeus calls Christ the Logos, in the Johannine
rather than the Pauline manner (95). He foreshadowed later
dogmatic definition by his implication that the divine Son
took to Himself a human soul as well as a body (98).
Irenaeus can see the human and divine blending in a new

Being. Here is a Christ who is more than an assemblage of heterogeneous elements. This is a better conception than the involved doctrine of the 'two natures' (99). The union of man with the Logos gave to him the full divinity originally designed for him. When Christ was undergoing temptation the Logos was temporarily inactive. Irenaeus quits metaphysics, and takes his stand upon the religious need for a Christ who as man can suffer with us, and who as God can forgive (100).

In the Saving Work of Christ the emphasis is upon the Incarnation as bringing Eternal Life, rather than upon the redemptive death (102). There is thus a certain minimization of the conception of Grace (104). From the historic point of view Recapitulation denotes that Christ went through experiences parallel to those of Adam, but with the opposite result (105–6). From the philosophic aspect this represents the realization of the original goal of the human race, by Christ as Man (107–8). However, the ecclesiastical interest prevents him from pressing this point to the conclusion of a doctrine of the ultimate salvation of every individual man. From the religious point of view Recapitulation reflects the fact that Christ's victory is for all, on account of the solidarity of the race. S. Irenaeus uses Pauline language regarding the expiatory and reconciling death of Christ, but does not share the Apostle's thought. Christ's death is not more than part of His obedience and humiliation, and does not move Irenaeus to love (112). Certain passages, however, appear to speak of redemption as a purchase, the price going either to God, or to the devil (115), but the idea of expiation is not present. Sin has not the gravity for S. Irenaeus that it has for S. Paul (116). This defect springs from the circumstance that God is conceived of mainly as the Creator and Governor of the world, while the attribute of Justice, the Pauline 'Righteousness of God', is effaced (117). According to the optimistic Irenaeus the great need of man is not for regeneration, but for the restoration of the lost Likeness of God. The Son of God became Man so that man could come to the source of perfection, and realize that which was in the first man potentially (119–20). Satan, the lord of death, over-reached himself in trying his power on the Person of Christ, and was defeated. God would not take back by force those whom Satan had cajoled into servitude. Instead he persuaded man to accept escape in Christ, out-playing Satan at his own game (121–2).

In approaching the teaching of S. Irenaeus on the appropriation of salvation by man Beuzart warns us that we must remember that salvation was at that time thought of largely as a relationship to the Church (123). The essential thing is right belief: only traces of S. Paul remain (124). Of the Reformation exposition of saving faith as *notitia, assensus,* and *fiducia,* Irenaeus has the first two, of which *notitia* predominates. There is no question of a 'Mystical union' by faith (125). Faith is that which produces works, from which position it is a short step to salvation by man's own effort (127).

By contrast, when defending the Church Irenaeus moves with ease and passion. His work equals that of S. Cyprian (131). The Church is more than the society of believers: she is their mother. The Church is the outward organization to which the Spirit is attached (132). Irenaeus approaches the formation of a Canon of the New Testament by ceasing to quote apocryphal Gospels. The New Testament is for him authoritative equally with the Old Testament, and is authoritative by itself, this being a new stage of development (134, 140). The New Testament is the expansion of the Old, the difference between the two being quantitative, not qualitative (137). On the other hand, living tradition, which has the advantage of covering more cases, is necessary to interpret Scripture in defence of the Church (142–3). Scripture is not necessary if there be sound tradition, and to the false (secret) tradition of the Gnostics the Church opposes a universal and constant tradition (145), guaranteed by the successions of Bishops (146). S. Irenaeus makes great pretensions for the Church, and is not free from

the human failing of intolerance (149). The Church bears
the marks of universality, unity, antiquity, and apostolicity
(149–55). Rome is placed first in rank, so that the republic
of the Church is tending to a monarchy (156). However,
Irenaeus still treasures the old conceptions of a universal
priesthood and of a charismatic ministry, though this is
over-laid by the division of the faithful into clergy and laity
(158). Baptism, a means of regeneration, is connected in *The
Demonstration of the Apostolic Preaching* with the Catholic
Faith and the Trinitarian formula (162–3). The Eucharist
answers to the Old Testament sacrifices, though it is a
sacrifice of freedom, not of slavery (164). Irenaeus is a
stranger to the idea of Transubstantiation, nor is the Eucharist an offering as the equivalent of a victim (165). It is not a
transformation of elements, but a juxtaposition, which brings
divinization to those who communicate (166).

Beuzart concludes that S. Irenaeus was not a first-rate
thinker, but was of first-rate practical importance (169).
His theology was more Jewish-Christian and Johannine
than Pauline (170), as he betrays a lighter estimate of sin, a
failure to contrast Law and Grace, and a Christian legalism
that S. Paul would have repudiated (171). On the other
hand, he was animated by the ideas of Incarnation and
Eternal Life. However, his most original idea, Recapitulation, was of Pauline derivation (172). He was one of the
least hellenized of the ecclesiastical writers (173). He was
oriental in his doctrine of God, and of Christ, and Western
in his dogma of the Church, though not Western in his view
of sin and salvation.

It will be observed that Beuzart attempts a complete
survey of the theology of S. Irenaeus, writing from the
Reformed point of view. The work is of very real value,
being comprehensive and concise, though a number of
points are open to adverse criticism, as follows: (i) Beuzart
does not sufficiently emphasize that the doctrine of the Two
Hands of God answers to an exposition of God as in immediate contact with the created universe. He wrongly

limits the work of the Hands to the creation of man. (ii) The
doctrine of the Trinity for which Irenaeus supplies the raw
materials is hardly to be described as an Economic Trinity.
(iii) Beuzart seems to assume that the circumstance that
S. Irenaeus does not expound the atoning death of Christ
as a substitutionary or satisfactory offering to God necessarily involves him in an un-Pauline position, and betrays an
emasculated estimate of sin, of grace, and of faith. Thus
Irenaeus is charged with moralism. There are some grounds
for this charge, but serious disproportion on this issue is an
error typical of much Protestant work upon S. Irenaeus.
(iv) Beuzart's exposition of the conception of saving faith in
Irenaeus is far from just. (v) The Pauline tradition in
S. Irenaeus is unduly minimized, in contrast to a supposed
predominance of Johannine and also of Jewish-Christian
elements. (vi) There is a false contrast in the statement that
the doctrine of the Church in Irenaeus is Western rather
than Eastern. It is indeed true that his declaration on Roman
primacy is a great landmark in the history of the rise of the
Papacy, but his interest in the authority of the Church is
in the maintenance of dogmatic orthodoxy, not in central-
ized organizational discipline. In this matter Irenaeus
belongs as much to the East as to the West. (vii) To condemn him for intolerance is a harsh judgement, for in
establishing the exclusive position of the organized Church
he was defending the Catholic Faith with the only weapon
available in his day.

The aim of the present work is to establish the primitive
and Biblical character of most of the important ideas of
S. Irenaeus in a more comprehensive, connected, and definite
way than heretofore, yet with such provisos as may serve to
guard against over-simplification. The following particular
points may be mentioned as possible contributions to the
study of this subject. (i) The exegetical difficulties of Irenaeus in controversy are traced as the motive for the appeal to
ecclesiastical authority. (ii) The actual religious authority for
S. Irenaeus is defined, and justified. (iii) The doctrine of

The Two Hands of God is demonstrated as most distinctively Hebraic, and an attempt made to clarify the vexed and vital question of the relation of the thought of Irenaeus to the Logos-theology and Greek Christianity in general. (iv) The conception of Recapitulation is defined, and connected with S. Paul's rationale of Christ's saving work. (v) An attempt is made to show that the presentation of the Gospel, and in particular the apprehension of saving faith, in S. Irenaeus is substantially evangelical and Pauline. It is demonstrated that much of the alleged divergence of S. Irenaeus from S. Paul is due to the assumption of a traditional exegesis of the Apostle now widely dismissed as incorrect. (vi) The conception of the Church as the New Israel is displayed in the work of Irenaeus, and the significance of his Hebraic Millenarianism commented upon. (vii) The general conclusion is to defend Irenaeus as an exponent of catholic and evangelical Christianity at its best, and to show his central importance in the historical development of the Church's life and thought.

It will be noticed that in the present work S. Irenaeus has usually been quoted in the English translation of T. & T. Clark's *Ante-Nicene Christian Library*, as the version most generally available in this country. This translation follows the chapter divisions of Massuet and Migne, to which the references given consequently correspond. It must be admitted that the most exacting claims of scientific scholarship would perhaps demand that all quotations should be in the Greek, or in the ancient Latin where the original is lost. However, a treatment of one of the Fathers is bound to contain very numerous quotations unless a host of statements are to be left unsubstantiated. References without citation may suffice for the very careful reader, but the work then loses much of its value as a means of exciting interest in the writings in question in the mind of the newcomer. Very voluminous quotations in the original likewise make for arduous reading for all but the accomplished scholar. It therefore appears to be a justifiable compromise to cite in

English in all cases where nothing is lost to the argument thereby, but carefully to discuss the original wherever a point can be better made by such reference, or where the meaning of the text is in doubt. The course adopted is further justified by the circumstance that S. Irenaeus is a writer whose meaning is to be deduced from the general effect far more than from a discussion of minutiæ. In the first place, the bulk of his work exists only in a Latin version agreed to be crude. A discussion of minutiæ therefore is frequently inconclusive, and leaves the final judgement to be made from general considerations. Furthermore, S. Irenaeus is not an exact and systematic writer. He lived before the rise of most of the exact terminology of Christian tradition, and his writings also contain not a few formal contradictions. However, it is hoped that proper recognition will be found in the following pages of the rightful claim that the study of one of the Fathers must be firmly grounded upon the original. The Clark translation has been found very generally adequate as to the sense, though inelegancies of English style are not infrequent. A few of these have been corrected. Care has also always been taken to collect a full list of references to relevant passages, in addition to the citations of the most striking examples, so that the work may be as far as possible a sustained commentary upon the writings of S. Irenaeus.

PART ONE

Saint Irenaeus on the Use of the Bible

Chapter Two

INTRODUCTION

THE MOST casual reader of S. Irenaeus cannot fail to observe two things. The first is the extensive use made of Scripture. At times, chapter after chapter is nothing other than a mosaic of Biblical quotations. The second is that the interpretation of Scripture is most commonly allegorical. To modern eyes it is often strange to the point of the fanciful, or even the grotesque. These circumstances are pointers to the truest significance of the work of this great Catholic Father in the history of Christian life and thought.

It is clear that S. Irenaeus loves to regard himself as *homo unius libri*. With him it is fundamental that the Scriptures provide complete proof for all Christian doctrine. 'But our faith is steadfast, unfeigned, and the only true one, having clear proof from these Scriptures, which were interpreted in the way I have related.' [1,2] They are an independent authority, an authority that speaks for itself. A witness to this is the constant habit of quoting Biblical texts in final settlement of matters of all kinds. Irenaeus plainly believes himself to be founding everything upon 'the Book of God'. The Church's bulwark against error is the Bible. 'It behoves us, therefore, to avoid their doctrines; . . . but to flee to the Church, and to be brought up in her bosom, and to be nourished with the Lord's Scriptures . . . *et dominicis Scripturis enutriri.*' [3,4] We may cordially agree with Seeberg, that

[1] III.21.3, i.354; see also II.35.4, i.256; III.**Pref.**, i.257–8; III.1.1, i.258.

[2] N.B. III.21.3, i.354 represents *Adversus Haereses*, T. & T. Clark's translation; Book III, chapter **21**, paragraph 3; found on page 354 of Volume I of *The Writings of Irenaeus*. An Index to the full system of references is at the beginning (see pp. xiii–xv *supra*).

[3] V.20.2, ii.109; Harvey, ii.379; see also: III.12.12, i.310.

[4] The phrase '*dominicis Scripturis*' also occurs in II.30.6, i.235; Harvey, i.365. In his note here Harvey maintains that the original was κυρίων γραφῶν, making Irenaeus speak of 'the authoritative Scriptures'. However, to judge from

'Irenaeus is a Biblicist, and the first great representative of Biblicism'.[1]

However, the question of religious authority for S. Irenaeus is by no means so simple as this. Very many other passages speak of the unwritten tradition of the Church as the determinative voice. It is even maintained that the Faith could well have continued upon this ground alone, had the Apostles left no writings behind them. The missionary Bishop knows of unlettered tribes 'who believe . . . having salvation written in their hearts by the Spirit, without paper or ink, . . . carefully preserving the ancient tradition. . . . Those who, in the absence of written documents, have believed this faith, are barbarians, so far as regards our language; but as regards doctrine, manner, and tenor of life, they are . . . very wise indeed.'[2]

One is introduced forthwith to one of the leading characteristics of the man. In many-sidedness and in moderation between extremes his powerful intellect is admirable, but he is no systematist, though out of his varied statements a most comprehensive system may be derived. To the evident distress of some systematic German writers S. Irenaeus constantly leaves the diverse sides of an issue in apparent unresolved contradiction. It is therefore necessary carefully to probe the question of what is for him the constitution of religious authority. No study could better serve to illuminate his great significance.

[1] DG., p. 290.
[2] III.4.2, i.264–5.

---

ancient usage regarding 'the Lord's Day', ἡ κυριακή (ἡμέρα), 'dies dominica', and later, of the building used for worship, the likely original for the adjective 'dominicus' when found in the Latin of Irenaeus would be κυριακός. For the phrase 'Scripturis Dominicis' see also II.35.4, i.256; Harvey, i.387.

Chapter Three

ON THE INSPIRATION AND CANONICITY OF SCRIPTURE

THE CHURCH has always honoured the Bible as a book sacred and apart, of unique religious authority, and yet there has never been any dogma of Inspiration. No definition of that in which this authority consists, and how it came to be, and how it acts, has ever been agreed upon by the whole Church. S. Irenaeus foreshadows this historic phenomenon. Though he is so eminently a Biblical theologian he has no definite doctrine of the inspiration of the Bible.

That the Bible is a book not to be classed with even the noblest works of human genius is demonstrated negatively by the consideration that S. Justin Martyr's doctrine of ὁ σπερματικὸς Θεῖος λόγος was abandoned. In a famous and beautiful passage Justin can say of the classical Greek writers: 'For each man spoke well in proportion to the share he had of the spermatic Word....Whatever things were rightly said among all men, are the property of us Christians.'[1] By contrast, Irenaeus set little store upon the great works of pagan thought as a revelation from God. 'Certain of the Gentiles, who were less addicted to . . . voluptuousness, and were not led away to such a degree of superstition with regard to idols, being moved, though but slightly, by His providence, were nevertheless convinced that they should call the Maker of this universe the Father, who exercises a providence over all things, and arranges the affairs of our world.'[2] Damning him thus with faint praise, Irenaeus can admit that 'Plato is proved to be more religious than' the Marcionites, 'for he allowed that the same God was both just and good'.[3] No other name was

[1] *Apol.* II.13; see also *Apol.* II.8. [2] III.25.1, i.371.
[3] III.25.5, i.373.

25

singled out for even this meed of praise. Indeed, that views
similar to those of the Gnostics could be found in all the
philosophers and poets was related as reflecting great dis-
credit upon the former. The great Plato himself was severely
censured for teaching the transmigration of souls.[1] The
verdict upon the gallery of the Immortals runs: 'Did all
those who have been mentioned . . . know, or not know
the truth? If they knew it, then the descent of the
Saviour into this world was superfluous.[2] S. Irenaeus
clearly viewed the inspiration of the Bible as a unique act
of God.

A further point of great importance is the affirmation
that every part of the Bible was inspired by one and the same
God. We must, however, be cautious in drawing from the
statements of S. Irenaeus the consequence that he regarded
the New Testament writings as inspired and canonical
equally with the Old Testament. When he argues the point
he always has in mind those who would detract from the
authority of the Hebrew Scriptures. The position of the
Apostolic writings is thus in effect left open. Polemical needs
drew attention to this question. When the Church had grown
out of being a Jewish sect the authority of the ancient
Scriptures naturally did not pass everywhere unquestioned.
Some Greek Christians were unimpressed by the literary
style. Many more found Old Testament morality sub-
Christian. The least instructed could see that many ordinances were enjoined which the Church did not in fact
observe. Such questionings would naturally be ventilated in
those circles of critical or 'modernist' theologians who were
most forward in the enterprise of reconciling Christian
tradition with secular culture. The Gnostics were such. It is
therefore natural to find Gnostics denying the unity of the
Old Testament, so as to separate it into elements of greater
and of less authenticity and divine authority. The classic
example of an exposition of this theme is the *Epistle of
Ptolemæus to Flora* preserved by Epiphanius.[3] This was the

---

[1] II.33.2, i.248.   [2] II.14.7, i.165.   [3] *Haer.* XXXIII.3-7.

nearest approach of the ancient Church to the modern conception of progressive revelation. It is a real misfortune that such exposition grew up as a part of systems of thought rightly condemned as heretical.

S. Irenaeus firmly rejected any such method of evading Biblical 'difficulties'. He was 'in opposition to the Valentinians . . . who maintain that some parts of Scripture were spoken at one time from the Pleroma . . . but at another time from the intermediate abode through . . . Prunica, but that many are due to the Creator of the world'.[1] Marcion, though not accurately to be classified as a Gnostic, had also rejected the Hebrew Scriptures, as showing a picture of God and a morality deficient in the light of Christian ethics. It was against this wholesale rejection that there came to its most emphatic assertion the doctrine that the Old Testament was inspired throughout by the Christian's God. 'The prophets were sent beforehand from the same Father from whom also the Lord came.'[2] The one God is the God of both Dispensations.[3] Christ and the Apostles acknowledged their connexion with the old religion. Jesus used 'the first and greatest Commandment of the Law.'[4] He also cared for the Temple.[5] S. Peter likewise showed his regard for the Law.[6] So Irenaeus developed one of his major themes, namely, that there is one God of the Old Covenant and of the New. 'Men were taught to worship God after a new fashion, but not another God.' '*Propter quod et nove Deum colere docebantur, sed non alium Deum.*' [7]

Regarding the exact way in which God acted upon those whom He inspired there are no more than a few hints. The two main conceptions of religious authority in the ancient world were the literal inerrancy of a written oracle, and the Gentile idea of divination, ἡ μαντική. Rabbinical Judaism is the supreme example of the former. The latter is well

[1] IV.**35.**1, ii.22; see also II.**35.**2, i.254. [2] V.**26.**2, ii.127.
[3] III.**12.**11, i.309; IV.**11.**4, i.408; IV.**12.**3, i.410; IV.**27.**4, i.469; IV.**28.**1, i.471; IV.**34.**1, ii.18; IV.**34.**5, ii.22; IV.**36.**1,2,5,6, ii.26–7,32–3.
[4] IV.**12.**2, i.409; see also IV.**2.**2, i.379. [5] IV.**2.**6, i.381.
[6] III.**12.**15, i.313. [7] III.**10.**2, i.283; Harvey, ii.35.

exemplified by the lines aptly selected by Bethune-Baker from Virgil.[1]

> Struggling in vain, impatient of her load,
> And lab'ring underneath the pond'rous God,
> The more she strove to shake him from her breast,
> With more and far superior force he press'd;
> Commands his entrance, and, without control,
> Usurps her organs, and inspires her soul.[2]

Here is the conception of the human medium of divine revelation losing temporarily the use of her own faculties, and becoming the mechanical mouthpiece of the indwelling god. Each notion corresponds to an appropriate religious experience. To the Jew religion had gradually become the minute examination of, and obedience to, a book. The triumphs of faith were the feats of the Rabbis in reconciling apparent discrepancies in Scripture. The Gentile on the other hand had the tradition of the oracles and Corybantics. If not always a living tradition this was at least an established tradition. A more intellectual treatment of the same theme is the account of Plato listening to the music of the spheres, and of Archimedes rapt in meditation in presence of the soldier who had come to destroy him. At those points where the interests of Judaism and of Gentile religion ran together the two conceptions of authority could very easily and naturally be held together. Such stories as Saul among the prophets, the inspired dance of David, and the accounts given of their own inspiration by some of the prophets, notably Ezekiel, gave ample grounds within the Hebrew Scriptures themselves for the attempt to explain the inerrant inspiration and supreme authority of Scripture in terms of $\dot{\eta}$ $\mu\alpha\nu\tau\iota\varkappa\dot{\eta}$. From the Jewish side Philo actually did this. The same course would be natural in the Gentile Church, which had inherited the Hebrew Scriptures and the Hebrew attitude to Scripture. So to Athenagoras the prophets were men

---

[1] *Early History of Christian Doctrine*, p. 44.   [2] *Æn.* vi.77-80, Dryden.

'who, lifted in ecstasy above the natural operations of their minds by the impulses of the Divine Spirit, uttered the things with which they were inspired, the Spirit making use of them as a flute-player breathes into a flute'.[1]

S. Irenaeus does not, indeed, disown this theory, but he most significantly does not use it. The reason for this is perhaps not far to seek. Irenaeus knows of ecstatic 'prophecy' among the Gnostic followers of Marcus, and what he knows fills him with abhorrence. Impressionable women are worked up by incantations and spurious miracles into a state of violent emotion and frenzied speech, and the orgy ends in sexual licence.[2] Here is one branch of Gnosticism displaying a well-known aspect of pagan religion. We may well presume that distaste for anything savouring of this, rather than that inclination of sympathy toward Montanism which some have claimed to find in S. Irenaeus, conditioned the practical attitude of Irenaeus to individual and ecstatic prophecy.[3] The doctrine typical of and general to Irenaeus is not that of a Spirit who comes to dwell in an individual prophet and inspires him to declare new truth, but of a Spirit who indwells and lifts to perfection those who faithfully adhere to the established tradition of truth. According to him the χάρισμα of truth is that which enables the successions of Bishops to preserve unblemished the Rule of Truth.[4] This is an exposition of 'spiritual gifts' far removed from the conception of a 'charismatic ministry'. It is more akin to the Rabbinical idea of an authorized and authenticated succession of teachers. It is significant that the doctrine of authority framed in the Church by S. Irenaeus should have this Hebraic aspect.

Irenaeus is more akin in his teaching to Theophilus of Antioch. Theophilus seems to have found a place for human personality in Inspiration by his teaching that God chooses as His instruments those who by His grace have become fitted for their office by personal quality. 'But men of God

---

[1] *Legatio.* IX.
[2] I.13.2–5, i.51–4.
[3] See pp. 97–8 *infra.*
[4] IV.26.2, i.462; cf. p. 98 *infra.*

carrying in them a holy spirit and becoming prophets, being
inspired and made wise by God, became God-taught, and
holy, and righteous. Wherefore they were also deemed
worthy of receiving this reward, that they should become
instruments of God, and contain the wisdom that is from
Him.'[1] So, when Irenaeus is seeking to establish the authority
of the four Evangelists, he is content to do so upon the
natural ground of human knowledge, and has nothing to say
about ecstasy or other unusual phenomena. He shows that
these writers either knew the Lord, or were the intimates
of those who did.[2] This, indeed, illustrates the case only of
the Four Gospels. We have no certain evidence as to whether
S. Irenaeus would have defined the inspiration of Moses and
of the Prophets in more strictly supernatural, or as some
would say, more mechanical, terms. All we can say is that
Old Testament Scripture is constantly quoted simply as the
Voice of God, or of the Divine Logos, and as of plenary
authority. However, the voice of the Apostles is in effect the
Voice of God also. 'For the Lord of all gave to His Apostles
the power of the Gospel, through whom also we have known
the truth, . . . to whom also did the Lord declare: "He that
heareth you, heareth me."'[3] It is expressly stated that after
the Lord's Resurrection the Apostles were invested with the
power and filled with the gifts of the Holy Spirit, with the
result that they possessed 'perfect knowledge';[4] 'et habuerunt
perfectam agnitionem'.[5] This argument that the Apostles were
inspired to the fullness of knowledge is significantly being
used as an argument to vindicate 'the Scriptures'. It is
dangerous to lay too much weight upon the mere use of the
word γραφή, scriptura,[6] but it is clear that, whatever the word
mean, the Apostolic writings are 'Scripture'. Furthermore,
whatever other writings may be termed γραφή, this particular
γραφή, namely, the Four Gospels, is assumed by Irenaeus to
be the equivalent to the voice of the Son of God, and the voice
of the Spirit. It is important to notice that as a source of

---

[1] ad Autol. II.9.   [2] III.1.1, i.258–9.   [3] III.Pref., i.258.
[4] III.1.1, i.258.   [5] Harvey, ii.2.   [6] See p. 51 infra.

γραφή S. Paul is on the same level as S. Peter and S. Matthew. If the authority of S. Mark's Gospel rests upon the natural ground that he was 'the disciple and interpreter of Peter', the authority of S. Luke as an Evangelist is based upon his similar relationship to S. Paul.[1] It is difficult to resist the conclusion that if S. Luke's Gospel is γραφή, and an integral part of 'the ground and pillar of our faith', through the circumstance that it is the work of the Apostle's disciple, then at least as much must be true of the writings of the Apostle himself. This goes far to lift the Pauline Epistles to the same status as the Four Gospels.

In arguing that S. Irenaeus sees a distinction between canonical Scripture and the Pauline writings, the latter attaining only to incipient canonization, Werner observes that one passage[2] allows that 'the Apostle frequently uses a transposed order in his sentences, due to the rapidity of his discourses, and the impetus of the Spirit which is in him'.[3] We may agree that to acknowledge this of S. Paul is to make room for the human element in his writing, for *hyperbaton* is a characteristic of human speech, rather than of the inerrant word of a divine oracle. However, Werner clearly misjudges the significance of the passage in question when he treats it as evidence that to Irenaeus the Epistles were partly 'human', and therefore less than 'Scripture'. Irenaeus is not moved by any interest in the 'human' accident of the Apostle's literary style. He is trying desperately to explain away the awkward phrase, 'the God of this world' (2 Corinthians 4₄), by an utter wresting of the sense, because upon this text the dualist Gnostics had not unnaturally fastened. In doing this he plainly betrays an underlying assumption that S. Paul, when rightly understood, must display the fullness of divine truth in his every word. This attitude hardly answers to an apprehension of the human element in the Epistles.

The divine inspiration of the Evangelists clearly extends to the choice of particular words and phrases. For example, Matthew 1₁₈ was written 'Now the birth of Christ was on

[1] III.1.1, i.259. [2] III.7.1–2, i.273–4. [3] *Paulinismus*, pp. 34, 46.

this wise' so as to preclude the later Gnostic error that only
the man Jesus was born of Mary, which view would have
been tenable had the Evangelist written 'Now the birth of
Jesus was on this wise', as he might otherwise well have
done.[1] We may therefore agree that Beuzart is correct in
stating that had S. Irenaeus lived in later times he would
probably have been an upholder of the doctrine of Literal
Inspiration.[2]

We must now proceed to the most important but difficult
question of the evidence supplied by S. Irenaeus on the
development of the Canon of the New Testament. It will be
impossible to clear up this perplexed issue without first
giving a brief definition of Canonicity. In general one may
say that Canonicity is that which grows out of Inspiration
by virtue of the passage of time. It is a derived conception.
Inspiration is therefore logically treated first.

The stages by which certain books become the canonical
writings of a given religion are three. (i) A teacher, or school
of teachers, is inspired with new and living truth. The
inspiration is of an uncommon degree, and an uncommon
impression is made upon those who accept the teaching. A
written record is formed. Among the disciples these books
are agreed to be inspired, but not of authority in the proper
sense of the word. They are still human, and may be criticized. They are works of piety or theology to be compared
with other works, though to be preferred to others. (ii) If
the initial impression be such that time and experience
deepen it, the day will probably come when, within the
religious community in question, a unique degree of inspiration in the teaching of the founder(s) may be taken for
granted as axiomatic. The background to this development is
commonly the realization that the breath of present creative
inspiration is becoming fainter. Men are becoming aware
that no new work is forthcoming which it is proper to compare with the old. The Holy Books are now of authority.

---

[1] III.16.2, i.325.   [2] *Essai*, p. 138.

They are set apart from others by virtue of repute. However, they are still of authority *on account of their authorship*. (iii) The converse process may then naturally set in. The works of the authors are declared to be of authority *because they are in the recognized Holy Book*. Antiquity is an element necessary for the completion of this change. Antiquity both invests with a halo and obscures historical knowledge of the rise of the sacred literature. The authors whose repute originally gave repute to the Books become the subjects of hagiography, and cease to be thought of as ordinary men. The essence of their repute is now that they provide holy names for the Books. Only when the process is complete are the works Canonical in the full sense of the word, i.e. it is an article of faith that a statement must be accepted because it occurs in the text of a book the name of which figures in the recognized list or 'Canon'.

It must not be supposed, however, that this definition confuses Canonicity with Literal Inerrancy. The doctrine of the Literal Inerrancy of the Christian Bible is only one particular theory to explain the peculiar authoritative property of Canonical Scripture. In ages when faith did not have to take account of modern scientific knowledge it was a very natural and compelling theory. Hence it has been a very wide-spread one, which has received particular emphasis in those circles of traditional Protestantism which have felt controversial need of providing themselves with an organ of authority to be set over against the Papal system. However, this theory is not the only possible one. By way of comparison, Islam has claimed every possible perfection of Arabic literary style for the Koran. This is a somewhat different claim than that of Literal Inerrancy, but it has the same underlying intention, namely, to lift the canonical writings of a great historic religion above the level of human piety into the sphere of eternal truth. So too, the great traditional 'mystical' school of Christian exposition has in practice displayed a wide divergence of interest from the Literal school, but it has nevertheless been at one with it in drawing a sharp distinction between the Bible and even the noblest non-Biblical literature. Again, it is logically possible, though not perhaps usual, to reconcile science with the doctrine of a sharp distinction between authoritative Canonical Scripture and 'mere human piety' by asserting that the whole Bible is of unique and final authority in spiritual things, but fallible in matters of natural knowledge. This is actually the position which appears to be assumed with regard to our Lord by many modern theologians who would be both 'Liberal' and orthodox. As the Divine Son He has been acknowledged as God's last and perfect word to the world in morals and piety. As Man He has been regarded as sharing the defective knowledge of His times in other spheres.

We observe, furthermore, that in her tradition that the test of Canonical New Testament Scripture is Apostolic origin the Church has preserved a memorial of the day when the New Testament had only advanced to stage (ii) (see pp. 32–3). However, since an early date this tradition has been a memory only. Whatever the theory of the matter, the practice in dogmatic appeal has been to 'the Book'. The appeal is to the sacred text as authoritatively determined by the tradition of the Church. Consistent with this is the irresistible tendency to be observed in the early Church to apply Apostolic names to those books which piety demanded should have their position in the Canon maintained, yet which unfortunately lacked this title. The Epistle to the Hebrews, for example, first won a place of wide and merited repute, and then had its place as Canonical Scripture confirmed by attribution to S. Paul. This is evidence to what extent the vital force in the early Church was not appeal to S. Paul as such, but to 'the Book'. The actual fact was the Canon: the doctrine of Apostolic origin was the theory, though a theory founded upon a substantial measure of historical reminiscence. The New Testament has from the practical point of view been regarded in the same way as the Old Testament, in the case of which there has never been any theory that it owed its authority to authorship by a certain class of men. Presence in the traditional Canon has been seen as the self-sufficient ground for authority. This is essential Canonicity. In passing one has to state that modern liberal scholarship has in effect de-canonized Scripture, apart from such sayings and historical reminiscences of our Lord as pass muster as 'authentic'. Only the latter element in the Bible is an authority in the strict sense of the word, i.e. a text which may be expounded, but not questioned.

If this definition be applied to S. Irenaeus it is plain that he accepted the Old Testament without question as Canonical Scripture. This was the natural and original position of the Church, the heritage of her first days as a Jewish community. To vindicate the Hebrew Scriptures against the attack of Gentile Gnosticism is indeed one of the main interests of *Adversus Haereses*. The authenticity of the old religion was one of the major corollaries of anti-Gnostic polemic. Irenaeus regarded the Septuagint as an authoritative version, even to the point of preferring it to the original in the case of Isaiah 7₁₄.[1] In consequence the Apocrypha is occasionally quoted as Scripture, without any apparent distinction from the rest of the Old Testament.[2]

With regard to the New Testament we observe that S. Irenaeus is fully advanced in stage (ii), but that he is not quite far enough away in time from the Apostles to be found in stage (iii). To him it is an article of faith that the Apostles, as inspired by God, are an organ of supreme and unquestioned authority. However, they are still men and not names. In actual practice S. Irenaeus quotes the Apostolic writings as of equal authority with the Old Testament Scriptures. They are alike the Voice of God. However, in the case of the Apostolic writings he always bases their authority on the fact of the authorship, not on the simple circumstance that the book occurs in the Canon. The argument is always that the books were written by the Apostles, or by those who had trustworthy recollection of the Apostles. Thus the Apostolic

perhaps contributing to Irenaeus' understanding of apostolic succession

[1] III.21.1–2, i.351–3.   [2] IV.26.3, i.463; V.35.1, ii.152–3.

writings are to Irenaeus fully authoritative Scripture, but
they are also only the substitute for the fully authoritative
spoken word. One can rightly discuss what writings S.
Irenaeus knew as Apostolic, but it slightly savours of
anachronism to ask: 'How many New Testament books did
he regard as canonical?'

In the thinking of S. Irenaeus the distinction between New
Testament Scripture and other venerated Christian writings
is still slightly obscure. The books of the New Testament
are still not quite on a shelf by themselves in the Christian
library. Their prestige is a matter of degree, not yet of
principle. However, this in no way detracts from the Apostolic writings as of plenary and unquestioned authority. To
Irenaeus the whole body of tradition preserved by the
Apostles, and by their disciples, and by the Elders, is an
authority. The Apostolic writings are the supreme example of
what is the case generally. In light of this reconstruction the
various most important statements of Irenaeus regarding the
New Testament fall into place. His early date gives a unique
interest to his witness, as together with the *Muratorian Fragment* his writings constitute the main source of information for
the first stages of development of the New Testament Canon.

We have come to a point in the present study where the
interest is as much historical as doctrinal. It will therefore
be of advantage to introduce the evidence supplied by S.
Irenaeus by a brief survey of the historical background, and
of the development to date. Among the Apostolic Fathers
S. Clement of Rome (writing *c.* A.D. 95) states the doctrine
of Justification by Faith in a manner reminiscent of the
Pauline Epistles, and combines this with the rejoinder of
the Epistle of James. There are apparent allusions to the
Fourth Gospel and Hebrews. The *Teaching of the Apostles*
(end of first century or early second century) contains
extensive quotations of the words of Jesus, though without
any mention of names of Evangelists, or any explicit indication that distinct writings are referred to. Twice the Lord is
named as the source of a Saying, most notably when the

Lord's Prayer is recited. Here, at any rate, the introduction is such as to make reference to a written document altogether natural. At the same time it is also to be admitted that there is hardly any 'Word of the Lord' more likely to have been widely and accurately remembered and used independently of written sources than the Lord's Prayer. So we read: 'Neither pray ye as the hypocrites, but as the Lord commanded in His Gospel, thus pray ye: Our Father, etc.' ὡς ἐκέλευσεν ὁ Κύριος ἐν τῷ εὐαγγελίῳ αὐτοῦ.[1] The remainder of the Words of the Lord are cited as the Law of the Christian Church, and of Christian conduct, but without any reference to whom is being quoted.

The opening quotations illustrating the Way of Life are certainly of sufficient length and accuracy, judged by the standard of the Canonical Gospels, to make literary dependence on S. Matthew and S. Luke very natural. At the same time, simple, practical, and striking sayings of Jesus, such as those in question, are likewise such as we can best imagine being remembered in the Church without a written record. This illustrates a general difficulty in all the earliest Christian literature. An allusion to an Apostolic saying in a sub-Apostolic work is the strongest evidence of acquaintance with the work known to us, even in absence of the confirmation of literary dependence given by prolonged and accurate reproduction, or by explicit statement. A similar allusion to a saying of Jesus is less clear evidence of literary dependence on the Gospels, inasmuch as we may be certain that the more striking words of our Lord would be more widely remembered in the early Church than any words of an Apostle. The ipsissima verba of Jesus would be universally accepted by Christians, and from the beginning. They also have the eternal ring about them, and the universal appeal. By contrast, teaching such as that of S. Paul is more occasional, and adapted to particular persons and episodes. Very often an Apostolic voice is the voice of a section of the Church, or even of one contending party in a controversy. In any case,

---

[1] *Didache*, VIII.

Apostolic writings would not have the same measure of original universal acceptance among Christians as the words of Jesus Himself. When in a sub-Apostolic work an allusion is made to one of the sayings of Jesus we must hence be somewhat cautious in inferring knowledge of the same writings as have come down to us. The matter is clearer when the reference is to something in one of the remaining New Testament writings. After the sub-Apostolic period, however, one may with confidence assume that there was little accurate recollection of the words of the Lord, apart from written records.

The Epistles of S. Ignatius of Antioch (early second century) contain many typical Pauline words, while the allusions sometimes extend to definite but anonymous quotations. Some Johannine ideas are also reflected by Ignatius. Just after this, S. Polycarp makes more frequent references to New Testament writings, but without actual citation. There appears to be a particular kinship of the Epistle of S. Polycarp to 1 Peter. In the sub-Apostolic Church, therefore, one would judge that the Apostles were venerated as spiritual authorities, but not conceived of as the writers of 'quotable' Scripture. The words of the Lord were on a different footing. The Apostles have at this period deeply impressed the Church with their beliefs, and have filled her vocabulary with their words, but the natural appeal is still to their doctrine and general ideas, not to their writings as such. Clearly the Apostolic writings would be seen as substitutes for their words. The authors, indeed, were regarded as different from other men. The disciples of the Apostles never ventured to call themselves Apostles, and were never so called by those who later venerated them as 'The Elders'. Nevertheless their writings, *as writings*, were not different from other writings. The appeal of the sub-Apostolic Church is still to holy men, not to a holy Book. How long this very human and natural, but historically unreliable preference for oral memory over written records continued is witnessed by the celebrated case of Papias. 'For I did not' [he writes] 'like the multitude, take pleasure in those that speak much, but in those that teach the truth. . . . If, then, any one came, who had been a follower of the elders, I questioned him in regard to the words of the elders, what Andrew or what Peter said, etc. . . . For I did not think that what was to be gotten from the books would profit me as much as what came from the living and abiding voice.'[1] This position agrees with the outline given above of the natural progress from Inspiration to Canonicity. By contrast, however, how completely natural at this very early period was the appeal to the Hebrew Scriptures, as to canonical writings proper, is seen from the reserved rebuke S. Ignatius sees fit to give to certain in the Church. 'For I heard certain persons saying, "If I find it not in the ancients" [or as Westcott translates: 'in the charters': ἐν τοῖς ἀρχείοις] "I believe it not in the Gospel.". . . But as for me, my ἀρχεῖα is Jesus Christ.'[2] S. Ignatius seems to be feeling his way forward from the position as it exists in Acts, where 'the Scriptures' are the Old Testament, and where the Christian Scripture appeal is that the Crucified may be accepted as God's Messiah, because the inconceivable paradox had been prophesied.

It might be expected that much fuller evidence for the use of the canonical New Testament writings would be forthcoming from the Greek Apologists, for here we come to writers whose work may correctly be described as Christian theology. However, the portion of the Apologists' work that remains to us is somewhat disappointing in this respect. The reason for this is not far to seek. The accounts in Acts 14₁₄-₁₈ and 17₂₂-₃₁ of S. Paul's speeches at Lystra and at Athens appear correctly to represent the approach made by the first Christian preachers to a Gentile, as distinct from a Jewish or semi-proselyte, audience. The preacher then spoke much as if he were a missionary for Judaism. To the heathen the evangelist argued ethical monotheism, on the ground of the inherent reasonableness of this belief, and in contrast to the

---

[1] Cited in Eus. *H.E.* III.xxxix.3,4.   [2] *ad.Phil.* VIII.

grossness and impurity of paganism. Only when this initial
impression had been made could one proceed to the Gospel.
This is exactly the position of the early Apologists in writing
for their Gentile public. They argue first from philosophy,
from history, and from morals, and only afterwards from
Scripture. The one Scripture argument that might with
some confidence be used to the outer world was that the
most surprising and unforeseeable events had been fore-
casted in the Prophets, and literally fulfilled centuries later
in the life of Christ. This uncanny degree of prescience
answered to divine inspiration. This, however, is a mode of
argument that does not lead to citation of the New Testament.

Papias (early second century) claims only to be an
expositor. This is a distinct stage, for the activity of an
expositor presupposes some authoritative text which it is of
interest to expound. Papias witnesses to a supposed Hebrew
original to S. Matthew's Gospel, and also to the existence of
S. Mark's Gospel. He shows some knowledge of John,
1 John, and 1 Peter, but makes no allusion to S. Paul. From
the fragments of the Elders of this period preserved by
S. Irenaeus comes a reference to 2 Corinthians 12₄.[1] In the
Epistle to Diognetus (*c.* A.D. 150) there are clear allusions to
Johannine and Pauline Epistles. More substantial evidence
is forthcoming from the work of S. Justin Martyr (*fl.* around
A.D. 150). S. Justin quotes loosely and conflates, but nevertheless a great part of the Gospel stories, and particularly, of
the teaching of Jesus, is reproduced, and in a form which
agrees with the use of our present Gospels. The names of
the Evangelists are not mentioned, however. Added to this
there is the celebrated mention of the *Memoirs of the
Apostles,* Τὰ ᾽Απομνημονεύματα τῶν Ἀποστόλων as read in the
Liturgy.[2] This is evidence of an important stage of development, though there is unfortunately no information as to
what Apostolic writings are in mind. Justin connects the
Apocalypse with the name of John the Disciple,[3] and makes

[1] V.5.1, ii.66.   [2] 1 *Apol.* 66-7.   [3] *Dial.* 81.

allusions to the major Epistles of S. Paul. There is, however, no clear indication that Justin used a collection of Gospels and Epistles. Melito (c. 170) speaks of the Old Books (παλαιῶν) as if there were also a Canon of New Testament writings.[1] Theophilus of Antioch (Bishop, c. A.D. 180) makes allusions to S. Matthew's Gospel, and mentions S. John by name. In his work, also, are traces of the Pauline Epistles, Hebrews, and 1 Peter. Athenagoras (c. A.D. 180) contains full references to Matthew, John, Romans, 1 Corinthians, and Galatians.

Of singular importance is the Latin fragment of a Canon (c. A.D. 170) first published by Muratori of Milan in 1740. The *Muratorian Canon* indeed adds little to what has already been observed, but serves to connect isolated facts. It opens by placing Luke third, written by S. Luke the Physician, and John fourth, by S. John the Disciple. 1 John is also mentioned. It is expressly stated that the four Gospels are a unity in variety. Acts is a record by S. Luke. There are nine Pauline Epistles addressed to Churches, analogous to the Letters to the churches of the Apocalypse. These are placed in the order 1 and 2 Corinthians, Ephesians, Philippians, Colossians, Galatians, 1 and 2 Thessalonians, and Romans. There are also four Epistles to individuals, namely, Philemon, Titus, and 1 and 2 Timothy. The *Fragment* then proceeds to disputed books. To be rejected are an Epistle to the Laodiceans, and another to the Alexandrians, but Jude and 2 and 3 John are to be received, together with a book of Wisdom. The Apocalypses of John and Peter are likewise to be accepted by the Church, though it is admitted that some will not allow the latter to be read. *The Shepherd* of Hermas is then mentioned, and the document passes on to definitely heretical works. There is thus no special enumeration in the Canon of James, 1 Peter, 2 Peter, or Hebrews. The reason for these omissions is perhaps a break in the text. The Old Latin Version of the New Testament apparently agreed with the *Muratorian Canon*, with the addition

[1] Eus. *H.E.* IV.xxvi.13.

of Hebrews, though without the name of S. Paul. The
Syrian Peshitta omits 2 and 3 John, 2 Peter, Jude, and the
Apocalypse.

Of some interest is the indirect evidence of heretical
teachers. According to Tertullian, Valentinus accepted the
whole Christian Canon,[1] and the Valentinians also had a
Gospel of Truth.[2] Heracleon was a commentator, thereby
acknowledging the authority of that which he expounded.
Most notably, Marcion (at Rome in the middle of the
second century) formed the first Canon of which there is a
record. This was a Pauline Canon, consisting of '*The Gospel*'
(i.e. S. Luke 'criticized with a penknife'), and '*The Apostol-
icon*' of ten Epistles of S. Paul, with a few emendations, and
excluding the Pastoral Epistles and Hebrews. This attack
upon so many books customarily read in Christian worship
was doubtless a major stimulus to the definition of an
orthodox Canon.

In turning to the information provided by S. Irenaeus for
our understanding of this historical development we first
observe that he solemnly announces his task as to give proof
of all he has been saying from those *Scriptures* which are
'the ground and pillar of our faith'. Significantly he proceeds
forthwith to enumerate the writings of Matthew, Mark,
Luke, and John, and to demonstrate their apostolical authority.[3] The Four Gospels are to Irenaeus in consequence
clearly authoritative 'Scripture', though too much weight
cannot safely be laid upon the mere use of this name. The
celebrated passage runs: 'Matthew also issued a written
gospel among the Hebrews in their own dialect, while Peter
and Paul were preaching at Rome, and laying the foundations
of the Church. After their departure, Mark, the disciple and
interpreter of Peter, did also hand down to us in writing
what had been preached by Peter. Luke also, the companion
of Paul, recorded in a book the gospel preached by him.
Afterwards, John, the disciple of the Lord, who also had
leaned upon His breast, did himself publish a gospel during

[1] *de Praescr. Haeret.* 38.   [2] III.11.9, i.296.   [3] III.**Pref.**; III.1.1, i.257–9.

his residence at Ephesus in Asia.' Here is indeed a statement
of the greatest authority, in view of its early date, and the
status of its author. It is also a statement of fascinating
interest. It is somewhat outside the scope of the present
work to criticize it in detail, for the matter has long been one
of controversy, and it is a part of a study of great intricacy. It
must suffice to record in passing some main points. Modern
New Testament scholarship in general rejects the idea of an
Aramaic or Hebrew original to the first Gospel. The statement of Irenaeus is at most a hazy recollection that this
Gospel sprang originally from the Jewish-Christian section
of the primitive community. The fact that its author used
sources compiled by those who were not eye-witnesses of
the life of Christ is an almost insuperable objection to the
claim that it was composed by one of the Twelve. That
Irenaeus makes Matthew earlier than Mark is presumably a
reflection of his opinion regarding authorship. On the other
hand, modern scholarship would very generally agree that
there is real insight displayed in the observations upon
the second and third Gospels. S. Mark's Gospel certainly
seems to reflect a personal interest in S. Peter. Even more
certainly, S. Luke's Gospel speaks for the Christianity of
the great Gentile mission, i.e. for the Gospel as understood
by S. Paul and his circle. The nature and authorship of the
Fourth Gospel is the most perplexing problem of New
Testament scholarship. Not a few would stoutly defend the
statement of S. Irenaeus, but many more would attribute
the Gospel to some disciple who cherished a tradition
derived from the Beloved Disciple. That the Gospel was
written in Asia Minor is widely accepted. From our point
of view the important thing is that Irenaeus admits our
four Gospels, and them only, and states their traditional
authorship.

Very interesting is the passage where it is argued that
there are and by the very nature of things can only be four
genuine Gospels. With some justice Kreyenbuhl has dismissed as 'a poor allegory' the argument that 'since there

are four zones of the world in which we live, and four principal winds,[1] while the Church is scattered throughout all the world, and the "pillar and ground" of the Church is the Gospel and the spirit of life; it is fitting that she should have four pillars'.[2] Gutjahr is, however, right in his rejoinder that the allegory does not pretend to show the ultimate reason for the four-fold nature of the Gospels. It only exhibits the cosmic propriety of the accepted facts.[3] The four-fold Gospel is simply an historic fact enshrined in the tradition of the Church, as witness the passage quoted above.[4]

It has been argued that S. Irenaeus felt that he could safely take it for granted that within the true Church there were recognized four, and only four Gospels, and that this indicates that those four must by that early date have been firmly established in long and universal custom. However, the fact that to Irenaeus a difference of opinion among the faithful regarding a matter of spiritual importance is a thing inconceivable is sufficient to vitiate this method of argument. We cannot doubt that once Irenaeus had been led to assent to the doctrine of the Four as essential he would inevitably have gone on to denounce as a heretic any person who entertained doubts about one of them, however orthodox and loyal to the Church he might be in other matters. The voice of this believer would be ignored in the *consensus fidelium*. For S. Irenaeus, anything that is established is taken for granted as established in long and universal custom. It is accordingly precarious to argue that what he takes for granted as universal is necessarily so in fact.

A sounder statement of the argument is based on the

---

[1] It is worthy of note that this passage provides evidence that neither S. Irenaeus nor his Latin translator used the word 'Catholic' in its later specific sense, despite the circumstance that the corresponding idea is so prominent in these writings. τέσσαρα καθολικὰ πνεύματα has here been rendered 'quatuor principales spiritus'. Harvey, ii.47.

[2] III.**11.8**, i.293; cf. III.**11.9**, i.296.

[3] *Die Glaubwürdigkeit des Irenaeischen Zeugnisses über die Abfassung des vierten kanonischen Evangeliums* (Graz. 1904), pp. 8–10.

[4] III.**1.1**, i.258–9.

proposition that S. Irenaeus was of a very comprehensive genius. He was in intellectual contact with the Church in several lands, and showed a strong sense of veneration for whatever was customary. We can safely judge that he would never have been happy in disowning any position that he knew to be traditional among any body of reputable Christians, simply on the grounds that his own religious interests carried him in a different direction. Judging by what is observed in other cases we may rather assume that he would have preferred comprehension to strict formal consistency. We may say with some confidence that had Irenaeus been aware of the existence of some minority of accepted Christians who professed reverence for some Gospel outside the Four he would have found some way of making a sympathetic salute to that writing, even at the expense of inconsistency with his own statements elsewhere. A case in point is the position of the Apocryphal Gospels. Many notable early Fathers, such as Hegesippus, Tertullian, Clement of Alexandria, and Origen, make a limited use of some of these. In general, they allow them a less weighty authority than the Four, and permit them to be used in private, though not to be read in public worship. That Irenaeus so pointedly makes no use whatever of any of these works, but rather stresses the exclusive position of the canonical Gospels, is by no means a token, as some have claimed, that he is in reality a controversialist contending against a view held by some within the Church. If there had been such teachers he would either have accommodated himself to them, or else have unchurched them. Rather does he appear in the role of a conservative who is unaware of or unaffected by individual innovations. His failure to make even a guarded use of any of the Apocryphal Gospels is therefore valid evidence that these cannot have enjoyed any prominence in the period up to his day. An argument from silence may perhaps be in this case upheld, though not an argument from what is taken for granted. The traditional evaluation of S. Irenaeus as a witness to the original four-fold nature of the written

Gospel is to be upheld, though not one of the traditional grounds for this evaluation.

The position of the Pauline writings has given rise to more debate. The Epistles are all quoted, save that to Philemon; the major ones very extensively. Werner has maintained that Irenaeus is a witness to the incipient canonization of the Pauline Epistles, though not to the completion of the process.[1] One argument used is that Pauline quotations are introduced almost as personal words, with an introductory 'the Apostle said', while Scriptural quotations proper are introduced directly as words of the Logos, or of God.[2] The evidence adduced for this distinction does not however appear to be satisfactory. It is true that Pauline citations are not unusually introduced in the way stated, but there are also numerous passages where S. Paul's words are quoted direct as divine authority, in the same manner as the prophets. A Greek example is the use of Romans 5_19 in a portion preserved in Theodoret, *Dial.* I. Ὥσπερ γὰρ διὰ τῆς παρακοῆς τοῦ ἑνὸς ἀνθρώπου, τοῦ πρώτως ἐκ γῆς ἀνεργάστου πεπλασμένου, ἁμαρτωλοὶ κατεστάθησαν.[3] A most striking example of a quotation of Ephesians 4_10 linked with one of Isaiah 7_11, without any mark of distinction of usage is: *Quod autem dixerit Esaias, 'In profundum deorsum, vel in altitudinem sursum,' significantis fuit, quoniam 'qui descendebat ipse erat et qui ascendebat'.*[4] In another passage Romans 3_30 is represented not quite explicitly as the very utterance of the divine Logos, but the thought is not far off. Certainly Werner's claim falls down upon such a passage, as upon a number of others. *Omnia enim nova aderant, Verbo nove disponente carnalem adventum, uti eum hominem qui extra Deum abierat, ascriberet Deo: propter quod et nove Deum colere docebantur, sed non alium Deum, quoniam quidem 'unus Deus, qui iustificat circumcisionem ex fide, et praeputium per fidem'.*[5] Similarly, while texts from the Old Testament and

---

[1] *Paulinismus*, p. 46.   [2] ibid. p. 33.   [3] III.18.7, Harvey, ii.101.

[4] III.21.5, Harvey, ii.117–18; see also I.10.3, Harvey, i.97.

[5] III.10.2, Harvey, ii.35. See also Harvey, i.239, i.272, i.308, i.330, ii.20, ii.43, ii.106, ii.129, ii.211, ii.228.

the Four Gospels are constantly woven into the work as 'the very voice of God', one quite frequently also reads: 'Moses said', 'David said', 'Isaiah said', and 'Jesus said'. This is the same usage as with S. Paul.

Werner has further argued that S. Irenaeus used the allegoristic exegesis upon Scripture proper, but did not do so upon the Pauline Epistles. This again is evidence that Paul was regarded as less than Scripture.[1] In the main this difference of treatment is actually to be observed, though there are places where Irenaeus approaches allegorism in Pauline exegesis.[2] However, the conclusion drawn from this distinction is quite unsound. The use of allegoristic exegesis does not of itself presuppose a regard for the text as Scripture. The reason for the use of allegorism rather lies in the obscurity of meaning in, or in the objectionable character of the plain sense of, a writing presumed to be sacred.[3] Irenaeus has in the main a competent understanding of S. Paul, and what he reads he finds edifying. The occasion to resort to this exegesis is therefore proportionately less than in the case of the Prophets. Werner continues by arguing that the following passage places S. Paul outside the category of Scripture: 'For that there are spiritual creatures in the heavens, all the Scriptures loudly proclaim; and Paul expressly testifies that there are spiritual things when he declares that he was caught up into the third heaven.'[4] A contrast between 'the Scriptures' and 'Paul' may certainly be read into the first sentence, but equally the passage may be taken as treating Paul as an example of Scripture. Finally it is asserted that the Pauline writings are only secondary Scripture, which must be shown to conform to 'the Scriptures'.[5] It is difficult to uphold this from the passages advanced by Werner. For example, III.**6**.5, i.272, and IV.**41**.4,

[1] *Paulinismus*, p. 35.

[2] e.g. Romans 10₁₅ in III.**13**.1, i.314; Romans 5₁₇ in III.**16**.9, i.332; and the use of the word 'Christ' in III.**18**.3, i.338–9.

[3] See p. 85 *infra*.

[4] *Paulinismus*, p. 44. II.**30**.7, i.235; see also Schmidt, *Kirche b.I.* p. 47.

[5] *Paulinismus*, p. 45.

ii.53, go no farther than the statement that S. Paul taught
the same doctrine as the Old Testament, namely, that there
is but one God, the Creator. It is hardly necessary to assume
from this that the Old Testament is quoted to give weight
to the testimony of the Apostle.

Werner is quite right in saying that the view of S. Irenaeus
that S. Paul possessed the Spirit on the ground of his
apostolic calling does not of itself involve an estimate of his
writings as 'inspired'.[1] The Elders also possessed the Spirit,
but their writings are not Scripture. It may be granted to
Werner that to the mind of the times an Epistle would seem
a 'modern' and profane form of writing, a mere substitute
for the spoken word of the author.[2] It by no means follows
from this, however, that Irenaeus would necessarily be
inclined to regard the Pauline Epistles as something other
than sacred oracles. It is difficult to see how a letter, mere
substitute for the spoken word though it be, could be
adequately described in any term less than 'the inspired
Word of God' when it is from the pen of one to whom is
ascribed such excellent authority as that of S. Paul. The
Church herself is of plenary authority because she has
received the truth from the Apostles. The Apostles are
therefore collectively a paramount religious authority.
Among this august company there are two who occupy so
exalted a place that the Church of Rome herself rises to her
pre-eminent authority through foundation in their ministry.
One of these great ones is the writer of the Epistles. It is but
natural to find that in practice S. Paul is quoted in the same
authoritative manner as are the Old Testament Scriptures.

The Pastoral Epistles are also frequently quoted, relatively to their length, and in a manner similar to that already
considered. If the first Pfaffian Fragment be accepted as
genuine, the name of Paul is attached to an indistinct
reference to 1 Timothy 6₄₋₅.[3] The Second Epistle to Timothy
was certainly regarded by Irenaeus as of Pauline authorship.
'Paul has himself declared also in the Epistles, saying:

[1] *Paulinismus*, p. 30.   [2] *Paulinismus*, p. 31.   [3] *Frag.* XXXVI. ii.175.

"Demas hath forsaken me . . ." etc.' (2 Timothy 4₁₀-₁₁).[1]
The same is true of the Epistle to Titus: 'and these men
Paul commands us, "after a first and second admonition, to
avoid" ' (Titus 3₁₀).[2] Contrary to the assertion of Vernet, there
appears to be no secure evidence that Irenaeus used the
Epistle to the Hebrews.[3]

The Acts of the Apostles are extensively cited as of full
authority. S. Luke is known as the author, and the authority
of his work rests upon his intimacy with S. Paul. The 'we-
passages' are observed as evidence 'that this Luke was
inseparable from Paul, and his fellow-labourer in the
Gospel'.[4] The Epistle of James is represented in Irenaeus
by two allusions,[5] and by one definite quotation of James 2₂₃.
It is noteworthy that this occurs in a chapter dealing with
circumcision, and in a context rather out of keeping with
the legalistic atmosphere of James. 'And that man was not
justified by these things . . . this fact shows—that Abraham
himself, without circumcision, and without observance of
Sabbaths, "believed God, and it was imputed unto him for
righteousness; and he was called the friend of God".'[6] This
very limited use hardly bears out Ritschl's statement that
the use of the formula, 'the Law of Freedom' (James 2₁₂), in
IV.34.4, ii.21, to connect the legalistic interest with Pauline
Christian freedom proves that this Epistle is in the hands of
S. Irenaeus an original factor in the legalistic development
of Gentile Christianity.[7] The First Epistle of S. Peter is
quoted some twelve times, with two further possible allusions.
On three of these occasions it is described as the work of
S. Peter, this being important as the first known statement
in Christian literature connecting this Epistle with the
Apostle: 'and Peter says in his Epistle: "Whom, not seeing,

[1] III.14.1, i.317.
[2] I.16.3, i.71; see also III.3.4, i.263.
[3] *Dictionnaire*, VII, col. 2416.
[4] III.14.1, i.316-7.
[5] James 1₂₁ in V.10.1, ii.79; James 2₂₃ in IV.13.4, i.416; see also an uncertain allusion to James 1₁₈ in V.1.1, ii.56.
[6] IV.16.2, i.422-3.   [7] *Entstehung d.a.K.* pp. 316-7.

ye love." '[1] The Second Epistle of Peter is represented by two citations of 2 Peter 3s.[2] In neither case is an author's name given. The First and Second Epistles of John are both quoted as the work of the Apostle: '"and every spirit which separates Jesus Christ is not of God, but of antichrist." These words agree with what was said in the Gospel, that "the Word was made flesh, and dwelt among us".'[3] It is of interest to note that the text of 1 John 4₁,₂, given here by Irenaeus, differs materially from the *Textus Receptus: Et omnis spiritus qui solvit Jesum Christum, non est ex Deo.*[4] Socrates in the Greek (VII.32) and Origen practically agree with this, as also Tertullian in *Adv. Marc.* V.16, and the Vulgate: hence the Revised Version margin. The Third Epistle of John, and also the Epistle of Jude, are not apparently used. As is natural in a millenarian writer, the Apocalypse is extensively quoted and given high authority, being also described as the work of S. John the Apostle.

The question has been raised as to what estimate S. Irenaeus placed upon *The Shepherd* of Hermas. The passage in question runs: *Bene igitur pronuntiavit scriptura quae dicit: Primo omnium crede, quoniam unus est Deus, qui omnia constituit, et consummavit, et fecit ex eo quod non erat, ut essent omnia.*[5] 'Truly, then, the Scripture declared, which says, "First of all believe that there is one God, who has established all things, and completed them, and having caused that, from what had no being, all things should come into existence".'[6] However, Eusebius preserves this quotation in the Greek[7]: Καλῶς οὖν εἶπεν ἡ γραφὴ ἡ λέγουσα· Πρῶτον πάντων πίστευσον ὅτι εἷς ἐστιν ὁ Θεός, ὁ τὰ πάντα κτίσας, καὶ καταρτίσας, καὶ ποιήσας ἐκ τοῦ μὴ ὄντος εἰς τὸ εἶναι τὰ πάντα.[8] In this, the assertion that *The Shepherd* is Scripture is not definite, though the context of Eusebius appears to imply that Irenaeus is to be taken in this sense, as this writing figures in a list of

---

[1] 1 Peter 1 s in IV.9.2, i.401 and in V.7.2, ii.72; also 1 Peter 2₁₆ in IV.16.5, i.425.

[2] V.23.2, ii.118; V.28.3, ii.132.　　　[3] III.16.8, i.331–2.

[4] Harvey, ii.90.　　　[5] Harvey, ii.213–14.

[6] *Mand.* 1, quoted in IV.20.2, i.439–40. [7] *H.E.* V.viii.2. [8] Harvey, ii.213–14.

works claimed to be known to S. Irenaeus as Scripture.
However, too much weight should not be placed upon the
mere use of the word γραφή. As Werner has demonstrated,
Irenaeus is not consistent in his usage.[1] In the passage
relating the legend of the translation of the Septuagint by
the Seventy Elders at the request of Ptolemy we certainly
find what looks like a distinction between συγγράμμα as
profane and γραφή as sacred writing. Πτολεμαῖος ὁ Λάγου,
φιλοτιμούμενος τὴν ὑπ' αὐτοῦ κατεσκευασμένην βιβλιοθήκην ἐν
'Αλεξανδρείᾳ κοσμῆσαι τοῖς πάντων ἀνθρώπων συγγράμμασιν, ὅσα
γε σπουδαῖα ὑπῆρχεν, ἠτήσατο παρὰ τῶν Ἱεροσολυμιτῶν εἰς τὴν
Ἑλληνικὴν διάλεκτον σχεῖν αὐτῶν μεταβεβλημένας τὰς γραφάς.[2]
Also, the solemn ἡ γραφή λέγει introduces canonical Scripture.
However, S. Irenaeus can speak of Gnostic γραφαί. Πρός δὲ
τούτοις ἀμύθητον πλῆθος ἀποκρύφων καὶ νόθων γραφῶν, ἃς αὐτοὶ
ἔπλασαν.[3] The Epistle of S. Clement to the Corinthians is also
scriptura. Hunc Patrem Domini nostri Jesu Christi ab ecclesiis
annuntiari, ex ipsa scriptura, qui velint discere possunt.[4] Indeed,
the same word can be applied to Irenaeus to his own work:
da omni legenti hanc scripturam, cognoscere te quia solus Deus
es.[5] These facts all serve much to reduce the significance of
the circumstance that a Pauline citation is on one occasion
explicitly called 'Scripture', γραφή. We read that the Gnostics
'addict themselves without fear to all those kinds of for-
bidden deeds of which the Scriptures assure us that "they
who do such things shall not inherit the Kingdom of God"'
(Galatians 5 21); περὶ ὧν αἱ γραφαὶ διαβεβαιοῦνται, τοὺς ποιοῦντας
αὐτὰ βασιλείαν Θεοῦ μὴ κληρονομήσειν.[6] In consequence, one is
left to decide from the usage of the word, rather than from
the mere use of the title, whether or no a particular book is
authoritative 'Scripture'. The circumstance that the tradition
of the Church, and in particular, of the Elders, can also be
quoted by S. Irenaeus as of plenary religious authority, must

---

[1] *Paulinismus*, pp. 36–7.   [2] III.**21**.2, Harvey, ii.111–13.
[3] I.**20**.1, Harvey, i.177.   [4] III.**3**.3, Harvey, ii.11.   [5] III.**6**.4, Harvey, ii.24.
[6] I.**6**.3, i.26; Harvey, i.55. The published English translation appears to
give another example in I.3.4, i.14. The word 'Scripture' is, however, here
supplied.

have served to dull the sharp distinction between canonical
and extra-canonical, so far as the writings of the Apostles
and of their disciples are concerned.

In short, while S. Irenaeus gives fuller information than
anyone before him of the use as an authority of distinctive
character of those New Testament books later regarded as
'Canonical', in the exact sense of the word, it savours of
anachronism to inquire whether he himself regarded this or
that Apostolic writing as 'Canonical Scripture'. In this
sense, at least, we may assent to Werner's proposition that
S. Irenaeus is a witness to the incipient canonization of the
Pauline Epistles, though not to the completion of the process.[1] However, one could not easily find any basis for a
distinction between the Epistles and the Gospels in this
matter, apart from the circumstance that Irenaeus sees fit to
enumerate Four Gospels, and to emphasize the essential
four-fold nature of the Evangelical Tradition. Unlike the
author of the *Muratorian Canon*, he does not attempt to give
an established number of Pauline Epistles, and a doctrinal
reason for that number. Thus one might say that in Irenaeus
the Four Gospels are a degree nearer to canonicity than are
the Epistles, though this does not affect the measure of
authority attributed to the two sections, or the use which
may be made of them. Both are an inspired authority, but
in the former case the Church is nearer to a consciously-held
dogmatic theory of the necessity of a certain defined list of
the writings in question.

Beuzart states that for S. Irenaeus the New Testament is
authoritative in itself, apart from the Old Testament, this
being a new stage.[2] This is correct, apart from a false contrast between the Old and the New Testaments. It would
never have occurred to Irenaeus, as it would to a modern
critical scholar, to estimate the position of the Apostolic
writings apart from the ancient Scriptures or, for that
matter, to contrast the words of Jesus with the words either
of the Prophets or of the Apostles. To him, all God-ordained

---

[1] *Paulinismus*, p. 46.   [2] *Essai*, p. 134.

authority is one. He is not in the habit of considering the possibility of one religious authority superseding or even contradicting another. Rather would one say that the Gospels are the natural climax and inevitable consequence of the Prophets, and belonging to one another they together form one authority. Our Lord Himself has indeed a supreme and unique place in the religion of S. Irenaeus, but this reflects what He did as Champion to conquer the spiritual foes of man, rather than what He taught as the climax of divine revelation. The doctrine of Christ was known before in the Prophets. What He brought new was Himself, who was prophesied.[1] We may feel that this position does not entirely do justice to our Lord's teaching. In the words of Jesus ethics and piety rise to a level of purity, consistency, clarity, and winning loveliness, which transcends all that had gone before. However, if Irenaeus errs he errs on the right side. Such doctrines as the Fatherhood of God and such pronouncements as the Golden Rule were not new to the world when Jesus spoke, though He spoke of them with a new emphasis. The really new thing in the Gospel is redeeming power divine, whereby man can live as if God were indeed his Father, and can receive spiritual strength to obey the Golden Rule. Thus we clearly see that for S. Irenaeus the New Testament writings have a spiritual authority which is all one with that of the venerable Hebrew Scriptures themselves, even though the former are not yet ancient enough to have attained to as definite a degree of canonicity.

Finally, we must take notice of Vernet's claim that these New Testament writings were already gathered together into a sacred collection.[2] The basis of this is a gradation of titles supposed to be found in certain passages: Law, Prophets, Gospels, Apostolic Writings. 'He it is whom the Law proclaims, whom the Prophets preach, whom Christ reveals, whom the Apostles hand down (*tradunt*) to us, and in whom the Church believes.'[3] The most that can be said is

---

[1] See pp. 238-9 *infra*.   [2] *Dictionnaire*, VII, col. 2417.
[3] II.**30**.9, i.239; see also I.**3**.6, i.15; II.**35**.4, i.256.

that S. Irenaeus would have found this manner of expression quite natural if he had had to hand an officially-recognized collection divided into these sections. This does not amount to proof, however. We cannot disprove Werner's statement that a collection of Pauline writings to be set alongside the Four Gospels was not known at this time.[1]

[1] *Paulinismus*, p. 28.

Chapter Four

ON THE EXEGESIS OF THE BIBLE

THE MANNER in which S. Irenaeus expounded the Bible and the justice he did to it are studies of the most far-reaching consequence for the understanding of a Christian Father who was so largely a Biblical theologian. It is unfortunate, therefore, that this aspect of his work has been so commonly dismissed in a perfunctory way with the rather obvious remark that he was an exponent of 'mystical' or 'allegoristic' exegesis. It remains to investigate this matter more carefully.

So numerous are his citations of Scripture that to examine in detail the use made by Irenaeus of every book of the Bible would be a vast task. The crucial points are, however, his evaluation of Old Testament prophecy and his relation to Pauline thought. Therefore the field of study may with advantage be narrowed by considering only the most important item of each category. Of all the prophetical books, Christian theology has used Isaiah more than any other. S. Irenaeus foreshadows this historic development, for this was his favourite Old Testament writing. Quotations from Isaiah will be found to be four times as numerous in proportion to the length of the book as from the Psalms and Jeremiah, which come next in order of frequent use. There is one citation for every five verses in the whole. In his use of Isaiah, if nowhere else, Irenaeus will show his ability to explore 'the dark wood of prophecy'.

S. IRENAEUS ON ISAIAH

We may first notice that S. Irenaeus did not show himself interested in the prophet as a man, or as an author. Only a scanty glance is given at the nature of the prophetic call. No

comment is made upon the literary style of the work. The
first element to receive a measure of attention is Isaiah's
conception of God.

In some eight passages Irenaeus cited the Book of Isaiah
as witness that God is an all-glorious and all-powerful
transcendent Being, the Creator and the Lord of all, great
nations being but His tools. All but one example come from
Deutero-Isaiah, where the theme of the majesty of God
receives perhaps its most sublime expression. Irenaeus here
shows himself inspired by his source. Isaiah 40₁₂, 'Who hath
measured the waters? . . . ' is quoted to prove that there is no
God superior to the One known to us.[1] In *Dem.* 45 the same
text is used to distinguish between the God of Creation and
the Logos: 'It was not He that came and stood in a very small
space, and spake with Abraham, but the Word of God.'[2]
Irenaeus interprets Isaiah 43₇, 'Every one that is called by
my name, and whom I have created for my glory,' to show
that God calls man not at all because his service is needed to
enhance His glory, but that the service may glorify man.[3]
Isaiah 45₇, 'I make peace, and create evil', speaks to Irenaeus
of God 'making peace and friendship with those who repent
and turn to Him . . . but preparing for the impenitent . . .
eternal fire and outer darkness'.[4] The use made of Isaiah 51₆
is particularly interesting. The Gnostics argued that the
Christian teaching that the Supreme Being was the Creator
was absurd, because He would undergo change when the
heavens which are His throne and the earth which is His
footstool should vanish away. In answer S. Irenaeus cites:
'and the earth shall wax old like a garment, and they that
dwell therein shall die in like manner. But my salvation
shall be for ever . . .'[5] The appeal from Hellenistic pantheism is made with perfect rightness to Hebrew transcendent-
alism. In marked contrast to this usage is the treatment
of Isaiah 55₈, 'for my thoughts are not your thoughts'. The
comment runs: 'For the Father of all is at a vast distance

---

[1] IV.**19**.2, i.437.   [2] cf. *Dem.* 45 on Isaiah 66₁.   [3] IV.**14**.1, i.417.
[4] IV.**40**.1, ii.49.   [5] IV.**3**.1, i.383.

from those affections and passions which operate among men. He is a simple uncompounded Being, without diverse members, and altogether like, and equal to Himself, since He is wholly understanding, and wholly spirit, and wholly thought, and wholly intelligence . . .'[1] The Latin is difficult, the Greek of this important passage being lost. *Multum enim distat omnium Pater ab his quae proveniunt hominibus affectionibus et passionibus: et simplex, et non compositus, et similimembrius,*[2] *et totus ipse sibimetipsi similis, et aequalis est, totus cum sit sensus, (νοῦς) et totus spiritus, et totus sensuabilitas, (νόησις) et totus ennoea . . .*[3] Here is a substantial departure from the original, for though the conception of the awful chasm which separates the Being of God from that of man is preserved, that conception is completely transported out of the Hebraic into the Hellenistic idiom. In general we may say that one inclines to the view that S. Irenaeus was not without some real grasp of the Hebrew conception of the Living God.

Upon the doctrine of the Sovereign God of the nations Isaiah built a Gospel and a practical policy. National safety and honour, he insisted, lay neither in alliance with the Gentiles nor in building the walls of Jerusalem. The nation was to live by faith in God. This theme provides a number of texts of which the Christian preacher can make ready use, but S. Irenaeus hardly shines here. The exposition of Isaiah 7₉ is most interesting, yet a little disappointing.[4] The text is read from the Septuagint: καὶ ἐὰν μὴ πιστεύσητε, οὐδὲ μὴ συνῆτε : 'But if ye believe not, neither shall ye understand.' The quotation is part of an argument which certainly displays the first two stages of faith, namely, conviction of the truth and committal of one's life to that truth, but which does not rise to the full idea of faith as personal trust in a

---

[1] II.13.3, i.155.

[2] In Grabe's view this word is used in an attempt to express ὁμοιομερής. In this case Irenaeus would be using the term coined by Anaxagoras to express the identity of the molecules, of which any substance was formed, with the substance itself. Feuardentius would regard it as the translation of an unknown compound, ὁμοιόκωλος, which would give the same meaning.

[3] Harvey, i.282.   [4] *Dem.* 3.

God of power and love.[1] Thus so far as this particular piece of exegesis is concerned Irenaeus falls short of the faith of which the prophet spoke to King Ahaz. However, as a counterpart to this is the evidence of the exposition of the post-exilic text Isaiah 35₃₋₄ (LXX): 'Be ye strengthened, ye hands that hang down: . . . behold, our God has given judgement with retribution. . . . He will come Himself, and save us.' S. Irenaeus is surely right in his comment: 'Here we see that not by ourselves, but by the help of God, we must be saved.'[2] It is noteworthy that Irenaeus has just given a clear witness to the fact that, owing to human infirmity, man's salvation is to be by the grace of God, on the basis of Romans 7₁₈, ₂₄. 'In me . . . dwelleth no good thing. . . . Who shall deliver me out of the body of this death?' Here is a token that when he speaks of faith, on the basis of the prophets, S. Irenaeus can rise to an adequate conception of saving faith.

The next element to be considered in this composite prophetic book is the prophet's zeal for righteousness. This strain makes a certain appeal to Irenaeus. Several times he turns to Isaiah when he is casting about for telling words of exhortation or rebuke. In connexion with several texts he strikes the genuine prophetic ethical note: God is righteous; sin is awful in its guilt, ruinous in its consequences; repentance is therefore demanded, and is possible. An example of this usage may be given: 'And those who do not believe, and do not obey His will, are sons and angels of the devil . . . And that such is the case He has declared in Isaiah: "I have begotten and brought up children, but they have rebelled against me." . . . According to nature, then, they are children, because they have been so created; but with regard to their works, they are not His children.'[3] In enforcing the unity of the religion of the Old and of the New Covenants, S. Irenaeus seeks to show that Christ treated the genuine Mosaic commandments as of perpetual obligation. To this

[1] See pp. 240–2 *infra*.   [2] III.**20**.3, i.350.
[3] Isaiah 1₂,₁₀,₁₆, in IV.**41**.2, ii.51.

end Isaiah 29₁₃, 'this people honoureth me with their lips, but their heart is far from me, . . . teaching the commandments of men', is quoted with the explanation: 'he does not call the Law given by Moses commandments of men, but the traditions of the elders themselves, which they had invented.'[1] S. Irenaeus is at one with the prophet here, in asserting that true religion is essentially ethical, and in the proposition that Law is the eternal principle of true morality, the only proviso being that the Law must be authentic, God-given, and ethical. Springing from this idea of the perpetual obligation of true ethical commandments is the exposition of Christianity as the 'New Law'. We notice that Isaiah 2₃₋₄, 'for out of Zion shall go forth the law etc.,' is interpreted as a prophecy of 'the new covenant which brings back peace, and the law which gives life', *vivificatrix lex*.[2] This is certainly an applied meaning read into the text, yet also certainly true to the spirit of the original. The prophet was looking to the day when a reformed and truly ethical Judaism should become the universal religion. If Christianity be viewed as a religion of ethical Law, this expectation has been fulfilled in its spread.

The Book of Isaiah, particularly 'Deutero-Isaiah', is a missionary book. It might have been expected that this would have appealed to Irenaeus, for he was very much a missionary bishop himself. There is, however, but one missionary message cited with the prophet's missionary zeal in view, though several others are quoted in other connexions. The main interest of S. Irenaeus in Isaiah 49₅f. is indeed to draw from it the Christian doctrine of the Person of Christ, but the original intention of the text is not lost, for he does mention that Christ came for all, both Jew and Gentile. 'So then right fitly Christ says through David that He converses with the Father . . . as in other instances, so also after this manner by Isaiah: "And now thus saith the Lord, who formed me as His servant from the womb. . . . A great thing shall it be to thee to be called my servant, to

[1] IV.12.4, i.411.   [2] IV.34.4, ii.20; Harvey, ii.271.

stablish and confirm the tribe of Jacob: . . . and I have set
thee for a light of the Gentiles, that thou shouldst be for
salvation unto the end of the earth." Here, first of all, is seen
that the Son of God pre-existed, from the fact that the
Father spake with Him; . . . and that He is the Lord of all
men, and Saviour of them that believe on Him, both Jews
and others.'[1] Two of the main missionary outbursts of
Irenaeus are curiously centred round passages which in the
original refer not to the Gentiles, but to the Jews. 'And that
these promises the Calling from among the Gentiles should
inherit . . . Isaiah says thus: "These things saith the God of
Israel: In that day a man shall trust in his Maker: . . . and
they shall not trust in altars, nor in the work of their own
hands." '[2] We conclude, therefore, that the strong sense of
the Church's universal mission treasured by S. Irenaeus was
not vitally connected with his reading of Isaiah.

Another great prophetic theme was the coming restoration of Israel. Many texts with this reference were used by
Irenaeus, but always with a secondary Christian application.
In some cases the prophecy was regarded as already fulfilled
in the coming of Christ or of the Holy Spirit, or in the
historic Church as the New Israel.[3] In others the prophecy
was read as of the future Advent and the Millennial Kingdom.[4]

The last element of importance in the Book of Isaiah is
'Trito-Isaiah's' emphasis on correct religious observance.
One might have expected that this would have appealed to

---

[1] *Dem.* 50,51.

[2] Isaiah 17₇₋₈ in *Dem.* 91; see also Isaiah 54₁ in *Dem.* 94.

[3] The chief examples are: Isaiah 9₆ in III.**19.**2, i.346; 11₁₋₄ in III.**9.**3,
i.280; 11₂ₐ in III.**17.**1, i.334; 11₂ᵦ in III.**17.**3, i.336; 11₂₋₃ₐ in *Dem.* 9; 11₁₋₁₀ in
Dem. 59; 26₁₉ in IV.**33.**11, ii.14, and in *Dem.* 67; 43₁₉₋₂₁ in IV.**33.**14, ii.17,
and in *Dem.* 89; 45₁ (LXX) in *Dem.* 49; 49₅₋₆ in *Dem.* 50; 50₅₋₆ in *Dem.* 34
and 68, and in IV.**33.**12, ii.15; 50₈₋₉ in *Dem.* 88; 52₁₃₋53₈ in many places;
and 60₁₇ᵦ (LXX) in IV.**26.**5, i.464.

[4] 13₉ in V.**35.**1, ii.151; 25₈ (LXX) in V.**12.**1, ii.83; 26₁₉ in V.**15.**1, ii.95, and
in V.**34.**1, ii.148; 30₂₅₋₆ in V.**34.**2, ii.148-9; 32₁ in V.**34.**4, ii.150; 54₁₁₋₁₄ in
V.**34.**4, ii.150-1; 65₁₇₋₁₈ in V.**35.**2, ii.154; 65₁₈₋₂₂ in V.**34.**4, ii.151; and 66₂₂ in
V.**36.**1, ii.156.

an eminent advocate of episcopal discipline. This is not so, however. The only text of this type used is cited as part of an argument that he who has righteousness written on the heart has no need of external commandments. 'Wherefore also we need not the Law as a tutor. . . . And there will be no command to remain idle for one day of rest, to him who perpetually keeps sabbath, that is to say, who in the temple of God, which is man's body, does service to God, and in every hour works righteousness. "For I desire mercy", He saith, "and not sacrifice; and the knowledge of God more than burnt offerings" (Hosea 6₆). "But the wicked that sacrificeth to me a calf is as if he should kill a dog; and that offereth fine flour, as though he offered swine's blood." '¹ By this exegesis S. Irenaeus goes far toward reversing the writer's original intention.

There yet remains a consideration of the main interest which drew the attention of Irenaeus to Isaiah, as to the other prophets. He saw the book as a mysterious oracle, to which one could turn to provide divine sanction for what one had to say. This attitude is not the scientific and historical, which approaches an ancient author with the question: 'How may I understand what this writer has to say?' It is the polemic attitude which argues: 'Here is a venerable book of acknowledged authority. How may I best use it to establish my position?' It is not that there is anything wilfully unscientific or unhistorical in so arguing. This attitude was so much part of the traditional mental background of S. Irenaeus that he was quite clearly unconscious that he was so arguing, and was of the opinion that all he was able to find in Isaiah came straight from the Prophet himself. This usage presupposes, and is indeed one aspect of, that tradition of subjective or allegorical exegesis which is so important an element in the work of Irenaeus.²

The citations already investigated are those which display a measure of appreciation for the historic message of the Prophet. These are the cases where the allegorical

---

¹ Isaiah 66₃ in *Dem.* 96.   ² See pp. 82–5 *infra.*

exegesis is more or less in the background. It is, however, much otherwise with the great bulk of the quotations from Isaiah. Constantly one finds the severing of texts from contexts, and the artificial union of such severed texts. With this goes the seeking of 'types', and the extraction of meanings from the accidents of composition. It goes without saying that results are frequently produced fantastically removed from the intention of the original. There is little to be gained by making a collection of extreme examples, and a single one will stand for very many. 'They shall beat their swords into ploughshares, and their spears into pruninghooks' is rendered as follows: the plough and the pruninghook represent 'the creation exhibited in Adam', while the plough shows the salvation of the world: 'for this reason, since He joined the beginning to the end, and is Lord of both (i.e. the Adamic creation and the fruit of the Gospel), He has finally been displayed in the plough, in that the wood has been joined on to the iron, and has thus cleansed His land; because the Word, having been firmly united to flesh, and in its mechanism fixed with pins, has reclaimed the savage earth'; *quoniam firmum Verbum adunitum carni, et habitu taleis*[1] *confixus emundavit sylvestrem terram.*[2]

We may rather turn to some happier and less astonishing results. 'For out of Zion shall go forth the Law' refers to the fact that the Apostles were to start the preaching of the New Law in the land of Judea.[3] There is real insight in forcing a connexion between the prophet's 'they shall beat their swords into ploughshares' and the Lord's command to turn the other cheek.[4] There is also a quaint but profound comment on Isaiah 10₂₃ (LXX), Λόγον συντελῶν καὶ συντέμνων ἐν δικαιοσύνῃ, ὅτι λόγον συντετμημένον Κύριος ποιήσει ἐν τῇ οἰκουμένῃ ὅλῃ, which is rendered: 'A word brief and short in righteousness: for a short word will God make in the whole

---

[1] Harvey restores this word for '*talis*'; see an interesting foot-note to this passage.

[2] Isaiah 2₄ in IV.**34**.4, ii.21, Harvey, ii.272.   [3] Isaiah 2₃ in *Dem.* 86.

[4] Isaiah 2₄ in IV.**34**.4, ii.21.

world.' This indicates that men are to be saved 'not by the much speaking of the law, but by the brevity of faith and love'.[1] Again, upon 'Behold I make new (things) which shall now spring up. . . . And I will make in the wilderness a way, and in the waterless place streams:' we have the following: the promise of a 'new thing' is a prophecy that Christ will not call all men back to the legislation of Moses, but will bring a new Covenant of faith. The 'wilderness' and the 'desert' are the Gentiles, 'for the Word had not passed through them'; the 'streams' are the Holy Spirit, who is to be poured out over the earth by the Logos.[2]

So also the second 'Servant Song' provided the details of a doctrine of the Person of Christ. That the Father spoke indicates that the Son was pre-existent. That the Lord 'formed Him from the womb' shows that He must become incarnate by a special action of God through the Holy Spirit. Furthermore, 'the Son of the Father' calls Himself 'Servant' on account of 'His subjection to the Father'.[3] As was but natural, the fourth 'Servant Song' was also given a most extended allegorical exegesis by S. Irenaeus. Quotations are very frequent, and in every case the reference is to Christ. It is important to notice that Irenaeus did not find here any notion of a Penal Substitution theory of the Atonement.[4] This is obviously no mere accident of omission, for he takes Isaiah 53s-6 so far as to assert that the tortures of Christ came upon Him by the will of the Father, and that this was for our salvation. Significantly he does not take the last step.[5] An interesting confirmation of this is that both citations of 'Surely He hath borne our griefs and carried our sorrows' are made to refer to our Lord's miracles of healing.[6] On three occasions Irenaeus finds a prophecy of the divine begetting of the Son in 'who shall declare His generation?' (Isaiah 53s, LXX.) The first is notable as an approach to the doctrine of eternal generation. 'But ye (Gnostics) pretend to

[1] *Dem.* 87.   [2] Isaiah 43₁₉ in *Dem.* 89.   [3] Isaiah 49s-6 in *Dem.* 50,51.
[4] See pp. 193–4 *infra.*   [5] *Dem.* 69.
[6] Isaiah 53₄ in IV.**33.11**, ii.14, and in *Dem.* 67.

set forth His generation from the Father, and ye transfer the production of the word of man which takes place by means of a tongue to the Word of God, and thus are righteously exposed by your own selves as knowing neither things human nor divine.' Actually God's Word is native to Him. *Deus autem totus exsistens Mens, et totus exsistens Logos* there is no separation between God and Original Mind.[1] The significance of this argument is that S. Irenaeus disowns as Gnostic emanationism the familiar Stoic distinction of λόγος ἐνδιάθετος and λόγος προφορικός. In the second case Irenaeus connects the phrase both with Christ's Godhead, as begotten of the Father, and with His manhood, as born of the Virgin.[2] Thirdly, 'This was said to warn us, lest on account of His enemies and the outrage of His sufferings we should despise Him as a mean and contemptible man. For He who endured all this has a generation which cannot be declared . . . for He who is His Father cannot be declared'.[3] It is of interest to notice that in *Dem.* 68 Irenaeus begins 'The Song of the Suffering Servant' at Isaiah 52₁₃, and continues straight through to the following chapter. This certainly shows a better sense for the construction of the text than that exhibited by those responsible for the unfortunate chapter-division familiar today.

Two passages of Isaiah are interpreted as prophecies of the Virgin Birth. On Isaiah 66₇, 'before she that travailed (gave birth . . .) she escaped and was delivered of a man child', the comment runs: 'Thus He showed that His birth from the Virgin was unforeseen and unexpected.'[4] There is also the inevitable use of Isaiah 7₁₄₋₁₆ in a number of passages, of which the chief may be noted. 'The Lord Himself shall give you a sign' refers to 'a sign . . . which man did not ask for, because he never expected that a virgin could conceive'.[5] In antithesis to the views of modern scholarship is: 'For what great thing or what sign should have been in this, that a young woman conceiving by a man should bring

---

[1] II.**28**.5, i.224; Harvey, i.354.   [2] III.**19**.2, i.345.   [3] *Dem.* 70.
[4] *Dem.* 54.   [5] III.**19**.3, i.346.

forth—a thing that happens to all women that produce off-spring.'[1] There are two signs of Christ's divinity, the name Immanuel,[2] and the Septuagint rendering of vv. 15b–16a: Διότι πρινὴ γνῶναι τὸ παιδίον ἀγαθὸν ἢ κακὸν, ἀπειθεῖ πονηρίᾳ, ἐκλέξασθαι τὸ ἀγαθόν: 'For before the child shall know good or evil, he refuses evil, to choose the good.'[3] Likewise appear two signs of Christ's real manhood: 'Butter and curds shall He eat', and the use of the phrase 'child' in verse 16a.[4]

There remain four notices of Isaiah 61 1, 'the Spirit of the Lord is upon me'. In the first S. Irenaeus is at pains to make it plain that the reference is to Christ's manhood, and not to His divine nature.[5] This appears to be an effort to avoid an Adoptionist reading. It is certainly noteworthy that this text is associated in the writer's mind with the baptism of Jesus. In another place the point is made that the Holy Spirit descended upon One who was the incarnate Son of God.[6] This is aimed against the Gnostic theory of the descent of the heavenly Christ upon the man Jesus. A third reference is of general application,[7] while for the fourth Irenaeus has a most interesting statement which serves as a kind of key to his appreciation of Scripture. The fact that Jesus was able to apply this ancient Scripture to Himself made faith easier for His hearers. In the same way, the circumstance that the Apostles had ancient prophecy which 'even prefigured our faith' to which to appeal, so worked that the world 'might easily accept the advent of Christ'.[8] This is a significant witness to the mentality of the age. Experience showed that the plea that ancient prophecies were literally fulfilled in the life of Christ served effectually to convince many that the Christian preaching was true. It was natural to attempt to make the most of this appeal. This was the incentive behind much working out of ingenious examples of 'prophecy ful-filled'. It was this that demanded the allegoristic exegesis. The argument was doubtless reciprocal and cumulative. That the prophets were able wonderfully to forecast

---

[1] III.21.6, i.356.   [2] *Dem*. 54.   [3,4] III.21.4, i.355.   [5] III.9.3, i.280.
[6] III.17.1, i.334.   [7] *Dem*. 53.   [8] IV.23.1, i.455-6.

events of future centuries proved the fact of their inspiration by an all-knowing God. The inspiration of Scripture having thus been confirmed, one could use Scripture as a mine of authoritative proof-texts to enforce the Church's contentions about Christ. This method of argument has had a most providential result in preserving the Old Testament for the Church. Beneath there is a deeper gain. The prophetic movement did indeed educate the People to which God could send His Son. S. Irenaeus spoke wisely when he said that 'posterity, possessing the fear of God', did 'easily accept the advent of Christ, having been instructed by the prophets'.[1]

In turning from the exegesis of the Old Testament to that of the New we find that the first Gospel is the favourite book. S. Irenaeus has one quotation for every three verses. Next in order of frequent use come Romans, 1 Corinthians, Galatians, and Ephesians, each with about two citations to nine verses. A long debate has raged regarding the question whether or no Irenaeus was faithful to the Pauline Gospel, and in particular, whether he had a competent understanding of the conception of saving faith. This is one of the most important issues affecting our estimate of him as a Biblical Christian. In seeking an example of New Testament exegesis it will therefore be as well to pass over the first Gospel in favour of the Epistle to the Romans, that weighty and considered letter of S. Paul.

Once again a survey may be made of the various theological elements which S. Irenaeus might have extracted from the Epistle. In the first place we find that one of the largest groups of quotations occurs in contexts where he is engaged in establishing the doctrine of God. In all but three of these cases S. Paul is used to overturn the Marcionite antithesis between the grudging God of bare legal justice of the Old Testament, and the generous Father of mercy of the New. This heresy was a perversion of the strong contrast Paul had made between the religion of Law and the religion

---

[1] IV.23.1, i.455–6.

of Grace. It is therefore natural that in countering the Marcionites Irenaeus should largely use those same portions of Scripture of which they had made such ill-use. In one place this polemic interest is made explicit. 'How beautiful are the feet of them that bring glad tidings of good things' is wrested to show that 'it was not merely one, but that there were very many who used to preach the truth'. This shows S. Paul himself disowning the Marcionite proposition that Paul alone had the genuine tradition.[1] Akin to this is the use made of Romans 4₃, 'Abraham believed God'. The witness of Paul, who was accepted by the Marcionites as an inspired Apostle, overthrows the doctrine of another God of the Old Testament, by speaking of the salvation of Abraham by faith in the true God.[2] Several other passages are quoted with the simple observation that they prove the unity of the God of the Old Testament with the God of the New.[3]

One or two interesting extensions of this theme remain to be noted. There is the citation of Romans 1₁₈: 'For the wrath of God shall be revealed', to dispose of Marcion's assertion that only the God of the Jews visited with Wrath, the Christian God visiting only with mercy.[4] This is legitimate exegesis, reproducing the sense of the original, in so far as S. Paul certainly taught that the Wrath was still at work in the world, even in the period when God had manifested His saving Grace. Furthermore, the heretic had fastened upon God's 'hardening the heart of Pharaoh' as evidence that that God was the reverse of good. The difficulty is curiously avoided by joining Romans 1₂₈: 'God gave them up to a reprobate mind', to the quotation of Isaiah 6₁₀: 'make the heart of this people gross', in Matthew 13₁₁₋₁₆, and also to 2 Thessalonians 2₁₁: 'God shall send them the working of error', with the comment: 'If, therefore, in the present time

---

[1] Romans 10₁₅ in III.**13**.1, i.314.

[2] IV.**8**.1, i.396.

[3] Romans 3₃₀ in III.**10**.2, i.283, and in V.**22**.1, ii.114-15; Romans 4₃ in IV.**5**.3, i.388; Romans 8₁₅ in III.**6**.1, i.269-70.

[4] IV.**27**.4, i.471.

also, God knowing the number of those who will not believe, since He foreknows all things, has given them over to unbelief, . . . leaving them in the darkness which they have chosen for themselves, what is there wonderful if He did also at that time give over to unbelief Pharaoh, who never would have believed?'[1] Thus the disharmony is resolved by a bold importation of the apparent difficulty of Exodus into Romans also. Hereby S. Irenaeus shows that he did not understand that Hebrew manner of thought which had no room for the conception of indirect divine causation, as it comes to expression in Romans 1 28, Exodus 9 35, and the other passages referred to.

At the close of the section, Romans 9–11, there is a passage whence Irenaeus draws a doctrine of God much more in accordance with S. Paul's intention. He commands our confidence as an exegete in picking upon Romans 11 32, 'For God hath concluded all in unbelief that He may have mercy on all' as the occasion for a statement that the purpose of God in showing mercy is that man might love Him the more.[2] Paul himself would surely have answered in this spirit had he been questioned concerning these chapters, which have proved so great a stumbling-block to many. Romans 11 33 is also most appropriately used as the climax of all the deep mysteries of the Faith, which the Church alone understands: 'Oh! the depth of the riches both of the wisdom and knowledge of God'.[3] The rhetoric of Romans 11 34, 'For who hath known the mind of the Lord?', draws the response that 'no other being had the power of revealing to us the things of the Father, except His own proper Word'.[4] God is in fact the transcendent One, who is to be known through the Son. The conception of divine transcendence is most properly derived from the utterance of the Apostle when his mind flies back from soaring speculation upon the secret purposes of God to the simple numinous approach of religious worship. In conclusion we may observe that, so far

---

[1] IV.29.1–2, i.475.   [2] III.20.2, i.348–9.   [3] I.10.3, i.45.
[4] V.1.1, ii.55.

as the doctrine of God is concerned, S. Irenaeus made worthy use of the Epistle to the Romans.

A further considerable group of citations deals with the doctrine of the world and of man, and of the origin of evil. Romans 13₁-₇, with its exhortation of loyalty to the Imperial Government, was manifestly a favourite passage with Irenaeus. This is for an interesting reason. If 'the powers that be are ordained of God' the implication is that this world does not belong to the devil. Thus a useful proof-text is provided to give answer to the dualism of the Gnostic.[1] It is further observed that this text is not to be explained away as referring to the angelical rulers, for taxes are to be paid to them.[2] In another place Romans 13₁-₆ comes in for an involved exposition.[3] The forces referred to are identified by Irenaeus with 'the armies' sent out in retribution in the Parable of the Marriage Feast. Thus 'the King' is symbolical of God, but 'the armies' literal, being those of Rome. These Roman armies are of God, 'because all men are the property of God'. S. Irenaeus is of course far from S. Paul's sense here, but his exegesis is legitimate to a certain extent. The patriotic Apostle is by anticipation repudiating the later apocalyptical identification of the Roman Empire with the Antichrist. Irenaeus is on not dissimilar ground in his assertion that the civil order of this world is not the domain of the devil.

Other texts in Romans deal with the nature of man as a moral agent. Romans 2₄-₅,₁₀: 'Or despisest thou the riches of his goodness . . . not knowing that the goodness of God leadeth thee to repentance?' is incorporated in an argument that men are morally responsible, seeing that they are possessed of a free will.[4] This application is justified in so far as S. Paul's chapter assumes moral responsibility, but one is disappointed that S. Irenaeus passes over the deepest truth here present, namely, that God's forbearance is aimed at winning man to penitence. He proceeds with a deduction

---

[1] Romans 13₁ in V.24.3, ii.120.   [2] Romans 13₁,₄,₆, in V.24.1, ii.119.
[3] IV.36.6, ii.33–4.   [4] IV.37.1, ii.37.

that reflects the optimistic view that man's power of moral
choice remains substantially intact. 'Those who do it [good]
not shall receive the just judgement of God, because they
did not work good when they had it in their power so to do.'
Romans 3₂₃ is given an interesting treatment in a passage
dealing with the sins recounted of Old Testament worthies.[1]
The Christian should not be puffed up with pride, and lay
undue blame upon sins committed in less happy ages,
before the coming of Christ, 'for "all men come short of the
glory of God", and are not justified of themselves, but by the
advent of the Lord'. There is, however, another side. The sins
af the Patriarchs 'have been committed to writing that we
might know, in the first place, that our God and theirs is one,
and that sins do not please Him although committed by men
of renown'. This is surely Pauline ground. S. Paul is arguing
that, 'as there is no distinction' between the more and the
less favoured parts of the human race, for none can keep
himself from sin, so there is no room for recrimination and
odious comparison. S. Irenaeus is on similar ground in
teaching that evil deeds of old time were indeed wrong, but
are not to be judged by full Christian standards.

Another legitimate use made of Romans is in countering
dualist Gnostic heresy, even though anti-dualist polemic
forms no part of S. Paul's direct purpose in this Epistle. For
example, to avoid the Gnostic reading of 'flesh and blood
cannot inherit the Kingdom of God', and to prove the salvation of the body as well as of the soul, S. Irenaeus refers to
'Let not sin therefore reign in your mortal body', with the
remark: 'It has not been declared that flesh and blood, in the
literal meaning of the terms, cannot inherit the Kingdom of
God; but [these words apply] to those carnal deeds already
mentioned.[2] This is apt, in that Paul is attacking Antinomianism, which is a dualism of practical life, while
Irenaeus adapts his words to oppose a system of speculative
dualism. It is worthy of note that in general an exact
understanding is displayed of the Pauline term 'the

---

[1] IV.27.2, i.468.   [2] On Romans 6₁₂₋₁₃ in V.14.4, ii.94.

flesh',[1,2] though S. Irenaeus does not notice the special usage in the text in question.

Under the heading of the doctrine of the Person of Christ there are also a number of citations. All save one of these are in passages where S. Irenaeus is rebutting the Gnostic distinction between Jesus and the Christ. As S. Paul does not treat of this subject the exegesis is in each case a drawing out of implications. The short Christological introduction to Romans comes in for two notices. Romans 1₁-₄, 'Who was born of the seed of David according to the flesh, who was declared to be the Son of God with power', is quoted to prove that the One who was born was the Son of God made man, and not merely the man Jesus.[3] Romans 1₃-₄ is likewise cited in another place as evidence that Christ assumed actual flesh of the Virgin.[4] Romans 5₆,₈-₁₀ proves 'that the same being who was laid hold of, and underwent suffering, and shed His blood for us, was both Christ and the Son of God, who did rise again, and was taken up to heaven'. The Apostle knew nothing of the Gnostic Christ 'who flew away from Jesus'.[5] One would have been more satisfied had Irenaeus made some recognition of the circumstance that the text in question is essentially a noble utterance on the love of the redeeming God. However, this content is not altogether lost, for the true antithesis to the utterly remote and unknown Supreme Being of the Gnostic systems is the God who loves, and who will therefore suffer. There are other passages cited as evidence for the unity of Christ, but the theme of the original is largely lost.[6]

There remains the place where mention is made of Romans 5₁₄. 'Hence also was Adam himself termed by Paul "the figure of Him that was to come" . . . God having predestined that the first man should be of an animal nature, with this view, that he might be saved by the spiritual one.

---

[1] See also on Romans 8₈-₁₁ in V.**8.1**, ii.73, and in V.**10.2**, ii.80.

[2] See also pp. 231–2 *infra*.   [3] III.**16.3**, i.325–6.

[4] III.**22.1**, i.359–60.   [5] III.**16.9**, i.333.

[6] Romans 6₃-₄,₉, in III.**16.9**, i.332–3; Romans 8₃₄ in III.**16.9**, i.333; Romans 9₅ in III.**16.3**, i.326.

For inasmuch as He had a pre-existence as a saving being, it was necessary that that which might be saved should also be called into existence, in order that the being who saves should not exist in vain.'[1] This is a speculation quite foreign to S. Paul, but the idea underlying it, that the dispensation of salvation through Christ is not a mere contingency, but a part of God's eternal purpose, is certainly one that is presupposed by what Paul says in this text.

Relating to the doctrine of Christ as derived from S. Paul, there is at first sight some force in Werner's objection that S. Irenaeus makes a strikingly external use of the text.[2] For example, upon Romans 14$_{14-15}$ the comment runs: 'And everywhere when [referring to] the passion of Our Lord, and to His human nature and His subjection to death, he employs the name of Christ, as in that passage: "Destroy not him with thy meat for whom Christ died".'[3] It is obvious that it is by way of an accident that the word 'Christ' is here used, for the Apostle could as well have written 'for whom Jesus died'. On the surface, therefore, this is a typical example of unsound exposition, for a distinction is read into the text where none is. In answer it may be claimed that the circumstance that this usage can be accidental is itself not without significance. Had S. Paul known anything of a Gnostic distinction between Jesus and the Christ he would certainly not have written as he did, for the Gnostic doctrine is definitely precluded by his system. Had he been faced with Gnostic error S. Paul would surely have made it plain that the use of the word 'Christ' for the suffering One was no mere accident of composition. The text in question does speak of the suffering of a divine Being, so S. Irenaeus is not without some justification in his exegesis. Werner clearly errs by overstatement.

Most of the quotations from Romans are accounted for when these three foundation doctrines of speculative theology have been dealt with. However, S. Irenaeus takes up various elements in the evangelical message of the Epistle.

---

[1] III.22.3, i.360.   [2] *Paulinismus*, p. 87.   [3] III.18.3, i.339.

First among these is the doctrine of the universal moral impotence of humanity, apart from the grace of God. Irenaeus does not show a very positive appreciation of this. Against the Gnostics he had to be very firm that moral failure in man is a matter of wrong personal choice, and not merely of inherent constitution. He is so dominated by this interest that his statements on free will sometimes sound almost Pelagian. Allowance must consequently be made for this. The assertion of some[1] that Irenaeus was a Pelagian is to be rejected. For example, Romans 2₄₋₅,₁₀, 'But dost thou despise the riches of His goodness?' etc. is thus expounded: 'God therefore has given us that which is good, as the apostle tells us in this epistle, and they who work it shall receive glory and honour, because they have done that which is good when they had it in their power not to do it; but those who do it not shall receive the just judgement of God, because they did not work good when they had it in their power so to do.'[2] At first sight the last phrase of this, taken out of the context, would certainly appear to give a non-Pauline exegesis. A more careful reading, however, gives at least some good ground for supposing that this is not so. The general intention of the chapter is to safeguard the freedom of the human will. The earlier part of this paragraph indicates that what is here called 'the good' is the grace of God. It is God's good-will, which is the antithesis of coercion. This is described as 'good counsel'. It must be confessed that this latter, taken alone, is quite inadequate as a definition of grace. However, in general Irenaeus rises well above this in his teaching regarding the saving grace of God.[3] Free will has been given 'so that those who had yielded obedience might justly possess that which is good, given indeed of God, but preserved by themselves'. That 'working of good' which is in man's power would therefore appear to be nothing other than a steadfast holding on to the grace of God. If this supposition be well founded S. Irenaeus rises above mere

---

[1] See pp. 223–5 *infra*.   [2] IV.37.1, ii.36–7.
[3] See pp. 228–9 *infra*.

moralism if anything more clearly than does S. Paul himself
in this particular chapter.

Irenaeus continues with a comment upon Romans 13₁₃,
'Let us walk honestly, as in the day', which here forms part
of a chain of ethical exhortations drawn from Pauline
sources. 'If then it were not in our power to do or not to do
these things, what reason had the apostle . . . to give us
counsel to do some things, and to abstain from others? But
because man is possessed of free will . . . advice is always
given to him to keep fast the good, which thing is done by
means of obedience to God.'[1] It may be agreed that one who
was unfailing in scrupulous care to safeguard the doctrine
of Grace might have expressed himself with some necessary
added proviso, but Irenaeus is not more at fault than this.
He has also the excuse that he wrote long before controversy
taught the Church the necessity of careful utterance. For all
his emphasis upon man's need of grace, S. Paul, like all
other prophets, does inevitably and rightly exhort to good
works. The deduction that moral responsibility is pre-
supposed is entirely legitimate, and the pre-supposition of a
real measure of free will is not far from this.

S. Paul gave the great historic witness to the futility of
religion based upon the hope of man earning forgiveness
and righteousness in the sight of God by his own efforts. It is
disappointing to find that S. Irenaeus made so little of this
vital element in Romans. Romans 10₃₋₄, 'For Christ is the
end of the law' is indeed noticed once, but is used in a sense
directly opposite to that probably intended by Paul.[2] At this
point, at least, Werner has raised an objection which may be
upheld in his efforts to demonstrate that the thought of
Irenaeus was un-Pauline.[3] S. Irenaeus is here arguing that
there is one God of the Old and of the New Covenant from
the fact that Christ condemned the traditions of men, when
they were contrary to the Law of Moses, and that He
established its main precepts. He asks: 'And how is Christ
the end of the law, if He is not also the final cause of it? For

left margin handwritten note: continued discussion on free will

---

[1] IV.37.4, ii.39.   [2] IV.12.4, i.411.   [3] *Paulinismus*, p. 101.

He who has brought in the end has Himself also wrought in the beginning.' From the context it appears that S. Paul's τέλος γὰρ νόμου Χριστός is rendered as: 'Christ is the culmination of the Law.'[1] This is very far from what must be assumed to be Paul's intention: 'Christ is the termination of Law (as a principle of religion).' That Christianity is identical with Judaism in that it is founded upon the principle of Justification by the works of the Law, differing only in that the Gospel is a correct and pure Law, is clearly an un-Pauline position. This is what would appear to be involved by the present exegesis of Irenaeus, and he is here in error. In venturing upon this unsound ground, drawn by zeal to establish the unity of the Old and New Covenants, S. Irenaeus has this excuse. He shows that he was led on by the authority of the Matthaean 'the Scribes and Pharisees sit in Moses' seat, etc.'.

The counterpart of man's impotence is the assurance of divine help. S. Paul taught that God would show His righteousness, that is, would come to vindicate the distressed cause of the right. This is His act of grace, a gift of helping power which man has done nothing to earn or deserve. S. Irenaeus thrice takes up this theme. Upon Romans 7 18, 'for I know that there dwelleth in my flesh no good thing', he comments: 'our salvation is not from us, but from God.' Owing to human infirmity man can do nothing to save himself. He must depend upon the grace of God in Jesus Christ.[2] The response to the outburst of Romans 7 24, 'Who shall deliver me from the body of this death?', likewise rings true to the spirit of S. Paul. 'Here we see, that not by ourselves, but by the help of God, must we be saved.'[3] To this is to be joined the comment on Romans 10 6-7,9: 'as it was also impossible that he could attain to salvation who had fallen under the power of sin,—the Son of God effected both these things,...descending from the Father, etc., upon whom [Paul] exhorting us unhesitatingly to believe, again says ...

---

[1] The Latin version runs: *finis enim Legis Christus;* Harvey, ii.179.
[2] III.20.3, i.349–50.   [3] III.20.3, i.350.

"If thou shalt believe in thine heart that God hath raised Him from the dead, thou shalt be saved".[1] Here is an evangelical note which goes far to counter-balance the tendency noticed above.

The 'righteousness of God' is also for S. Paul partly eschatological. The present triumph of the Saints over evil, through the power of God, is something which is to culminate in 'the Day of the Lord'. This note is not prominent in Romans, but the millenarian Irenaeus not unnaturally fixes upon such mention as is made of it. When speaking of the earthly millennial Kingdom he says of Romans 8₁₉₋₂₁: 'the creation itself also shall be delivered from the bondage of corruption' etc.: 'It is fitting, therefore, that the creation itself, being restored to its primeval condition, should without restraint be under the dominion of the righteous.'[2] S. Irenaeus has, however, not got the whole sense of this text. The transformation of the Creation is not merely the preparation of conditions under which the righteous may 'receive the reward of their suffering' in that same world in which they toiled. S. Paul has something deeper than this. His faith is that God's loving purpose extends to all His works, and that His redemptive activity will in the future work outward from mankind to every creature.

The consideration of statements about the saving work of Christ made as expositions of texts from Romans is a study of special interest and importance. It is at this point that the treatment given by S. Irenaeus is most nearly adequate to the thought of S. Paul. The latter part of Romans 5 comes in for ample notice. There is a passing allusion to Romans 5₁₄, 'death reigned from Adam to Moses, etc.', in the course of an argument, quite in accord with Pauline thought, that those who deny that Christ became man are 'holding out patronage to sin: for, by their showing, death has not been vanquished'.[3] Romans 5₁₉, 'through the one man's disobedience the many were made sinners', is twice quoted. It is asserted that it was necessary for Christ to become man,

---

[1] III.18.2, i.338.   [2] V.32.1, ii.141–2.   [3] III.18.7, i.343.

because man's bondage to sin had to be destroyed by a man for men.[1] In relation to the doctrine of Recapitulation it is also cited as one of several parallels between Adam and Christ.[2] Romans 5₂₀ appears on behalf of a belief in the salvation of Adam. Irenaeus identified Adam with the human race. He was the sheep that was lost. Therefore, 'if it has not been found, the whole human race is still held in a state of perdition'. Against the salvation of Adam, Tatian had quoted 'In Adam all die'. The answer is: 'But where sin abounded, grace did abound more exceedingly.'[3] A kindred reference is that upon Romans 1₁-₄: 'the Son of God being made Son of Man, that through Him we may receive the adoption.'[4]

In S. Paul's scheme this deliverance is appropriated by faith. S. Irenaeus once develops this idea in exposition of a text from this Epistle. Upon Romans 4₃, 'Abraham believed God', he writes: 'In like manner we also are justified by faith in God . . . not by the Law, but by faith, which is witnessed to in the Law.'[5] The best definition of this faith is contained in another comment on the same text. The faith of Abraham was 'the undoubting and unwavering certainty of his spirit', when confronted with the promise that his seed should be as the stars in number.[6] The idealized Abraham of Scripture tradition is a good example of a life lived by that which the Christian knows as saving faith. He responded to the divine call by committing his whole life and future to God, in the steadfast conviction that despite all appearance to the contrary God was altogether sufficient. He was prepared to accept the offer of grace, and God's promises of good-will toward him, and to live as if they were valid. In a powerful chapter S. Irenaeus draws from Romans 4₃ an important part, though perhaps not the whole, of this conception of faith.[6] Werner goes too far in maintaining that Irenaeus had little conception of the faith of Abraham.[7] Certainly, 'to

---

[1] III.18.7, i.344.   [2] III.21.10, i.358.   [3] III.23.8, i.368.
[4] III.16.3, i.326.   [5] *Dem.* 35.   [6] *Dem.* 24.
[7] *Paulinismus*, p. 102.

believe in things future, as if they were already accomplished, because of the promise of God' is by itself inadequate as a definition of faith. However, it is not necessary, in the light of the above, to assume that S. Irenaeus by 'the faith of Abraham' meant nothing more than this, any more than it is to deduce from the same passage that the content of the Christian faith is exhausted in 'beholding the future kingdom'.[1]

Other references are less hopeful. Another note on Romans 4₃ savours of the idea of faith as no more than intellectual assent to a proposition.[2] This is clearer still in an exposition of Romans 4₁₂, 'who also walk in the steps of that faith of our father Abraham', where Irenaeus writes of 'Jesus . . . bringing us over from hard and fruitless cogitations, and establishing in us a faith like to Abraham'.[3] An allusion to Romans 3₃ is worthy of careful note. 'Yet the scepticism of men of this stamp shall not render the faithfulness of God of none effect.'[4] The 'scepticism' is that of those who 'oppose their own salvation, deeming it impossible for God, who raises up the dead, to have power to confer upon them eternal duration'. Such are sceptical because they do not receive the signs of God's power to preserve life, the tokens of which are the miraculous longevity of the Patriarchs, the translation of Elijah, and the preservation of Jonah. One would be inclined to infer that 'saving faith' is here built upon the foundation of acceptance of these stories. Furthermore, it is not without significance that in one of those passages where S. Irenaeus strikes a clear evangelical note he should fall back, rather inappropriately, upon Romans 10₆₋₉, 'If thou shalt confess with thy mouth the Lord Jesus, etc.', the one passage in Romans where faith at all approximates to 'acceptation of a proposition'.[5] In conclusion, the witness to the conception of saving faith in S. Paul's Epistle is of unequal adequacy. If this were characteristic of all that S. Irenaeus has to say upon this subject there

---

[1] On Galatians 3₅₋₉ in IV.**21**.1, i.451.   [2] IV.**5**.3, i.388.
[3] IV.**7**.2, i.395.   [4] V.**5**.2, ii.67.   [5] III.**18**.2, i.338.

would be some ground for the doubts that have been expressed under this head.

Another major theme of Romans is the nature of the Christian Church. This is represented as the legitimate spiritual successor of the Hebrew nation, the new and true Israel of God. Considering the importance of the idea of the Church in S. Irenaeus it is a little surprising that his treatment of the relevant texts is so inadequate. He follows S. Paul in his application of Hosea 2₂₃, 'I will call that my people which was not my people', to the call of the Gentiles into the Church, with the interesting difference that he is conscious that the words apply to himself, as a Gentile Christian. 'God . . . by His Son Jesus Christ has called *us* to the knowledge of Himself, from the worship of stones.'[1] He also follows Paul in the claim that the Christians are the true children of Abraham.[2] Two other passages are quoted against Marcion. Romans 3₂₁, 'the righteousness of God has been manifested, being witnessed by the Law and the prophets', is used to prove that the prophets made reference to the coming Christ.[3] Here only the secondary thought of the original is reproduced. Still less apposite is the use of Romans 11₂₆ to prove that the Father preached by Jesus was one with the God of the Old Testament. In arguing that the Law is good Irenaeus writes: 'And Paul likewise declares, "And so all Israel shall be saved" . . . Let them not therefore ascribe to the Law the unbelief of certain of them. For the Law never hindered them from believing in the Son of God; nay, but it even exhorted them so to do.'[4] This argument is not really sustained by the text, though it would be by the accompanying Galatians 3₂₄, 'the Law has been our tutor to bring us unto Christ'. There is, however, a certain propriety in resisting Marcion's effort to sever the Church from its Jewish root by an appeal to this text. The verse is the climax of S. Paul's protestation of affection for the Jewish people,

---

[1] Romans 9₂₅ in III.**9**.1, i.278.
[2] Romans 4₁₂ in IV.**7**.2, i.395.
[3] IV.**34**.2, ii.19.   [4] IV.**2**.7, i.382.

and of his certainty that they yet have a special part to play
in God's purposes.

Regarding the problems of Christian ethics, S. Irenaeus
seems to pass over one of the great arguments of this Epistle,
namely, that the sufficient foundation for all Christian
morality is love in the heart, worked by the gift of the Holy
Spirit. Ethical exhortations are, however, cited in warning
against spiritual and worldly pride,[1] and to show that
believers ought to obey the government.[2]

A final use of the Epistle to the Romans is one similar to
that observed to be dominant in the case of Isaiah. S. Irenaeus could regard it as a mysterious oracle of proof-texts.
The New Testament is not used in this way to anything like
the same extent as the Old. In most cases a quotation from
Romans is given a meaning with at least some approach to
the original. Irenaeus had therefore a much firmer grasp of
the real meaning of the Epistle than he had of the Prophecy.
The reason for this is not far to seek. In the case of S. Paul
he had some solid background of knowledge for his understanding of the writing, for it originally went out into a
world mentally similar to his own. In the case of the Prophets
no such knowledge was available at the time.

Of the nine texts from Romans rendered allegorically
there is only one example of a passage interpreted in disparate senses in different places. Romans 11 17b, from the
allegory of the Grafted Olive Tree, is on one occasion further
allegorized to refer to the salvation of the body. The wild
branch is the body; the grafting on to the good stock is the
joining to the Spirit of God.[3] However, in another place this
same text, united with Romans 11 21, is taken in the original
sense of S. Paul's allegory.[4] The lesson here drawn is that
the Christian must not be puffed up with pride when he
reads of the failings of Old Testament worthies. One of the
more interesting examples of a significance read into words
the form of which is a mere accident of style is the rendering

---

[1] Romans 12₁₆ in V.22.2, ii.115.   [2] Romans 13₁,₄,₆ in V.24.1, ii.119.
[3] V.10.1, ii.78.   [4] IV.27.2, i.468.

of Romans 10₁₅. 'And again, when Paul says, "How beautiful are the feet of those bringing glad tidings of good things and preaching the gospel of peace", he shows that it was not merely one, but that there were many who used to preach the truth.'[1] This disproves Marcion's thesis that S. Paul was the only true Apostle.

In summing up the value of the work of S. Irenaeus as an exegete, on the basis of the examples taken, tribute must first be paid to his powers. Irenaeus shows that he appreciated aright the vision of the transcendent God in Hebrew prophecy. He echoed the prophetic zeal for ethical religion and righteous conduct. The conviction that Israel must trust only in God for salvation received some notice, though only in a secondary and applied sense as referring to Christian salvation. Likewise, large justice is seen to have been done to the hope of the coming restoration of Israel, but only as applied to the glorified Church of the Millennial Kingdom. This represents a substantial measure of comprehension for the message of the prophets.

S. Irenaeus fared better with S. Paul. This is indeed a matter of the first importance. He found the Hebrew Living and Righteous God in Romans. This God is the Creator. His providence and His possession extend to this created world, and to the bodies as to the souls of men. Irenaeus, furthermore, was able to demonstrate his doctrine of the divine Son, who for love's sake became incarnate and suffered, as something firmly grounded upon S. Paul. To some extent, however, this aspect of the work is spoiled by the polemical interest of establishing the identity of Jesus with the Christ. A somewhat more optimistic view of human nature is perhaps taken than that characteristic of S. Paul, though Irenaeus was not a Pelagian. Justice was done to man's need of grace. Here again the exegesis suffers by an incautious attempt to demonstrate the identity of the divine Source of the religions of the Old and New

[1] III.13.1, i.314.

Covenants by means of the doctrine of the New Law.
The Apostle's eschatological hope was fully reproduced.
Upon the saving work of Christ the exposition is
satisfactory, though Irenaeus was not altogether clear-
sighted in drawing from the Epistle the conception of that
faith by which are appropriated the fruits of this saving
work. He did not fall back as much as might have been
expected upon Romans for the conception of the Church as
the New Israel. Hence it is not too much to claim that in
general S. Irenaeus was a fairly sound expositor of S. Paul.
Werner has given a detailed discussion of this exegesis, with
the damaging conclusion that the crucial passages of Paul
are either ignored or interpreted contrary to the writer's
intention, and that the Pauline Epistles are not used as a
source for thought, but as mere external props.[1] This is to be
rejected as a serious overstatement. Individual unfortunate
examples can certainly be produced, but this is very far
indeed from being the general rule.

We now pass to the consideration of the so-called
'allegorizing' or 'mystical' exegesis. In the proper sense
allegorism consists in making the characters or scenery of a
story 'stand for something'. A celebrated example occurs in
Galatians 4 21-31, where S. Paul makes the sons of Hagar and
of Sarah represent respectively the Jewish and Christian
communities. A distinctive activity along these lines is the
seeking of 'types of Christ', such as the Melchizedek of
Hebrews. Other exegetical practices are very naturally
associated with allegorism, by virtue of a common mental
background. Like allegorism these spring from the axiom
that Scripture is in every phrase and word an oracle packed
with open or hidden divine revelation. Such practices are:
seeking passages which may be construed as forecasts of the
future (i.e. 'prophecies'), now fulfilled; detaching phrases
from the context, and expounding them apart from the
determinative effect of that context upon the meaning; connecting such detached phrases one to another in continuous

[1] *Paulinismus*, p. 98.

narrative by the link of some common word or association, as, for example, the several texts mentioning 'a stone' in 1 Peter 2₅-₈; and the reading of a significance into the accidents of grammar or composition, as exemplified by the distinction found by S. Paul between 'seed' and 'seeds' in Galatians 3₁₆. When, in the present discussion, 'allegorism' is spoken of, we have in mind also these allied practices in general.

Schmidt makes a rather surprising statement when he ventures to assert that in general S. Irenaeus avoids allegorism, that when he uses it the exegesis is mostly typology, and that allegoristic passages are not for him determinative for faith.[1] This is manifestly incorrect, for all the practices enumerated above are constantly used. There is, however, a kernel of truth in this statement. It has been demonstrated that allegorical exegesis is much less prominent in the case of the New Testament, and this is also the part of the Bible which provides the passages most significant for distinctive Christian doctrine. There is, however, no definite separation in usage as suggested by Schmidt.

There is perhaps more truth in Harnack's statement that S. Irenaeus was the first to apply the mystical interpretation to the New Testament.[2] Harnack gives as his examples a case of exposition of the Parable of the Good Samaritan, where the victim is the human race, and the two pence the gift of the Spirit;[3] and also the explanation that Christ administered food to the disciples at the Last Supper in a recumbent posture 'indicating that those who were lying in the earth were they to whom He came to impart life'.[4] So also the sleep of the disciples in Gethsemane is a type of the sleep of mankind. We have also observed allegorical exegesis of Romans.[5] However, Harnack probably goes too far. That Irenaeus appears as the first who practised this method upon the New Testament is probably due to the circumstance that he is the first from whom we have inherited any

[1] *Kirche b.I.* p. 43. [2] *H.D.* II.252. [3] III.**17**.3, i.336.
[4] IV.**22**.1, i.454. [5] See pp. 80–1 *supra*.

considerable exposition of this part of Scripture. The quotations from the Gospels in S. Justin Martyr are almost purely descriptive. Allegoristic exegesis was a part of the heritage of the original Christians from Judaism, and had already been practised upon the sayings of Jesus in the composition of the Four Gospels.[1]

We cannot agree with Beuzart, who in zeal to find Scripture as the supreme proof of doctrine in S. Irenaeus maintains that allegorism is an inconsequential accident of the times.[2] Plainly, allegoristic exegesis is almost purely subjective. He who uses it can find in the Holy Book anything he already has in mind, so that every conceivable system of doctrine may be substantiated from Scripture. Past and present Christian history clearly shows this. The acid test of the unhistorical and unscientific nature of this method is that a given writer can be found to interpret one and the same text in opposite senses in different parts of his work. This will be found the case with Irenaeus, within the scope of his quotations of Isaiah alone. For example, Isaiah 11 6f., 'And the wolf shall dwell with the lamb', is in *Dem.* 61 given a spiritualized rendering, as referring to righteous men. This view is in 5.33.4 (ii.147) noticed as one held by some, but is politely disowned by Irenaeus as being beside the point. Furthermore, Isaiah 26 19 (LXX), 'the dead which are in the grave shall arise', is twice cited as referring to Christ's miracles of healing,[3] and twice as of the Millennial Resurrection.[4] Again, Isaiah 35 5-6, 'then the eyes of the blind shall be opened', can be read of these healing miracles,[5] yet in another place of the salvation of the soul.[6] An example from the Epistle to the Romans has been mentioned already.[7] As Vernet has to admit, S. Irenaeus is not a sure guide to the historic sense of the Old Testament.[8] An accident of the

critical of allegorism

---

[1] The interpretation of the Parable of the Sower, Mark 4 14-20, is probably later allegorism. Many passages in the Fourth Gospel are also probably of a similar nature.

[2] *Essai*, p. 31.   [3] IV.33.11, ii.14–15; *Dem.* 67.

[4] V.15.1, ii.95; V.34.1, ii.148.   [5] IV.33.11, ii.14; *Dem.* 67.

[6] III.20.3, i.350.   [7] See p. 80 *supra*.   [8] *Dictionnaire*, VII, col. 2422.

times this allegorism certainly is, but it is an accident of infinite consequence.

The more historical treatment of S. Paul's writings is a measure of greater knowledge and mental affinity. S. Irenaeus had some actual knowledge of Paul's life, and of its background. Above all, he lived in a community which still spoke the religious language of the Apostle. He therefore had no difficulty in 'making sense of' most parts of Paul's writings. With the old prophets it was quite otherwise. Irenaeus had not, and in his day could not have had, any adequate historical knowledge of the religious or social background of their lives, nor of the religious issues of their day. Neither had he such knowledge of Hebrew psychology or literary style as would allow the interpretation of one mode of expression into another. There was therefore chapter after chapter in the Old Testament which had no obvious religious sense, or which even contained that which was offensive to the piety of the Church. The more strongly it had to be maintained that every part of these writings was a plenary revelation from God the darker became the mystery. The only way to wrest crumbs of spiritual food from the sordid story of the incest of Lot's daughters, for example, was to turn the old legend into a parable of the Old and of the New Israel.[1] S. Irenaeus himself unconsciously confesses to the difficulty which was the mainspring of such exposition. To those who have not a knowledge that prophecy is fulfilled in Christ the Old Testament reads like a fable.[2] The mental process which is at work is perfectly exemplified by the instruction of a presbyter quoted by Irenaeus. The believer should not censure wicked actions recorded in Scripture without specific blame, but 'should search for a type. For not one of those things which have been set down in Scripture without being condemned is without significance.'[3] The Church therefore did as the Rabbis had done before when in the same position, and carried on the

---

[1] IV.31.1–2, ii.1–3.   [2] IV.26.1, i.461.
[3] IV.31.1, ii.1.

allegoristic tradition. At the expense of launching into subjectivity she put to silence the Gnostic scoffer.

In closing we may observe that at one point S. Irenaeus makes a slight approach to the conception of progressive revelation, which scientific doctrine is the true resolution of the difficulties referred to above. He teaches that God, on account of their hardness of heart and idolatry, subjected the Hebrew People to the whole Mosaic Law.[1] This hard discipline was, however, temporary, and is done away in Christ.[2] In appearance Irenaeus is not far from the Gnostics here. He agrees with them in separating in the Scriptures precepts which were fulfilled in Christ, and precepts which were abolished. The former are the fundamental rules of moral life, the 'natural precepts'.[3] The latter are the added ritual commandments of the Law. In one important respect, however, he rises above the heretical systems, which saw the inferior commandments as the work of an inferior god. The precepts of merely temporary validity were just as certainly an authentic revelation of the Supreme God as were the eternal and absolute. The temporariness and imperfection of some of the commandments of the Mosaic Law was the provision of the true God in pursuit of an eternal and unchanging purpose, yet by methods temporarily adapted to the frailty of mankind. S. Irenaeus had here grasped the essential principle of progressive revelation. When he allowed himself to be inspired by Christ's words about divorce,[4] rather than by theories about 'Scripture Types', he was well in advance of the Gnostics, both in religious insight and in historical appreciation of the Old Testament.

---

[1] IV.**15**.1–2, i.419–20; IV.**16**.3, i.423–4; IV.**16**.5, i.425; *Dem.* 8.

[2] III.**2**.2, i.260; III.**12**.14, i.313; IV.**15**.2, i.420; *Dem.* 35, 89, 95.

[3] IV.**13**.4, i.415; IV.**16**.5, i.425. For this phrase see also IV.**13**.1: *Et quia Dominus naturalia Legis, per quae homo iustificatur, quae etiam ante legisdationem custodiebant qui fide iustificabantur et placebant Deo, non dissolvit, sed extendit et implevit, ex sermonibus eius ostenditur.* Harvey, ii.180–1.

[4] IV.**15**.2, i.420–1.

Chapter Five

ON UNWRITTEN SCRIPTURE

ACCORDING to S. Irenaeus, the available authentic information from the Apostles regarding the life, teaching, and saving work of the Lord was not wholly written. There was also an oral tradition handed down by the Apostles and their successors. We may most accurately describe this tradition as the unwritten New Testament. It will be seen that in the system of Irenaeus it occupies a position of dogmatic value equivalent to that of the Epistles, save only that ink and paper is absent. The Apostolic Tradition may therefore most correctly be given the paradoxical title of 'Unwritten Scripture'.

We may first return to a passage already quoted. 'For how should it be if the apostles themselves had not left us writings? Would it not be necessary to follow the course of the tradition which they handed down to those to whom they did commit the Churches? To which course many nations of those barbarians who believe in Christ do assent, having salvation written in their hearts by the Spirit, without paper and ink, and carefully preserving the ancient tradition. . . . Those who, in the absence of written documents, have believed this faith, are barbarians, so far as regards our language; but as regards doctrine, manner, and tenor of life, they are, because of faith, very wise indeed.'[1] It is clear from this that the determinative factor for faith is simply the preaching of the Apostles, whether written or unwritten, and that New Testament Scripture is essentially this witness as preserved in writing. This is further borne out when S. Irenaeus discusses the authority of the written Four Gospels.[2] The argument is essentially an historical one. It does not proceed from any theory that would separate this

---

[1] III.4.1–2, i.264–5.   [2] III.1.1, i.258–9.

authority from its human origin, such as, that the Apostles went into a trance and uttered oracles 'straight from God', or that an angel brought a mysterious manuscript from heaven. Despite the assertion that the Holy Spirit in coming upon the Apostles endowed them with 'perfect knowledge',[1] the main weight of emphasis rests upon the fact that the Evangelists either had personal human contact with Jesus, or had intimate friends that had. This does not raise the contents of the Gospels to a higher level of authority than any other authentic information about the Lord. Such information is available from tradition.

The argument is also that of historical probability. In the first place, it is asserted that the inspiration of the Holy Spirit granted to the original Apostles the gift of 'perfect knowledge'. *Postea enim quam surrexit Dominus noster a mortuis, et induti sunt supervenientis Spiritus sancti virtutem ex alto, de omnibus adimpleti sunt, et habuerunt perfectam agnitio-nem.*[2] This step may be allowed. While the first Christians were certainly not infallible, they are the final authority for the facts about Jesus. If they are not to be trusted the Church knows nothing at all about Him for certain, and historical criticism indicates that they are to be trusted. One may therefore concur that 'if anyone does not agree to these truths, he despises the companions of the Lord; nay more, he despises Christ Himself the Lord'.[3] A second stage is legitimate: 'For if the Apostles had known hidden mysteries, which they were in the habit of imparting to "the perfect" apart and privily from the rest, they would have delivered them especially to those to whom they were also committing

---

[1] Doubtless based upon John 14₂₆ and 16₁₃.

[2] III.1.1, i.258; Harvey, ii.2. See also III.12.7, i.305. *Perfectam agnitionem* probably represents τέλειαν γνῶσιν. This may mean 'complete knowledge' rather than 'perfect knowledge'; i.e. 'complete' in the sense in which Article VI declares that 'Holy Scripture containeth all things necessary to salvation'.

[3] III.1.2, i.259. It is to be noted that S. Irenaeus slips in a fresh turn to the argument here. The 'perfect knowledge' is that of the facts concerning Christ. 'These truths' are, that there is one Creator God, and one Christ, His Son. The assumption is made that those who are authorities in the former sphere are thereby constituted authorities in the latter.

the Churches themselves'.[1] There is therefore no appeal to secret tradition. The third step is false. 'It is not necessary to seek among others the truth which it is easy to obtain from the Church, since the Apostles, like a rich man (depositing his money) in a bank, lodged in her hands most copiously all things pertaining to the truth.'[2] The analogy assumes that a learner of truth is in the same state of passive receptivity as the bearer of a cheque. A duly-accredited pupil has received the truth intact from his master as surely and inevitably as one who presents a good cheque receives good money. Truth cannot be handed on like this. No tutor can 'certify' his pupil on the ground that he has been properly taught, for learning depends also on the taught. The fourth step of argument is consequently vitiated. A complete list of bishops, showing a continuity of authorized teachers and pupils from Linus to Eleutherus, is not an absolute guarantee of the Church of Rome in the days of the latter. Irenaeus speaks of 'the presbyters . . . who . . . possess the succession from the Apostles; those who, together with the succession of the Episcopate, have received the certain gift of truth, according to the good pleasure of the Father'.[3] It is certainly the purpose of God for His Church that Christian office and Christian truth should thus go together, but the facts of history and of human life do not always and everywhere bear out the *'together with'*. Howbeit, the preaching of the truth cannot take place without human instruments, and does not exist apart from the prophetic community. Though due succession to office cannot in principle absolutely *guarantee* the tradition, it yet remains a cardinal fact of history that it is in the organized and visible Church, and not among well-meaning *individuals* elsewhere, that the truth has been preserved. With justice, therefore, can S. Irenaeus claim for the Church that: 'that

[handwritten marginal note: apostolic succession]

---

[1] III.3.1, i.261; see also II.22.5, i.201–2.   [2] III.4.1, i.264.
[3] IV.26.2, i.462; see also III.Pref., i.258; III.2.2, i.260; III.3.1, i.260; IV.26.5, i.464–5; IV.27.1, i.465; IV.33.8, ii.11; V.Pref., ii.54; V.20.2, ii.109; *Dem.* 98.

well-grounded system which tends to man's salvation . . .
we do preserve . . . as if it were some precious deposit in
an excellent vessel.'[1,2]

It is therefore impossible to accept without modification
Werner's thesis that what Irenaeus calls 'the apostolic' was
not built out of reminiscence of the Apostles, but out of the
doctrine of the Church.[3] Certainly the underlying reason for
the appeal to ecclesiastical authority was not historical, but
born of polemical necessity. However, in appealing to
apostolic tradition, S. Irenaeus clearly intended to base
himself upon the actual history of the Church, and not solely
upon a dogma. This intention is not vitiated by the circumstance that some of his historical reminiscence was in fact
inaccurate.

It must be confessed that this inaccuracy is apparent.
Nowhere is the work of Irenaeus more seriously at fault
than where he avowedly bases himself upon oral tradition to
establish facts about the life of our Lord, or of the activity of
His first Apostles. That this could be so even in the case of

---

[1] III.24.1, i.369.

[2] It would appear that Irenaeus did not *originate* the activity so closely
associated with his name, that is, the compilation of lists of Bishops as a mark
of the authenticity and authority of the Churches. Hegesippus was probably
the pioneer here. Eusebius reports him as writing γενόμενος δὲ ἐν Ῥώμῃ
διαδοχὴν ἐποιησάμην μέχρις Ἀνικήτου (*H.E.* IV.xxii.3). The interpretation
of this obscure sentence has been much disputed, but the opinion of
many scholars, including Lightfoot, is that the only possible rendering is :
'Being in Rome, I composed a catalogue of bishops down to Anicetus,'
despite the circumstance that '*catalogue*' is not the accepted meaning of
διαδοχή, and that the catalogue in question is not reproduced by Eusebius,
as one would expect. However, this interpretation is in accord with the sense
of the context. Eusebius has just stated of Hegesippus that 'on a journey to
Rome he met a great many bishops, and that he received the same doctrine
from all'. Corinth, of which Hegesippus says, 'we were mutually refreshed
in the true doctrine,' is then mentioned ; 'and the church of Corinth continued in the true faith until Primus was bishop in Corinth.' Hegesippus was
evidently seeking to verify the orthodox tradition by the method of inquiring
after the bona fides and unanimity of the Bishops. It is hardly to be disputed,
however, that to Irenaeus belongs the credit of taking the matter the decisive
further stage. He made the Church fully conscious of the far-reaching
theological and ecclesiastical consequences of this appeal to 'lists of Bishops'.

[3] *Paulinismus*, p. 23.

one so relatively near in time to the first days of the Church
is a standing warning to any who would lay undue store upon
the unwritten tradition of the Church as a source of authentic
information.

One such judgement that has been seriously challenged
by historical investigation is the statement by S. Irenaeus
that the First and Fourth Gospels were written by members
of the Twelve.[1] Much more remarkable is the opinion
recorded that Jesus attained to the age of fifty years. This
piece of 'tradition' self-evidently owes its place in the
teaching of the circle to which Irenaeus belonged to a stupid
misunderstanding of John 8:57: 'Thou art not yet fifty years
old.' He can yet claim that the information came from the
disciples of S. John in Asia.[2] This is indeed an unhappy
example for Battifol to have chosen as illustrative of the
unwritten heritage of the Apostles witnessed to by the
Elders.[3] So also the quaint and celebrated picture of
millenarian fertility is given an impossible attribution to our
Lord on the authority both of the word of the Elders who
saw John, and of the writings of Papias.[4] We cannot agree
that 'these things are credible to believers', but prefer the
judgement of Eusebius, that Papias 'appears to have been of
very limited understanding, as one can see from his discourses'.[5]

As the Canon and interpretation of the written tradition
is to be determined by authority, so also is the unwritten.
The Gnostics asserted that they alone possessed the true
tradition.[6] Once granted that there was such a thing as
unwritten information to which valid appeal could be made,
the only answer to the heretic was the plain assertion that
true oral tradition was the exclusive possession of the Church,
just as was the written tradition. This was seconded by the
assertion that, as the Church was alone competent to expound the Scripture, so also she alone could determine the

[1] III.1.1, i.258–9. [2] II.22.5, i.201. [3] *L'Église*, p. 243.
[4] V.33.3–4, ii.145–6. Cited on p. 283 *infra*.
[5] *H.E.* III.xxxix.13. [6] I.8.1, i.31; III.2.1–2, i.259–60.

meaning of that which was not written. As with the Bible, these assertions were backed by the sanctions of solidarity. The lists of Bishops were produced in vindication of the claim that present Church leaders were the recognized heirs to the Apostles. It was maintained that all, in every place, agreed with one another.

It was the teaching of S. Irenaeus that the witness to tradition is collective, and, indeed, by inherent nature universal. It is not individual, for individualism is the mark of heresy. According to Irenaeus the erroneous subjectivity of Gnostic allegoristic exegesis is sufficiently shown by the variety of their opinions, in which they resemble the Schools of pagan philosophy. Hence the voice of the Church is always for practical purposes regarded as the voice of her official and recognized leaders. Vernet[1] is essentially right in dismissing as alien to the intention of Irenaeus Beuzart's portrait of the free spiritual man, not of necessity in office, as a sovereign spiritual judge, on the basis of IV.33.1–7, ii.6–10.[2] These things may be so in theory, but in practice the appeal is always to the bishops, as the passage in question shows in the succeeding paragraphs. As Beuzart has to agree, the spiritual equality of all the faithful is overlaid by the division of the Church into clergy and laity.

There remains for examination the claim of Vernet that S. Irenaeus did not invent the appeal to tradition, but only defined as apostolic that which he found in current and original usage.[3] We may agree to this extent, that the appeal to tradition in defining the uncertain meaning of Scripture was a part of Judaism, and hence original in the Church. Further, it was inevitable that this appeal should continue to be made so long as the embarrassments of controversy made it necessary. However, the work of Irenaeus certainly represents an element of development as well as of definition. It cannot be denied that in these times the Church attained to a heightened consciousness that she had a unique

---

[1] *Dictionnaire*, VII, col. 2429.   [2] *Essai*, p. 158.
[3] *Dictionnaire*, VII, col. 2424.

Christian tradition to which to appeal. The reason for this was two-fold. There was the increased controversial pressure of the times, and furthermore, the Church was beginning to arrive at an age when the passage of time was providing a gallery of ancestral portraits to be venerated. The course of years had sufficed to lift the first great Apostles above the tide of controversy and the memory of personal idiosyncrasy. Harnack is correct in stating that the work of Irenaeus and Tertullian was to justify theoretically what had already been done.[1] However, that the current usage could be justified in this way was itself the mark of a momentous step.

[1] *H.D.* II.26.

Chapter Six

ON THE RECOURSE TO ECCLESIASTICAL AUTHORITY

AT HEART S. Irenaeus was aware of the subjective nature of allegoristic exegesis. It distressed him to behold the manner in which his Gnostic opponents, who shared with him these methods, could substantiate their heresies from the Bible. In consequence there comes naturally enough from his pen one of the classic exposures of un-scientific 'Scripture-proofs'. 'Their manner of acting is just as if one, when a beautiful image of a king has been con-structed by some skilful artist out of precious jewels, ... should rearrange the gems, and so fit them together as to make them into the form of a dog or of a fox, and even that but poorly executed; ... and by thus exhibiting the jewels, should deceive the ignorant who had no conception what a king's form was like, and persuade them that that miserable likeness of the fox was, in fact, the beautiful image of the king.'[1]

Perhaps S. Irenaeus had forgotten these admirable senti-ments when he later came to write: 'I came to the prophetess, and she bare a son, and His name is called Wonderful, Counsellor, the Mighty God.'[2] A powerful, ingenious, and completely convincing chapter is furthermore devoted to the folly of Gnostic arguments derived from 'mystic numbers' in Scripture.[3] 'For this is an uncertain mode of proceeding ... because every sort of hypothesis may at the present day be, in like manner, devised by anyone.'[4] How-ever, the three (!) spies entertained by Rahab in Jericho are a type of the Trinity.[5]

In this confusion may be seen the pressing need for an

---

[1] I.8.1, i.32; cf. also the amusing medley of Homeric lines in I.9.4, i.40-1.
[2] Isaiah 8₃ and 9₆ in IV.33.11, ii.14.　　[3] II.24.1-6, i.204-12.
[4] II.25.1, i.213.　　[5] IV.20.12, i.450.

94

authority which could be brought to bear upon the interpretation of the Bible. Historical ignorance forced the Catholic Christian into the same fast-and-loose game as the heretic, well aware though he was of the perils of religious subjectivity. If the resultant controversial frustration was to be avoided there had to be provided a set of rules for the game. Here was the motive behind the retreat to the authority of the Church. The Church roundly asserted that certain historical and certain allegorical interpretations, and they only, were legitimate. For sanction in her judgement she appealed to her numbers, her manifest good character, her continuity in different times, and her unanimity in different places. In unfavourable contrast to this was placed the variety and novelty of those who asserted other interpretations. Thus a commanding voice was raised to bear down the cavils of the heretic.

The consequence of this in practical application is made most explicit by S. Irenaeus. In dealing with the moral difficulties that the simple believer may find in parts of the Old Testament, and to show that the two Testaments, rightly understood, are at one, he writes: 'And then shall every word also seem consistent to him, if he for his part diligently read the Scriptures in company with those who are presbyters in the Church, among whom is the Apostolic doctrine, as I have pointed out.'[1] Of the presbyters 'who possess that succession of the Church which is from the apostles, and among whom exists that which is sound and blameless in conduct' it is said: 'they expound the Scriptures to us without danger.'[2] This is the happy régime at work in detailed act. The large-scale policy of which this is an expression is a succession of bishops and presbyters who are guardians of a fixed 'rule of truth'.

Harnack's well-known judgement is that what was needed to combat the Valentinians was an apostolic Creed *definitely interpreted*, because, possessing the art of explaining a given text in whatever way they chose, they could **give formal**

[1] IV.32.1, ii.5.   [2] IV.26.5, i.464–5.

recognition to such Creed-forms as may then have existed.[1] With this we may agree, for it is a particular instance of the wider principle. The primitive baptismal Confessions were not dogmatic, but descriptive, like the Apostles' Creed, being simply digests of New Testament phraseology. The meaning of a brief phrase in the Creed had in any case to be sought in the wider content of the Apostolic writings whence it was derived. The problem regarding the interpretation of the full form in the New Testament also arose in connexion with the concise form in the Confession.

[1] *H.D.* II.26.

Chapter Seven

ON THE SEAT OF RELIGIOUS AUTHORITY

WE MAY NOW return to the problem stated in the Introduction.[1] The most divergent opinions have been maintained as to what was for S. Irenaeus the actual seat of religious authority. This is not surprising, for he makes various statements which, in form at least, appear to contradict one another. Investigators have commonly shown a natural desire to find the attitude distinctive of their own religious communion substantiated in a writer so revered.

It is first to be observed that Scripture and the tradition of the Church are not the sole possible alternative foundations for religious authority. Claims may be advanced for both charisms and reason. Harnack seems to go a little too far when he writes that in Irenaeus tradition and reason take the place of charisms as a proof of doctrine.[2] S. Irenaeus certainly writes as though the Spirit-given charismatic ministry reflected in the Pauline Epistles was something with which the Church of his day was still familiar.[3] In the Church was the witness of adoption, the power of prophecy, speaking with tongues, exorcism, and foreknowledge; the power of seeing visions, of healing the sick, and even of raising the dead. Irenaeus followed S. Paul in teaching that the 'speaking with tongues' should be for the edification of the Church, and not a mere riot of individual self-expression. 'We also hear many brethren in the Church ... who through the Spirit speak all kinds of languages, and bring to light for the general benefit the hidden things of men, and declare the mysteries of God.'[4] This certainly seems to speak of 'prophecy' as a legitimate foundation for authoritative doctrine. At the same time one would incline to the view that

[1] See pp. 23-4 *supra*.　　[2] *H.D.* II.232.
[3] II.32.4, i.245-6; III.11.9, i.295-6; V.6.1, ii.68.　　[4] V.6.1, ii.68.

these utterances reflect loyalty to what the New Testament
has to say of the charismatic ministry, and to the witness of
the sub-apostolic period, rather than any actual living
experience or strong personal conviction. It is notable that
these statements are never produced for the purpose of
basing a doctrine upon the authority of any particular living
'prophet'. The aim is always simply to vindicate the claim of
the Church that it is herself, and not the heretics, who
possesses the Spirit of God. Thus recognition of these 'gifts
of the Spirit' did not involve Irenaeus in belittling the
ecclesiastical orders as a seat of authority.

The voice of established corporate authority within the
Church was, in fact, a charism.[1] 'It is incumbent to obey the
presbyters who are in the Church—those who, as I have
shown, possess the succession from the apostles; those who,
together with the succession of the episcopate, have received
the certain gift of truth (*charisma veritatis*),[2] according to the
good pleasure of the Father.'[3] The legitimate individual
prophetic and wonder-working ministry can and must co-
operate with the social, administrative, and disciplinary
ministry. There was indeed another prophecy, that of those
'wretched men . . . who wish to be pseudo-prophets'.[4]
Against this S. Irenaeus set his face. The test was that
legitimate prophecy edified the Church. 'Those who give
rise to schisms, who are destitute of the love of God, and
who look to their own special advantage rather than to the
unity of the Church; and who, for trifling reasons . . . cut
in pieces and divide the great and glorious body of Christ
. . . who prate of peace while they give rise to war (are)
false prophets.'[5]

---

[1] III.24.1, i.369; IV.26.5, i.464–5.

[2] Harvey, ii.236. It is, however, with justice that Dr. A. J. Mason observes :
'It would be unfair to Irenaeus to credit him with believing in a transmission
from bishop to bishop of a power of finding out the truth by personal inspiration. This is not the meaning of his *charisma veritatis*. The truth is received
by tradition, not evolved from an inner consciousness.' (In *Essays on the Early
History of the Church and the Ministry*, ed. H. B. Swete (1918), p. 46.)

[3] IV.26.2, i.462.   [4] III.11.9, i.295.   [5] IV.33.6–7, ii.10.

S. Irenaeus recognized charismatic prophecy as an original and authentic part of the life of the truth-giving Church. As such it was to be reverenced as an authority. That there was also a false prophecy no more detracted from the appeal to the true than did the existence of a spurious Gnostic tradition make void the appeal to the genuine Catholic one. In particular, this sympathy for prophecy by no means involves the assumption, made by some writers, that Irenaeus was a Montanist, or at least inclined that way. The texts commonly quoted to this end [1] are very ambiguous unless approached with a presupposition in mind. Other sects fit the description much better. In general, the bishop does not write as though the Phrygian heresy was a live issue among his flock. There is much justice in Harnack's observation that actually the appeal to 'prophecy' is but rarely made by S. Irenaeus. In principle it is not repudiated: in practice it is falling out of use. The reason for this is not far to seek. A charismatic ministry was accepted, for it was present as part of tradition. It was, however, of too individualist and innovating a character to be useful to conservative polemics, and was not congenial to the temper of Irenaeus.

Reason is hardly to be described as a seat of authority for Irenaeus. There is much sound and cogent reasoning in his writings, but it is polemic reason based on authority, not philosophical reasoning proceeding from postulated ideals or inherent probabilities. It is confined to drawing out the implications of tradition and Scripture, and to exposing the fallacies and self-contradictory arguments of those who would displace these authorities. S. Irenaeus is never an abstract thinker. He had the air of one who seeks and preaches the truth not so much for its own sake, but because he knows that the truth will preserve the health of the Church.

The tradition of the Church and Scripture must consequently between them enshrine the principle of religious authority. Several passages are forthcoming which lay much weight upon the part played by the Bible. The most

[1] III.11.9, i.295; *Dem.* 99, 100.

emphatic appears to be: Γνῶσις ἀληθὴς, ἡ τῶν ἀποστόλων
διδαχή· καὶ τὸ ἀρχαῖον τῆς ἐκκλησίας σύστημα κατὰ παντὸς τοῦ
κόσμου· Agnitio vera est Apostolorum doctrina: et antiquus
Ecclesiae status in universo mundo: et character corporis Christi
secundum successiones episcoporum, quibus illi eam quae in
unoquoque loco est Ecclesiam tradiderunt, quae pervenit usque
ad nos custodita sine fictione scripturarum[1] tractatione[2]
plenissima, neque additamentum neque ablationem recipiens,
et lectio sine falsatione, et secundum Scripturas expositio
legitima et diligens, et sine periculo et sine blasphemia: et
praecipuum dilectionis munus, quod est pretiosius quam agnitio,
gloriosius autem quam prophetia, omnibus autem reliquis charismatibus supereminens.[3] The passage is difficult, and somewhat
vague. It is not easy to give an agreed translation. The
published English translation may, however, be quoted.
'True knowledge is (that which consists in) the doctrine of
the apostles, and the ancient constitution of the Church
throughout all the world, and the distinctive manifestation
of the body of Christ according to the successions of the
bishops, by which they have handed down that Church
which exists in every place, and has come even unto us, being
guarded and preserved, without any forging of Scriptures,
by a very complete system of doctrine, and neither receiving
addition nor (suffering) curtailment (in the truths which she
believes); and (it consists in) reading (the word of God)
without falsification, and a lawful and diligent exposition in
harmony with the Scriptures, both without danger and
without blasphemy; and (above all, it consists in) the pre-
eminent gift of love, which is more precious than knowledge,
more glorious than prophecy, and which excels all the other
gifts (of God).'[4] The general drift of this obscure but
important passage would appear to be the assertion that the
doctrine handed down by the successions of bishops is

---

[1] According to Harvey, this word is to be rendered 'writings' simply,
marking the purely traditional character of the Regula Fidei.
[2] Harvey claims that the Creed is here meant.
[3] Harvey, ii.262–3.   [4] IV.33.8, ii.11.

nothing other than the content of authentic Scripture. We have to agree with Schmidt that this makes the Scriptures the principle which constitutes the Church the truth-bearer.[1] Another passage which may be read in much the same sense is: 'It behoves us, therefore . . . to flee to the Church, and be brought up in her bosom, and be nourished with the Lord's Scriptures.'[2] It is not certain from this, however, that Scripture is the sole nourishment the Church has to offer. It is not at all obvious how Schmidt can substantiate from this, or its context, the extreme position that the Scriptures are that within the Church wherein the Spirit dwells.[3]

In two passages S. Irenaeus lays down the entirely sound rule that texts of obscure meaning are to be interpreted in the light of those of an obvious meaning. If this be done, he claims, 'the entire Scriptures . . . can be clearly, unambiguously, and harmoniously understood by all, although all do not believe them'.[4] He appears to mean that Scripture expounded on historical lines will yield an obvious and determinate meaning. It is, in fact, an independent authority that speaks for itself. The difficulty is to know what passages have an obvious meaning. Irenaeus would have regarded 'prophecies of Christ' as of plain intention. Today these are among the more hotly-disputed parts of the Old Testament. Stories relating moral lapses of the Patriarchs are today of unambiguous import. Then they were seen as obscure parables of spiritual truth. In actual practice, then, S. Irenaeus loses the sound rule of this passage in the general tradition of allegorism, and does not succeed in raising Scripture to the level of an independent authority upon this basis. Another passage that has been quoted in this connexion is weaker. 'But our faith is steadfast . . . having clear proof from these Scriptures which were interpreted in the way I have related.'[5] Reference should be made to the context. The Jews Theodotion and Aquila had translated

---

[1] *Kirche b.I.* p. 39.   [2] V.20.2, ii.109.   [3] *Kirche b.I.* pp. 117–21.
[4] II.27.1–2, i.217–8; see also II.28.3, i.222.   [5] III.21.3, i.354.

Isaiah 7₁₄ as: 'Behold, a young woman shall conceive, and bring forth a son.' Irenaeus, though probably not a Hebrew scholar, seems to have been aware that this was the reading of the original, because he proceeds to justify the Church for taking the Septuagint text as the more authoritative. He is at particular pains to show that for a long period before the prophecy was vindicated by the miraculous birth of Christ the Jews themselves had accepted the Septuagint as Scripture. The implication of his argument is that the actual meaning of the original may rightly be passed over if the traditional exegesis of the Greek version can conveniently provide a prophecy of the Virgin Birth, for this doctrine is by all means to be upheld. On the other hand, it may be claimed that the present passage indeed shows Irenaeus basing himself on Scripture, because his ground for preferring the Septuagint version is that it conforms to the First Gospel, where παρθένος is read in Matthew 1₂₃. However, the continuation of the citation of III.21.3 given above shows that the appeal is not so much to S. Matthew as such, but to the authority of the whole company of the Apostles, with their successors. 'For the apostles . . . agree with this aforesaid translation; and the translation harmonizes with the tradition of the apostles. For Peter, and John, and Matthew, and Paul, and the rest successively, as well as their followers, did set forth all prophetical (announcements) just as the interpretation of the Elders contains them.' We cannot therefore agree with Beuzart, that the present passage shows that for Irenaeus Scripture was the foundation of the faith.[1] It merely shows that a 'proof-text' may be contrived to fit every doctrine. Traditional authority is determinative for Scripture.

For the other side it is to be said that the most casual reading of S. Irenaeus will serve to demonstrate that he constantly appeals to the tradition of the Church as the basis of religious authority. The most important passage, and one which has most usually been brought forward by investi-

[1] *Essai*, p. 136.

gators seeking to establish the primacy of tradition, has already been noticed.[1] It is there expressly stated that had the Apostles left no written records tradition alone would have sufficed to maintain the faith, as it actually did among illiterate tribes. Here ecclesiastical tradition is certainly represented as a self-sufficient authority.

However, to inquire whether tradition or Scripture is the primary authority is to obscure the mind of S. Irenaeus by asking the wrong question. To him both are manifestations of one and the same thing, the *apostolic truth* by which the Christian lives. The authority within the Church is all one, '*the Apostolic*', however transmitted. The truth hangs by two cords, and he can speak of either as self-sufficient without intending to deny or subordinate the other. The questions that arose when 'the Written Word' was pitted against 'priestly tradition' had not then been raised, and so they are not answered. To judge by his general temper one may surmise that had one approached S. Irenaeus for his verdict upon later controversial questions he would not easily have committed himself to either side. The two statements, that Scripture makes the Church the truth-bearer, and that Scripture is not as necessary to salvation as tradition, cannot indeed be formally reconciled. This is because Irenaeus was not careful to preserve a system in his every utterance. Each is a one-sided statement of the truth, and neither is to be taken alone at its face value. We may agree again with Schmidt, that apostolic tradition is not an independent quantity over against Scripture.[2] Nor for that matter is Scripture an independent quantity over against apostolic tradition.

Vernet's statement must now be considered, that the Rule of Faith is more than the baptismal Confession. Rather is it a body of doctrine capable of interpreting Scripture.[3] It has already been pointed out that S. Irenaeus is feeling after some canon which will serve to give a definite interpretation alike

[1] See p. 24 *supra*.   [2] *Kirche b.I.* p. 54.
[3] *Dictionnaire*, VII, col. 2412.

to Scripture and to the scriptural baptismal Confession.[1]
This he does by showing that the Church asserts that such-
and-such is the self-evident and only legitimate content of
scriptural language. This 'legitimate content' *is* the 'Rule of
Truth',[2] or rather, it is one manifestation of the 'Rule'. The
danger in fixing upon the ambiguous rather than the plain
passages of the Bible, so that everyone may discover for
himself as inclination leads, is that 'in this way no one will
possess the Rule of Truth'.[3] The whole Rule of Truth, in
all its possible manifestations, is nothing other than *'the
apostolic'*. It is that which the Church preaches, and which
she asserts upon her own authority to be the truth. S. Irenaeus has no idea, therefore, of a separate Rule of Faith
standing over against Scripture to interpret it. The interpreter of Scripture is always described as the Church, and in
particular, the company of authorized and apostolic bishops
and presbyters. Certainly the Rule is, in a sense, more than
the Baptismal Confession. On the one hand, the Confession
is only a brief compendious formula, requiring to be expounded. On the other, it is simple scriptural language,
which therefore needs to be interpreted. However, the Confession is nothing other than a manifestation of the one
teaching, the Rule, and may therefore be described simply
as 'The Rule of Faith'. So the Creed-like formula in the
Demonstration of the Apostolic Preaching is introduced as 'the
order and rule of our faith',[4] and the stately Creed in the
opening of *Adversus Haereses* as 'this faith'.[5] When we read
that 'the Rule of the Truth' is 'received by means of
Baptism'[6] we naturally presume that the writer is referring
to the custom of reciting at Baptism a doctrinal Confession
more or less fixed by custom, of which the Creed-like forms
referred to above are reminiscences. However, it is not to be

---

[1] See pp. 94–6 *supra*.

[2] 'The Rule of Truth' is the usual phrase in S. Irenaeus. The more generally
accepted formula, 'the Rule of Faith', is found only in *Dem.* 3.

[3] II.27.1, i.218.   [4] *Dem.* 6.

[5] I.10.1, i.42; cf. also I.22.1, i.84; III.4.2, i.265; IV.33.7, ii.10.

[6] I.9.4, i.41.

inferred from this that the Creed is identified with the Rule of the Truth in any sense other than that which may apply also to Scripture and tradition.

This demonstration of the views of S. Irenaeus must be concluded with the observation that there is a great gap between what he himself takes to be his principles and the way in which a dispassionate onlooker will find them to work out in practice. He is acutely aware of the perilous subjectivity of allegoristic exegesis, etc., when it is in the hands of the heretics. He is not so aware that these methods are also subjective in the hands of the Catholic Church. Hence he is unconscious of the fact that, expounded in the way he allows, the written tradition of Scripture and the 'unwritten Scripture' of tradition both fail to be standards of a completely fixed and obvious meaning. Religious authority as something fixed in historic and objective fact, whether enshrined in written documents or in the authentic memory of the faithful, is strongly asserted. In actual fact, however, it always dissolves, and is bound to dissolve, into the tones of the *present* voice of the Church, as she interprets her heritage afresh in every generation under the pressure of her active life. We may call this present voice the '*Living Voice*' of the Church. It is the resultant of the spiritual experiences, the reasoning, and the practical needs in piety and polemics of the main body of those who recognize one another as religious companions. This '*Living Voice*' is the actual religious authority for S. Irenaeus. We may candidly agree that he would probably not have recognized this as the truth about himself. He would have stoutly maintained that in all things he was solely and firmly grounded upon the joint foundation of fixed tradition and fixed Scripture. Irenaeus was, in short, one of those many who have professed a theory in the practice of which they have unconsciously fallen short. As Vernet rightly states, the Rule of Faith is the 'grand-mastership' of the Church, with Scripture and tradition coming after this.[1] Thus in a profound sense Irenaeus

[1] *Dictionnaire*, VII, col. 2424.

followed his master Papias, who left it on record that: 'I did not think that what was to be gotten from the books would profit me as much as what came from the living and abiding voice'.[1]

[1] Eus. *H.E.* III.xxxix.4.

Chapter Eight

ON THE LEGITIMACY OF THE LIVING VOICE

WE HAVE seen that S. Irenaeus, and with him the men of his time for whom he speaks, were conditioned by lack of historical knowledge. In consequence of this lack two assertions had to be maintained on the authority of the Church: first, that one reading of subjective exegesis was to be preferred to another: second, that one unwritten tradition was to be accepted and another rejected. The historical weakness was not realized, and those who retreated to authority were hardly conscious of what was happening to them. Nevertheless, the movement of thought was there, and was most significant. There remains, then, the question of the present-day view of the rightness of these developments.

To accept the '*Living Voice*' of the Church as authority is a way of admitting that religious knowledge is like other knowledge, and comes through the exercise of the faculties of the human mind and spirit. There would, indeed, be no knowledge of God unless He chose to make Himself known, but the revelation comes not through the supersession of human faculties, but through stimulation and guidance. The existence is also to be recognized of unusual exercises of human faculty, such as visions and other 'psychic' experiences. Divine truth may come through these. The history of religion is full of attempts to find a message from God which is completely independent of any human medium. So the old engravers decorated the frontispiece of the Family Bible with a picture of the Divine Hand piercing the clouds to convey the sacred volume to earth. Men of a less discerning spirit have received their heavenly letters from the 'automatic writing' of a medium, or have been led by an angel to the place where they might find the golden plates of

the Book of Mormon. Others have revered the oracles of the
ecstatic, or even the ravings of the insane. In plain light of
day all these constructions fall to the ground. A dispassionate
view of the history of religion shows that the authentic
revelation of God, which will stand the test of the long and
growing experience of the race, comes through the mind and
spirit of man. Men learn of God by responding aright in
thought and feeling to the pressure of events around them,
and to the experience of life. Divine inspiration is never
something that suspends the faculties of men, or that makes
searching with them superfluous. It is always a gracious
guidance to help, and an assistance to enable men to respond
aright. Thus the only possible religious authority is the
substantial consensus of conviction of all good men, of the
past and of the present, and from this there is no appeal.
So the Lord said to His Church: 'What things soever ye
shall bind on earth shall be bound in heaven.' This is the
essence of what S. Irenaeus taught. In this he was surely
right.

   Some will object that this is to make all things subjective.
In answer there are two weighty considerations. The first is
that the Church which learns and then teaches is indwelt by
the Holy Spirit, so that the whole process is an objective
work of the Living God. All too often Christian thought has
attenuated the doctrine of the Holy Spirit. The Spirit who
dwells in the heart of the believer, and in the company of
believers, has been described in terms of a 'divine spark'.
'The Spirit' has become little more than a name for the
higher and nobler faculties of human nature. The sense of a
majestic Presence, personal, very real, and the rightful
Object of religious adoration, has been lost. The guidance
of the Holy Spirit has been looked upon as something mild
and indeterminate, not as an effective operation which,
while certainly not automatic, is nevertheless to be regarded
as ultimately prevailing in the heart of whoever will continue
faithful. Any such erroneous attenuation cannot fail to shift
the balance of thought toward the purely subjective. The

second consideration is that the experience which teaches is not individual, but collective. The man who sees what others present cannot see, and then only when he is in a certain state of mind, is rightly in danger of being dismissed as the victim of a subjective delusion. It is when a thing is to be seen constantly, and by all competent observers alike, that the presence of objective fact is apprehended. So also in religion, the experience which is essentially private and fleeting, and which is denied by the collective experience of the noblest of all the ages, is under suspicion as a mere individual aberration, an unrestrained flight of subjective fancy. The individual religious experience which is echoed far and near in the company of the faithful, and which accords with the lessons of time, is declared thereby to be authentic, and to be founded firmly upon the objective facts of divine revelation. History shows that many undoubted Christians have erred at times, and that on occasion even the majority have gone astray through inexperience or lack of balance. However, a deep conviction that the Catholic Church at large cannot remain permanently in error is the only possible ground the race has for supposing that anything certain is known of God, for God is observed to speak to man through man. This basic conviction is an act of faith alike in the goodness of God and in the reasonableness of human life. So by way of parallel, all science is based upon a similar act of faith. The necessary postulate of science is that, while individuals may on occasion err, the race collectively is rational, and its physical senses to be trusted. So it is with the Christian Faith. The believer who will endeavour to preserve the universal fellowship, and who will, so far as in him lies, humbly try to learn of all his brethren past and present, may have an increasing confidence that he listens to the authentic voice of God. Nor is there any hope to short-circuit the discipline of learning from the 'Living Voice' of the Church by searching for a more immediate word which is not declared through human agency.

Battifol's reading of S. Irenaeus is that while Gnostic

traditions were various, being personal to the various masters, the tradition of the Church is one, being maintained impersonally.[1] This attempt to eliminate the human element is based upon a common confusion of thought. Just as there is no 'humanity' apart from *men*, save in an ideal sense, so there is no concrete Church apart from the company of actual Christians, including the Church Triumphant. However numerous be that company, and however continuous and unanimous their *consensus*, the doctrine is never held *impersonally*. It is held collectively by individual persons moulded by a common life.

The religious world today sees the growing embarrassment of schemes of external authority. Some religious communions have in the past laid great store by the inerrancy of the 'Written Word'. This inerrancy has now succumbed before the onset of science. Such communions are now left with no workable theory of religious authority, though the rank and file are frequently slow to realize this. Other communions have spoken more of ecclesiastical tradition. These likewise find themselves confronted by more adequate historical knowledge, which increasingly has to be evaded or ignored if certain traditional positions are to be maintained. Thus under the inexorable pressure of life the whole Church half-consciously stumbles away from the conception of a fixed Word, whether enshrined in tradition or in Scripture. She is increasingly driven to trust the '*Living Voice*' of the present. Historical science sheds ever-increasing light upon the nature of the ancient Scriptures. The 'offences' in the Bible can now be explained in the light of the theory of progressive revelation. Allegorism is thus no longer necessary to defend hard Scriptures, and this method must therefore pass away. We live in more fortunate days, when hope is rising for the perfecting of an exegesis which will give with increasing certainty one fixed historic meaning for every text, to the exclusion of all others. The process is not complete, and certain passages are likely to remain for

---

[1] *L'Église*, p. 256.

ever obscure, but in proportion as the process advances the Church escapes from that frustration which met S. Irenaeus as he approached the Bible. Historical science likewise illuminates the life of the primitive Church. We may perhaps claim to have more knowledge of the facts of the life of Jesus and of the Apostolic Church than Irenaeus himself, even at this greater distance in time. Thus a correction is applied to that information for which the Fathers had to rely upon tradition. The Church is again exercising her authority to interpret Scripture and to determine tradition. She therefore still treads in the path of S. Irenaeus, though with this difference. The Church of this age is more conscious of what is happening to her than was that of his.

PART TWO

The Theology of Saint Irenaeus as a Biblical System

Chapter Nine

INTRODUCTION

NOTE HAS already been made of Seeberg's dictum, that 'Irenaeus is a Biblicist, and the first great representative of Biblicism'.[1] There is much more in this than even that brilliant writer appears to have seen. It can be shown that every important and constructive element in the theology of S. Irenaeus is fundamentally of Biblical or Hebraic inspiration. Furthermore, he is essentially Pauline. This is perhaps the most important thing to be said of this Christian Father.

We have seen that there is a sense in which Irenaeus was not a Biblicist. What he said was determined not so much by the actual letter of Scripture as by the authoritative voice of the Church. He was not, indeed, completely aware of this, yet it was nevertheless so, and in the circumstances of the time it could not have been otherwise. However, many strains go to make up the '*Living Voice*' of the Church, and one of these is the influence of the Bible. The mental process here is reciprocal. Much reverent reading of the Bible cultivates a certain state of feeling and attitude of thought toward God and man. This in turn decides with what eyes a man will read, and thus largely determines what he will find in his reading. It is therefore possible, and indeed common, for a believer to be deeply Biblical in spirit and feeling without having much scientific knowledge of the actual and historical meaning of many parts of those Scriptures upon which he feeds. This seeming paradox is well exemplified in the religious life of certain individuals of the present day. Most Churchmen will have among their acquaintance someone who is a believer of a radically Hebraic type. This worthy man is commonly much misunderstood by 'superior people'

[1] See p. 24 *supra*; also *DG*. p. 290.

115

in the Church, and is probably referred to popularly as a 'Fundamentalist'. He makes much of 'the inspired Word of God', and has a phenomenal facility in quoting the Bible. It does not, however, follow from this that all his particular views are based upon the Bible, much as he may like to think so. He revels in all those subjective methods of exegesis we have observed in S. Irenaeus, and therefore his exposition is commonly far removed from the actual meaning of his text. He may, for example, be a convinced British Israelite. However, there will be a certain unmistakable cast in his temper, and this constitutes him a witness, despite manifest failings, to many authentic and most valuable elements in the Christian faith, which the Church dare not forget. There is in him an intense awareness of living under the eye of God the Judge, a rigid though rather legal ethical standard, a zeal for worship and a fidelity to the institutions of religion, an apocalyptical expectation, and on the less noble side, an insensitivity to intellectual curiosity and æsthetic satisfaction. All these qualities irresistibly remind one of those stern prophets and patriarchs whom this man so admires. He is a follower of James rather than of John, and would have been more at home in Jerusalem than in Alexandria. This is the type of the Biblical or Hebraic Christian. It is not an injustice to say that S. Irenaeus was such a one, though at a much loftier intellectual level than is commonly found in the type today.

This is borne out by the circumstance that Irenaeus will be found to show an instinctive appreciation for many of the great themes of the Bible. That this appreciation is indeed an instinctive one, a feeling, a 'way of looking at things', rather than a scholarly or contemplative grasp of the historical message of Scripture, is evidenced by the fact that he commonly does not reproduce the language of the Bible, but expresses the essential content of Biblical doctrine in words drawn from other sources. What he actually writes is based on the 'Living Voice' rather than on the 'Written Word', but what lives in him is largely the spirit of the Old and New Testament Scriptures. Thus there is in Irenaeus an Hebraic interest which acts as an effectual counterpoise to the Hellenic interest of Gentile Christianity, which is also there. This balance in S. Irenaeus is a matter of the greatest significance. Arianism was an attempt to approximate the Christian religion to the non-Christian philosophy of the day. It was Christianity stated in terms of a non-Christian and non-Biblical conception of God, and of His relation to the world. Irenaeus admirably represents that type of Christian faith, at once more robust and uncompromising, and more balanced, which condemned Arian heresy. We may almost say that by anticipation he rallied the forces for the long campaign which ended in the rejection of Arius.

With this in mind guarded assent may be allowed to Brunner's proposition that, though Irenaeus has more title than any other to be regarded as the founder of ecclesiastical theology, nevertheless in him the New Testamen twitness, Johannine and Pauline, the specifically New Testament and the whole-Biblical, are united as in hardly any other until Luther.[1] This statement is certainly better founded than is Beuzart's counterpart to it, namely, that the theology of S. Irenaeus is more Jewish Christian and Johannine than Pauline.[2] Irenaeus is Jewish Christian, but is Pauline also. There is no contradiction in this, for S. Paul himself was certainly an Hebraic Christian in his fundamental view of God and of the religious life of man, though he was not a legalistic Judaizer. On the other hand, Vernet's judgement is not hereby excluded, that S. Irenaeus is a Greek, but one whose Hellenism shows itself less in love of abstract speculation than in his good sense and love of concrete facts.[3] Irenaeus was certainly not uninfluenced by the culture of his day. He often used the terms of Greek thought to express his conception of God, but the conception expressed was fundamentally Biblical. He shows a moderation of spirit as between extremes, a certain measure of scientific attitude to the world, and an undeniable humane, and even humanist

[1] *Der Mittler*, p. 219 (E.T., p. 249).   [2] *Essai*, p. 170.
[3] *Dictionnaire*, VII, col. 2508.

and optimistic conception of human nature. Yet he is Hebraic, and utterly un-Greek, in his lack of care for abstract speculation as such. God is for him much more than an object of thought, a philosophical concept necessary to explain the universe. He is an omnipotent and creative Living God, who above all is to be worshipped in awe and trusted in obedience.

Chapter Ten

'THE TWO HANDS OF GOD'

ANY RELIGIOUS system is, and must be, determined by its conception of God. It is right, therefore, in demonstrating the Biblical theology of S. Irenaeus, to turn first to his doctrine of God. His most distinctive teaching will be found to be of a thoroughly Hebraic character, significantly advanced to combat a Gnostic doctrine of God of entirely Gentile inspiration.

The Gnostic theology that confronted Irenaeus as an alarming menace alike to the apostolic Gospel and the solidarity of the Church had a twin mainspring. On the nobler side was the speculative interest of Greek philosophy. This instinctively felt after God as an object of thought, and postulated Him as the Absolute, whose ineffable Being is the first cause and ultimate explanation of the phenomenal world. On the baser side was oriental despair of the world. This was a spirit bred of the disillusioning experience of the vanity of moral effort in this world, and of obsession with the grim and overmastering power of the lust of the flesh. Between these fundamentally alien strains there was a common interest which could serve to unite them. Both saw an unbridgeable gulf between the Supreme God and this world. Consequently it was the hopeless task of religion to bridge the gulf which by definition could never be spanned, and to provide mankind a road of mysterious knowledge along which he could escape from the world, and in particular, a means whereby he could shuffle off this mortal coil, a hated load.

Though there was an endless variety of Gnostics, and some were more extreme than others, all united in assuming that, so far as religion was concerned, the material was the antithesis to the spiritual. Material existence was, if not the

119

active enemy of spiritual living, at least inert, unprofitable,
and a hampering burden. The problem of evil as stated by the
Gnostic was not the moral question: 'How comes it about
that there can continue in existence wills in rebellion against
the divine good will?' It was rather the speculative question:
'Why is there a material creation?' Upon this premise the
only way to 'justify the ways of God to men' was to assert
that the creation and continued existence of the material
world was no part of the will and plan of the Supreme Being.
The Gnostic therefore taught that from the unknowable
Supreme there proceeded emanations or Æons. These were
exalted spiritual beings capable of a measure of communion
with the Supreme, and akin to the divine nature. As they
were more lowly than the Supreme they were imagined as
capable of contact with a plane of existence too mean to be
the concern of the Highest. This provided room for the
procession of secondary and humbler Æons from the primary, and from these in turn yet others. The lower ones could
have no direct contact with or knowledge of the Supreme
Being. It was Gnostic teaching that one of these lower
spirits was responsible for the Creation. In some systems
the Creation was accounted for as the direct or indirect
result of the rebellion of this Æon against the divine plan,
of her passion to rise above her proper station, and conse-
quent expulsion from the heavenly sphere. Otherwise the
Creation was an accidental miscarriage of the plan of the
Supreme God, or something that happened without His
knowledge. Thus the creator of the world, frequently called
the Demiurge ('Workman'), was, if not positively evil, at
least clumsy and ignorant. In every case the god of the
Creation was, to use the immortal phrase of S. Irenaeus, 'the
fruit of a defect'.

Irenaeus hence founded his creed by emphasizing that
the Supreme God is the Creator. This was the most important thing he had to say about God. 'It is proper, then, that I
should begin with the first and most important head, that is,
God the Creator, who made the heaven and the earth, and

all things that are therein (whom these men blasphemously style the fruit of a defect).[1] He constantly repeats the formula: 'One Creator God.' 'This God, the Creator, who formed the world, is the only God, and there is no other beside Him.'[2] Irenaeus seems never to assert the unity of God without as a matter of course passing on to say that He is the Creator. He finds it impossible too strongly to emphasize this fact. 'He is the Former, He the Builder, He the Discoverer, He the Creator, He the Lord of all . . . He is Father, He is God, He the Founder, He the Maker, He the Creator, who made those things by Himself.'[3] This is rehearsed again and again.[4] God has created everything that is.[5] He is the only Creator.[6] He is the Absolute Creator, who conceived the plan of Creation Himself, not having received it from any other being.[7] God created all things from nothing, not from pre-existent matter.[8] 'He did Himself make all things freely, and as He pleased.'[9]

This much said, S. Irenaeus carries the war into the enemy's camp. This he does first by demonstrating the *reductio ad absurdum* of all attempts to span the unbridgeable gulf. He appears thoroughly to enjoy this polemic exercise. Nowhere does he cover the ground more adequately. A Supreme Being who permits evil upon His own territory is not good,[10] but if the defect is not upon His territory He must be limited.[11] Nor can the difficulty be explained away by saying that 'inside' and 'outside' are not to be understood spatially.[12] That the world should be formed by angels contrary to the will of the Supreme Being denies His omnipotence.[13] Irenaeus sees that the whole speculative weakness of the Gnostic systems lies in this. Having for religious pur-

[1] II.1.1, i.117.
[2] II.16.3, i.171; see also III.1.2, i.259; IV.32.1, ii.4; *Dem.* 4, 5.
[3] II.30.9, i.238–9.
[4] I.10.3, i.43; I.22.1, i.84–5; II.9.1, i.143; III.25.1, i.371.
[5] I.22.1, i.84; *Dem.* 5.   [6] II.1.1, i.117.   [7] II.16.3, i.171.
[8] IV.38.3, ii.43.   [9] III.8.3, i.276.   [10] II.4.2, i.127; II.5.3, i.131.
[11] II.2.2, i.121; II.8.3, i.141; IV.19.3, i.438.
[12] II.4.2, i.127; II.5.2, i.130.   [13] II.2.1, i.120.

poses defined the gulf between God and matter as unbridgeable, the Gnostics then try to span the gulf with a bridge of
emanations. There is no end to the bridge that will be necessary. The philosophical dualism thus remains ultimate.
'Thus by that very process of reasoning on which they
depend for teaching that there is a certain Pleroma or God
above the Creator of heaven and earth, anyone who chooses
to employ it may maintain that there is another Pleroma
above the Pleroma, above that again another, and above
Bythus another ocean of Deity . . . and thus, their doctrine
disappearing[1] into immensity, there will always be a necessity to conceive of other Pleromata, and other Bythi, so as
never at any time to stop.'[2] The heretic would know the God
he had pronounced unknowable. In aiming his arrow at the
heavens he bends his bow till it breaks.[3]

Of more lasting worth than this polemic is a second line
of assault upon the Gnostic doctrine of God. The positive
method is adopted of expounding a Christian God who is not
separated from His world. This is done with admirable
insight. To combat these morally destructive pre-supposi-
tions about the nature of God S. Irenaeus has recourse to the
Hebrew conception of the Living God. This is possibly a
case where, impelled by sound Biblical instinct, Irenaeus
moves at depths more profound than he realizes. He appears
to treat the doctrine of *The Two Hands of God* simply as a
method of emphasizing that it is the Supreme God and none
other who is the God of Creation. Actually *The Two Hands
of God* is much more than a corollary of the doctrine of
Creation. It is itself the expression of the doctrine of an
immediately present and active God.

We must first examine a crucial passage, which gives the
clue to the significance of the many texts where the Son and
Holy Spirit are described as the creative Hands of God.
Having cited Isaiah 40$_{12}$: 'the heavens are meted out in
the palm of His hand', S. Irenaeus continues: 'Or who

---

[1] Or even 'perishing'; the Latin being *excidente*. Harvey, i.253.
[2] II.1.4, i.119; see also IV.**19.1**, i.437.   [3] I.**16.3**, i.72.

doth understand His hand,—that hand which measures
immensity; that hand which, by its own measure, spreads
out the measure of the heavens, and which comprises in its
hollow the earth with the abysses? . . . For His hand lays
hold of all things, and that it is which illumines the heavens
. . . and trieth the reins and the hearts . . . and does openly
nourish and preserve us.'[1] Continuing this great theme of
the transcendent greatness of the Creator God, Irenaeus
immediately makes one of his most striking references to
the Son and Spirit as *The Two Hands of God*. 'It was not
angels, therefore, who made us, nor who formed us. . . . For
God did not stand in need of these, in order to the accom-
plishing of what He had Himself determined with Himself
beforehand should be done, as if He did not possess His
own hands. For with Him were always present the Word and
Wisdom, the Son and the Spirit, by whom and in whom,
freely and spontaneously, He made all things.'[2]

The 'arm', 'hand', or 'finger' of God was a regular Old
Testament metaphor. It was descriptive of some special and
wonderful divine act or intervention, particularly in creation,
in protection of God's People or the vindication of the
right, in revelation, or in prophetic inspiration.[3] 'Yea, mine
hand hath laid the foundation of the earth, and my right
hand hath spread out the heavens' (Isaiah 48:13). 'His right
hand, and his holy arm, hath wrought salvation for him'
(Psalm 98:1). 'Awake, awake, put on strength, O arm of the
Lord' (Isaiah 51:9). 'So the spirit lifted me up, and took me
away . . . and the hand of the Lord was strong upon me. . . .
And it came to pass at the end of seven days, that the word
of the Lord came unto me' (Ezekiel 3:14,16). Dr. R. Newton
Flew observes that 'it is noticeable that the only references
to "the finger of God" in the Old Testament are to certain
epochal events, which to the Hebrew mind lit up the

[1] IV.**19**.2, i.437–8.   [2] IV.**20**.1, i.439.
[3] e.g.: Exodus 32:11; Numbers 11:23; Deuteronomy 5:15, 6:21, 7:8,19, 9:26, 11:2,
26:8, 34:12; 1 Kings 18:46; 2 Kings 3:15; Psalms 44:3, 71:18, 77:15; Isaiah 40:10, 51:5,
52:10, 53:1; Ezekiel 3:22, 8:1, 37:1.

meaning of history. Thus in Psalm 8₃ the heavens are the work of the finger of God. This is a reference to the creation. In Exodus 8₁₉, "the magicians said unto Pharaoh, This is the finger of God". God's activity is marked at the time of the signal deliverance of the nation from Egypt. In Exodus 31₁₈ we read: "And he gave unto Moses. . . the two tables of the testimony, tables of stone, written with the finger of God."[1] This metaphor of 'the hand of the Lord' is a parallel to 'the Spirit of the Lord'. They alike denote 'God in action in the world of men'. If anything, the metaphor of the 'hand' goes beyond that of the 'Spirit', in that it properly concerns the work of Creation also. It was with fine insight, therefore, that S. Irenaeus fixed upon the phrase 'the hand of God' when casting about in his mind for an expression with which to convey the truth that it is the Supreme God Himself who is engaged in creative activity in this world. In the context in question we most significantly see him adapting the metaphor straightway to the Triune Name of God, for the Christian Confession spoke not of one, but of two divine active Presences in the world. At once he goes on to speak of *The Two Hands of God*. The Spirit is a *'Hand'* equally with the Son. The same mental process is seen at work in the passage IV.7.4, i.396. The theme is there stated that creation was not effected through mediating angels, but by the Son. A few lines later, as if by way of afterthought and necessary correction, the Son and Holy Spirit, the Word and the Wisdom of God, are placed side by side as equal agents of creation.

The doctrine of 'The Two Hands of God' consequently denotes 'direct action' as opposed to the intermediary angels of the Gnostic systems. Possibly the identification of 'Hand' and 'Spirit' was made easier by suggestion from the Gospels themselves. Our Lord's phrase: 'But if I by the finger of God cast out devils, no doubt the Kingdom of God is come upon you' (Luke 11₂₀) is the very obvious parallel to: 'But if I cast out devils by the Spirit of God, then the Kingdom of

---

[1] *Jesus and His Church* (London, 1938), p. 32.

God is come unto you' (Matthew 12₂₈). There is indeed an actual passage where Irenaeus explicitly equates 'the finger of God' with the Holy Spirit. 'Ten Words on tables of stone, written with the finger of God. Now the finger of God is that which is stretched forth from the Father in the Holy Spirit.'[1] Mankind was formed by the hand of God,[2] and also 'moulded at the beginning by the hands of God, that is, of the Son and of the Spirit'.[3]

S. Irenaeus speaks of 'the Father planning everything well and giving His commands, the Son carrying these into execution and performing the work of creating, and the Spirit nourishing and increasing'.[4] At first sight the place given to the work of the Spirit in creation looks like that of an intermediary or subordinate. Actually the intention is the reverse. There is here an effort to preserve the equality of divine status between the Son and Spirit demanded by the trinitarian formula. This parallelism is better seen in the more rhetorical language of the following: 'that we should know that He who made, and formed . . . and nourishes us by means of the creation, establishing all things by His Word, and binding them together by His Wisdom—this is He who is the only true God.'[5] *The Two Hands of God* is an expression of the immediacy of creation, not of its mediacy. It is an unfolding of the implications of the phrase 'One Creator God'. It justifies the claim that S. Irenaeus taught the doctrine of creation 'by the whole Trinity'.

An interesting consequence of the identification of the creative Spirit with the Wisdom of God is pointed out by Dr. J. A. Robinson. S. Justin before (and Origen afterwards) regarded as referring to the Son the Old Testament texts which personify the Wisdom of God, such as Proverbs 8. S. Irenaeus always applies them to the Holy Spirit.[6]

It would further appear that Revelation and Inspiration

---

[1] *Dem.* 26.   [2] V.**16**.1, ii.99.   [3] V.**28**.4, ii.132–3.

[4] IV.**38**.3, ii.44; see also II.**30**.9, i.239; IV.**7**.4, i.396; IV.**20**.2, i.440; IV.**20**.4, i.441; *Dem.* 5.

[5] III.**24**.2, i.370–1.   [6] Introduction to *Demonstration*, pp. 50–1.

are also described as the work of the 'Two Hands'. These
aspects have, however, not received such careful thought
from Irenaeus as has the Creation, and consequently do not
come to such explicit formulation. The matter is clearer in
the case of Inspiration. In the first place, in a passage dealing
with the revelations to the prophets, the Son and the Spirit
are treated as parallel organs, though they are not termed
'hands'. 'God the Father is shown forth through all these,
the Spirit indeed working, and the Son ministering.'[1] Then
the deliverance of the Three Holy Children from the burning
fiery furnace, by a theophany described as an appearance of
the Son of God, is described as the work of 'the hand of
God'.[2] In the third place, a hint is given that prophetic utterances regarded as the words of Christ may be the work of the
Holy Spirit. In the place where Irenaeus develops his doctrine of the heavenly 'conversation' of the Father with the
Son, three illustrative texts are collected. There is Isaiah 451;
Psalm 27, 'The Lord said unto me: Thou art my Son, this
day have I begotten thee'; and Psalm 1101.[3] These are some
of the very texts that would certainly be advanced as examples
in any theory of prophetic inspiration by the Son-Logos.
Yet Irenaeus can conclude his chapter thus: 'the Spirit of
God . . . speaks in the prophets, and utters the words sometimes from Christ and sometimes from the Father.' That the
pre-existent Son can speak in the prophets is a work of the
Spirit. Once over, the proposition is explicitly stated. 'Now
the Spirit shows forth the Word, and therefore the prophets
announced the Son of God; and the Word utters the Spirit,
and therefore is Himself the announcer of the prophets.'[4]
S. Irenaeus is at this point very near to the primitive
Christian usage of the New Testament. Here is a definition
of the Holy Spirit in terms of the manifest Presence and
activity of the invisible Christ. This is the New Testament
'Spirit of Christ'. One is not surprised to find that the
prophetic Spirit is once actually called 'the Spirit of Christ'.[5]

---

[1] IV.20.6, i.443.   [2] V.5.2, ii.67.   [3] *Dem.* 49.
[4] *Dem.* 5.   [5] *Dem.* 73.

Immediately following is the creed of the *Demonstration*. In this one reads: ' The Word of God . . . who was manifested to the prophets according to the form of their prophesying . . . and the Holy Spirit, through whom the prophets prophesied.'[1] There are not two disparate theories of inspiration here, for the two halves of the proposition are complementary. As loyalty to the venerable trinitarian formula turned a single *'Hand of Creation'* into two, so here. Inspiration is the work of the Son-Logos, and also, of course, of the Spirit. It is in fact simply the work of God.

In the case of Revelation God's work is likewise described in two ways, at first sight contradictory. Men 'ascend through the Spirit to the Son, and through the Son to the Father'.[2] Alternatively, the Son brings the Spirit to man, and the spiritual man is united to God. The incarnate Christ has come to us in order that we 'may be able to contain in ourselves the Bread of Immortality, which is the Spirit of the Father'.[3] Men ascend through the Son to the Spirit, and through the Spirit to God.[4] There has been dispute whether Irenaeus regarded the Son or the Spirit as the first step. By analogy to the case of Inspiration considered above, it is probable that this debate has obscured the issue. The doctrine of *'The Two Hands of God'* represents immediate action by the whole Godhead, and consequently equality between the Son and the Spirit. However, when loosely stated this doctrine may look like a subordination of function, where none is intended. These two opposite arrangements of Son and Spirit in Revelation indicate essentially nothing other than that S. Irenaeus thinks of the two as equal and interchangeable in function. Though there is no passage forthcoming which unites the Spirit-Son-Father and Son-Spirit-Father revelation-sequences into a single text, thus showing their identity, as was found to be the case when Inspiration was discussed above, the interchangeability and equality are there. That

[1] *Dem.* 6.   [2] V.**36**.2, ii.156; see also IV.**20**.5, i.442; *Dem.* 7.
[3] IV.**38**.1, ii.42; see also IV.**20**.4, i.441–2; V.**1**.1, ii.56; V.**20**.2, ii.110.
[4] III.**17**.1, i.334; *Dem.* 9, 41.

the two 'steps' should be found in reverse order at times is a warning that they may not be steps at all, but rather, the loose statement of a doctrine of Revelation by 'The Two Hands of God'. This formula would represent immediate self-revelation by the Godhead.

It is impossible, in estimating the standing of S. Irenaeus as a Father of the Church, to over-estimate the importance of the circumstance that he is so firmly based upon the conception of a God who is Himself the immediate Creator of the world, and who immediately reveals Himself to man. The deep fact of consciousness in the lives of millions who have bowed in true worship is that 'the Lord spake unto Moses face to face, as a man speaketh unto his friend'. The Holy God, awful and ineffable, is near. He can be met. He can speak and act. He can be known as a Friend. This is the foundation of religion. The mature religious consciousness spurns dualism as alike irrational and immoral. It likewise outsoars in rapture any conception of a pale and remote God defined in abstractions and negatives. To the Christian, however, the heart of the matter is in the questions: 'Why is God near? Why can He speak? Why can He be known?' The touchstone of faith is the confident answer: 'Because He loves!' The greatest thing that man can say of his Maker is that God is love. The test of that love is that God is found to be near. The most profound and sustained treatment of the nature of God given by Irenaeus is perhaps that great chapter quoted above in illustration of the doctrine of 'The Two Hands of God' (IV.20.1–12). It is of great significance that this chapter opens by celebrating the love of God. 'As regards His greatness, therefore, it is not possible to know God, for it is impossible that the Father can be measured; but as regards His love (for this it is which leads us to God by His Word), when we obey Him, we do always learn that there is so great a God, and that it is He who by Himself has established, and selected, and adorned, and contains all things.'[1] At the heart of the religion of S. Irenaeus is the

[1] IV.20.1, i.439.

conception of the self-communicating love of God. It is because He loves that God freely gives Himself in Creation, in the prophets, and in the Son of His love who loved us and gave Himself up for us. This note rings out again and again throughout the work. Here is a mark that Irenaeus was a Christian indeed.

From the foregoing it will appear to some that S. Irenaeus held an economic or modalist view of the Trinity. This has indeed been maintained by some, though on other grounds than the considerations dealt with above. For example, Bousset claims that for Irenaeus Jesus Christ is God become tangible and visible, a doctrine akin to the ἐπιφανὴς θεός of Hellenistic piety; and also states that such a passage as *Dem.* 31 ('For so long as incorruption was invisible and unrevealed, it helped us not at all: therefore it became visible, that in all respects we might participate in the reception of incorruption'), yields a practical Modalism, because 'for belief and piety the Father and the Word who appeared on earth coincide'.[1] Seeberg also pronounces Modalist the celebrated phrase, so typical of Irenaeus, that the Son is the visible of the Father, and the Father the invisible of the Son.[2] Loofs likewise notices an economic trinitarian monotheism which keeps chiming-in in Irenaeus.[3]

An answer to this which has often been made, and which is valid so far as it goes, is that S. Irenaeus taught that the Son co-exists eternally with the Father.[4] In modification of this position it is to be admitted that Zahn can produce a passage which appears to teach that the economic form of trinitarian relationship has an end, when the Son hands over His perfect work to the Father.[5] However, as a counterpart

[1] *Kyr.Ch.* p. 347.   [2] *DG.* p. 322.
[3] *Studium DG.* p. 143; see also Beuzart, *Essai*, p. 55.
[4] e.g. Vernet, *Dictionnaire*, VII, col. 2444.
[5] *Marcellus*, p. 243. See V.36.2, ii.156: 'in due time the Son will yield up His work to the Father', coupled with citations of 1 Corinthians 20₂₅₋₆: 'For He must reign till He hath put all enemies under His feet', and of 1 Corinthians 15₂₇₋₈: 'then shall the Son also Himself be subject unto Him.'

to this isolated passage, which is not completely in accord with the general trend of the mind of Irenaeus, and which is manifestly drawn from him by 1 Corinthians 15$_{27-8}$, is the definite statement that Christ's Kingdom has no end.[1] A better answer to the charge of Modalism is made by Zahn in another place. He observes that while it does not come to mind to say anything of God apart from His revelation in the world, the distinction in the Economy is actual, i.e. eternal.[2] It is certain that S. Irenaeus teaches that in Christ, God is seen as He really is, and not merely as He temporarily appears.

A more radical answer is that '*The Two Hands of God*' is not a modalist doctrine because it is alien to Modalism in inward intention. The intention of the Modalist was at all costs to maintain the 'Monarchy' of God. This anxiety answers to the religious problem of Christianity as preached against the background of the polytheistic pagan world, a world in which the austere and morally salutary principle of the unity of God could not be taken for granted. This pagan world, furthermore, had the loosest idea of the Divine. It could speak of an emanation from God as God. Thus the motive of Sabellius and the Patripassians is seen in a reaction to pagan surroundings. At the same time, that Modalism could appear to them to be a satisfactory solution of the problem of the divinity of our Lord is likewise evidence of the clinging influence of that same paganism from which

---

[1] 'The Son . . . receives from the Father . . . the throne of the everlasting kingdom': *Dem.* 47; see also III.**10**.2, i.282; III.**10**.4, i.285; III.**12**.13, i.311; III.**16**.2, i.324; III.**21**.5, i.355; III.**21**.9, i.358; *Frag.* LIII.ii.183; *Dem.* 36, 56, 66, 95. All these are directly based on Biblical quotations.

[2] *Marcellus*, p. 238.

It is, however, difficult to see what evidence is forthcoming for Zahn's corresponding proposition, that the trinitarian relationship has also a beginning. The Son was with the Father in the beginning, before the Creation took form and time began (II.**22**.4, i.200; III.**18**.1, i.337; IV.**20**.1,3,7, i.439, 440, 444; *Frag.* XXXIX., ii.177; *Dem.* 30, 43). More strongly expressed is the statement that the Son is an 'uncreated Being', who did 'always co-exist with God' (II.**25**.3, i.214; see also II.**30**.9, i.239). Furthermore, Christ was *salvans* before the world (III.**22**.3, i.361; Harvey, ii.123).

they so wished to escape. Modalism, and to some extent also, more moderate and orthodox statements of a Christian economic Trinity, sprang from a mind which felt that the alternative lay between the confession of an Absolute who was so bare and abstruse as to be utterly separated in Being from this world, or else the degrading superstitious worship of 'gods many and lords many'. These doctrines likewise reflect the mind which could worship as divine a portion of the Divine proceeding from the Fullness. All this is very far from the spirit of the New Testament. A Hebrew Christian like S. Paul did not show himself particularly anxious to safeguard the 'Monarchy' of God. Say what he will about the divine nature of his Lord, he can take for granted as axiomatic the solitary grandeur of Jehovah. Nor was Paul exercised with any problem of bridging the gulf between God and the world. It is assumed that the utterly transcendent God is the creator of the world, and that He can visit it in power when He will. Furthermore, when Paul spoke of the Divine he meant what he said, for there was no place in his monotheism for a demigod, whether angel or Hero.

S. Irenaeus was of this mind. He could assume and powerfully assert that there is but one God, the Creator of all things. He is a Living God, in intimate contact with the world, though far above it. The Son and the Holy Spirit are His Hands; they are Very God at work in the world. Irenaeus was not too much concerned to explain to the troubled intellect how these things could be. They were the revealed truth. Thus he was not a complete theologian, but in inward spirit he was the very opposite to a Modalist, or to any theologian of an economic Trinity. We may therefore agree with Loofs, that it is not to be called the result of deep thought that Irenaeus appears to have anticipated the later doctrine of the Trinity.[1] The 'deep thought' of those days still retained its pagan background, and tended to demand that the Son and the Spirit be regarded as modes of God's

---

[1] *Studium DG.* p. 149.

appearing, or as emanations from God. Loofs, however, goes
quite astray when he writes that the conception of God found
in S. Irenaeus rests more on the philosophy of the time than
on the traditional revelation of God.[1] There is, in fact, no
emanationism in the doctrine of '*The Two Hands of God*'[2]
nor is there any subordinationism. The '*Hands*' indeed serve
God, but they are not thereby subordinate, for this service is
God's own activity in the world. So also the Spirit may be
described as a gift, but this does not place the Gift below the
Giver, for that which God gives is Himself.

We cannot leave the doctrine of God here, however, because
the teaching of S. Irenaeus has another side. Much of his
essential thought is indeed drawn from the Hebrew Bible,
but he can also express himself after the manner of the
culture of his day, that is, in the terms of Greek philosophy.
In respect not of one, but of many important themes, the
critical reader can easily collect passages from different
parts of these very profound but not completely systematic
writings, and, placing them side by side, demonstrate that
they formally contradict one another. The foregoing exposition of the doctrine of God in S. Irenaeus would be
justly condemned as one-sided if it stood alone. The writings
of Irenaeus are packed with statements about God and the
Logos which are quite after the manner of the Apologists,
and which could well have come from Alexandria.

By way of illustration we may turn to an exposition of
Isaiah 55₈. 'But if they had known the Scriptures, and been
taught by the truth, they would have known, beyond doubt,
that God is not as men are; and that His thoughts are not
like the thoughts of men. For the Father of all is at a vast
distance from those affections and passions which operate
among men. He is a simple, uncompounded Being, without
diverse members, and altogether like, and equal to Himself,
since He is wholly understanding, and wholly spirit, and

[1] *Studium DG.* p. 148.
[2] cf. Duncker, *Irenäus Christologie*, pp. 68–9; Beuzart, *Essai*, p. 50.

wholly thought, and wholly intelligence, and wholly reason, and wholly hearing, and wholly seeing, and wholly light, and the whole source of all that is good—even as the religious and pious are wont to speak concerning God.'[1] This Being is uncreated and perfect.[2] In contrast, all things else are created, and consequently imperfect.[3] The Godhead is static, unchangeable.[4] The self-existent One is self-contained and self-sufficient. A Being who is 'moved with any curiosity respecting the affairs of others . . . would be unjust, and rapacious, and would cease to be what God is'.[5] God does not need man's love.[6] The ground of existence of the universe is a thought in the mind of God. 'Let them cease, therefore, to affirm that the world was made by any other; for as soon as God formed a conception in His mind, that was also done which He had thus mentally conceived.'[7] God is One 'who, containing all things, alone is uncontained'.[8] Bonwetsch is so far right in stating that S. Irenaeus describes God in terms of negative abstraction.[9] It is clear that the doctrine of God in S. Irenaeus is not wholly Biblical.

There are two separate factors at work here. The first is that Irenaeus is a man of many-sided genius, but not a systematist. The interest that moves him is plainly the practical one of expounding the Christian Faith as a religion of moral redemption. His more powerful and constructive thought moves within this sphere, and here he is essentially Biblical and 'primitive'. At the same time, he does not repudiate or neglect the culture of his day as something dangerous or worthless. He is happy to express himself through it. This is in itself an admirable intention, but it does involve Irenaeus in occasional formal contradictions, which he perhaps did not notice, and certainly was not careful to resolve. The doctrine of God is a case in point. The history of thought shows that it is difficult to hold the

[1] II.13.3, i.155. [2] IV.38.3, ii.44. [3] IV.38.1, ii.42. [4] II.34.2, i.252.
[5] II.1.5, i.120. [6] IV.16.4, i.424. [7] II.3.2, i.124.
[8] *Dem.* 4; see also II.1.1, i.117.
[9] *Theologie d.I.* p. 51. On p. 53ff., however, Bonwetsch also finds stress laid upon the living Personality and the will of God.

balance between the conception of God as the remote and
unmoved One, defined in terms of abstraction or negation,
and the religious conception of a present and active Living
God. If a coherent philosophical theology is to be framed
one of these conceptions must be accommodated to the
other. The interests of Christianity as a religion of redemption are surely best preserved by defining God as the
Biblical Living God. The theologian can then rightly pass
on to observe that the undoubted moral and intellectual
values of the more severely philosophical conceptions can be
united with the religious doctrine. The conception of the
Living God is enriched and balanced thereby. Thus philosophy may be used both to amplify devotion, and to provide a
medium whereby religion may be expounded. We must admit
that S. Irenaeus does not rise to this level of systematic intellectual coherence. He does, however, preserve the materials
for this synthesis. The Hebraic and Greek strains are both
there in all fullness, with the Biblical, as it were, the rightful
senior partner. His witness is thus most valuable. It prefigures much of the healthiest and profoundest Christian
thought of later ages.

The other factor at work is doubtless loyalty to the
tradition of the Apologists. As the name implies, these first
theologians, who worked even before Irenaeus, were inspired by the aim of presenting Christianity in a manner
attractive to the Greek world. It is therefore natural that in
their work the Hellenic atmosphere should prevail. It would
appear, for example, that S. Justin Martyr had in his
theology less of Hebraic counter-balance than had S. Irenaeus. The men of that generation were now honoured by
Irenaeus and his fellows as the Elders, the Martyrs, and the
Saints. With his love of the solid tradition of the Church
S. Irenaeus would hardly have thought of going back upon
what they had said. This principle holds good even in cases,
like the present, where his own aim was divergent from that
of the Apologists. S. Justin attempted to expound Christianity as the fulfilment of everything that was best in Greek

thought. S. Irenaeus had to show wherein the Faith differed from certain of the less noble aspects of Greek thought, for the Valentinian Gnosticism he faced was nothing other than an amalgam of Christianity with elements drawn from the thought and religion of the Gentile world. The aim of Justin was most legitimate, and his work most valuable, but it must be admitted that the controversy with Gnosticism was the historical occasion for the better-balanced theology. The wider spiritual issues of the relation of Biblical to Hellenic thought are more easily illustrated from the doctrine of Salvation found in Irenaeus. This important matter will therefore be treated of again in a later part of this study.[1]

The contrast between the Biblical and the philosophical interest in Irenaeus may further be illuminated by a consideration of his Logos-doctrine. In the doctrine of '*The Two Hands of God*' he had his own way of expounding the connexion of God with the world, and so of providing a rationale of the Incarnation. This seems in strict logic to preclude the use of the Logos-doctrine, for if the Living God be in intimate contact with the world of men one may well ask what need there is for a Mediator of Creation and Revelation. On the other hand, the Logos-theology is in Christian tradition the language typical of precisely those who have felt the need of such a Mediator. A strong feeling that an intermediary between God and the world is necessary is presumptive evidence that consciously or unconsciously God is being defined as the eternal and impassible Being, remote and unmoved, rather than as the Living God. We have seen very plainly that S. Irenaeus conceived of God as present and active. Nevertheless, with his deep-seated instinct for tradition he constantly used the Apologistic Logos-theology also. 'The Word' is one of the commonest titles applied to our Lord. 'The rule of truth which we hold is, that there is one God Almighty, who made all things by His Word.'[2]

---

[1] See pp. 163-5 *infra*.
[2] I.22.1, i.84; see also II.2.4–5, i.122–3; III.8.2, i.276; III.11.1, i.287; IV.24.1, i.458; IV.32.1, ii.5.

Several writers may be found to have hinted at aspects of this problem. Most notably, Seeberg observes that S. Irenaeus differs from S. Justin in his conception of the Logos. To Justin the Logos is the hypostatized Divine Reason. On the other hand, Irenaeus thinks in the manner of the old Johannine tradition: the Logos is the revealed God. The consequence is drawn from this that for Justin the Logos is part of God, δεύτερος Θεός, for Irenaeus He is God, God self-revealed.[1] This well describes the position of S. Irenaeus. Harnack, likewise, correctly states that when Irenaeus speaks of the Logos or of God the Son he always thinks of Jesus, and therefore does not identify the divine element in Christ with the world-idea or Reason of God; and further-more, the circumstance that he makes the Logos the regular designation of the pre-existent Christ is due to the authority of the Apologistic tradition, and seemed also to be required by John 1₁.[2] We may also agree with Aall, who claims that S. Irenaeus customarily thinks within the scheme of the Biblical 'Word', who is a work-master of arbitrary will.[3] Aall continues that the idea of the Logos lands Irenaeus in speculative weakness, as he has already laid it down that God cannot have a mediator in the creation and government of the world. We may dismiss, therefore, Harnack's judge-ment, that Irenaeus only thought with systematic clarity within the scheme of the Apologists.[4]

In passing, notice must be taken of Loofs' interesting suggestion that the doctrine of 'The Two Hands of God' is an expansion by S. Irenaeus of a piece of tradition from Asia Minor, which contained the notion that the Logos is the Hand of God.[5] This is one aspect of Loofs' main thesis, worked out in painstaking elaboration of detail in *Theophilus von Antiochen adversus Marcionem, und die anderen theologis-chen Quellen bei Irenaeus* (Leipzig, 1930), namely, that the various and contradictory strains in Irenaeus are to be accounted for as due to a rather unintelligent reproduction

---

[1] *DG.* p. 325.   [2] *H.D.* II.262–3.   [3] *Logosidee*, p. 357.
[4] *H.D.* II.237.   [5] *Studium DG.* p. 149.

of a wide variety of sources and sub-sources, into which his writings may be analysed.[1] Most of these results appear to be somewhat speculative, but Loofs does seem securely to establish that Irenaeus knew and used the *ad Autolycum* of Theophilus of Antioch.[2] This is a link between Irenaeus and the theology of Asia Minor, additional to the circumstance of his birth and race. A theology of *'The Hands of God'* may well have been preached there. However, there does not appear to be any direct evidence that Theophilus spoke of the Logos as 'the Hand of God'. The distinctive doctrine of S. Irenaeus may therefore be more safely derived direct from the Bible. As is but natural, the Roman Catholic Vernet dismisses the whole notion of a 'theology of Asia Minor' in the interest of the doctrinal solidarity of the primitive Church.[3]

In conclusion, the question must be raised of the adequacy of *'The Two Hands of God'* as a Christian doctrine of God. We may say that if the Christian Trinity is an adequate doctrine, then S. Irenaeus is advancing on right lines. If he is to be condemned the Church Catholic is to be condemned also. In an atlas there will be found several systems of map-projection, each giving a map with its own proper use and its own inevitable error. One will give accurate compass bearings, but at the expense of distorting areas. Another will reproduce the relative areas of continents and oceans, but the true shape of each will be lost. The navigator and the statistician will consequently remain for ever at variance. This is a token that the surface of a spheroid cannot be converted into a plane surface. If a globe be chosen, as the only adequate form of map, the eye cannot obtain an undistorted view, save of a single point at a time. So it is

[1] *Theophilus*, p. 432.

[2] ibid., pp. 58–80. Not all the parallels quoted are convincing, but some are. For a brief and effective digest of this subject see J. A. Robinson's introduction to the S.P.C.K. translation of *The Apostolic Preaching*, pp. 53–60.

[3] *Dictionnaire*, VII, col. 2516.

with all efforts to convey the mystery of the Being of God to the mind of man. If a conception of God be framed in such a way as to form the most convenient basis for a neat and easily expounded doctrine of the world, the interests of religious worship and of salvation are almost bound to suffer. We would emphasize as a principle of fundamental importance the fact that reason is, equally with religious 'experience', a God-given faculty for the apprehension of truth. All true science and philosophy must therefore speak of the same God as does true religion. The perfect conception of God would completely satisfy alike the claims of religious faith and worship, and the claims of philosophy and science. However, seekers for truth and God do not rise to this level, save perhaps momentarily. In consequence, the order in which one seeks to satisfy various interests remains a circumstance of momentous importance. Ideally he who sets off to expound the universe should end by bowing before the same God who is worshipped by him who is first thrilled by religious awe, and who then goes on to investigate the world which God has made. In practice this is not always so. On the other hand, experience shows that reason, with its claims, assists in the distinctively religious apprehension of God by acting as a restraining corrective, as also the religious consciousness has much of importance to contribute to the study of philosophy and psychology. In consequence, the Deity of philosophical and scientific speculation will almost inevitably be found a bare Supreme Being, an impersonal Great First Cause. The incarnation of such a God is bound to be some form of emanationism. God inspires and indwells all men, and the Incarnation is the supreme example. Religion, on the other hand, demands a God who is a personal Being, at once gloriously transcendent and in intimate contact with the world. The active minds who must and will inquire 'How can these things be?' have never found easy answers to their questions. If a conception of God be framed to fulfil the interests of religion there are bound to be embarrassments and obscurities, or at the very least, a certain difficulty in lucid and simple exposition, when it is used as a basis for a doctrine of the natural universe.

The history of the Arian controversy is the story of how the theologians of the Church faced this hard choice. In that long conflict the scientific Logos-theology, which was nothing other than the form of theology congenial to the speculative mind of the day, revealed serious religious weakness latent within itself. It displayed an inherent tendency to slip, despite frequent excellent intentions, into subordinationism and emanationism. The Church therefore finally resolved to relegate the claims of speculation to a secondary place. First and foremost would she safeguard the interests of a religion of Redemption by Divine Incarnation, and then after that, and only then, would she do her best with Cosmology. Ever since then the Christian Trinity has been a 'Mystery', something to be contemplated with adoration, and to be understood only so far as the limitation of the human mind permits. The significance of S. Irenaeus is that he prefigures this preference. In his own day, and in his own way, he based himself firmly upon the God of the Bible, that is, upon the God of religious experience. In preaching '*The Two Hands of God*' he asserted that the Supreme God Himself both intimately indwells, and has incarnated Himself in, the world He had Himself created. This was his vital interest, and the constructive work for which he is remembered. At the same time, however, he did not neglect those other things which may rightly be said of God from the point of view of speculative thought.

Chapter Eleven

THE RECAPITULATION

Ita notio ἀνάκ. definiri potest: recapitulatio est iteratio Adami (per idem ac contrarium) a Christo eo consilio perfecta, ut omnia sibi subiceret.—MOLWITZ

S. IRENAEUS has a most distinctive exposition of the manner in which the Living God intervened in this world to work the salvation of man. This is the doctrine of the *Recapitulation*. Here again it will be found that Irenaeus is a profoundly Biblical and Pauline theologian.

There has been much discussion as to the meaning of the word ἀνακεφαλαίωσις, rendered in the Latin translation by *recapitulatio*. Gustav Molwitz opens his very useful Dissertation *De 'ΑΝΑΚΕΦΑΛΑΙΩΣΕΩΣ in Irenaei Theologia Potestate* (Dresden 1874) with a careful discussion of the derivation of this term. The verb κεφαλαιοῦν is derived from the substantive κεφάλαιον, i.e. 'the chief point, or summary' (p. 1). The sense of κεφάλαιον (= *capitulum*) is: 'that in which is the whole of a thing.' Κεφάλαιον is that in which the parts of a thing have unity, the whole containing the parts. Κεφαλαιοῦν expresses the action by which anything comes to its κεφάλαιον (2). In the verb ἀνακεφαλαιοῦν the preposition ἀνα has not the proper sense of *sursum*, 'upwards', but of the Latin *re*. 'Ανακεφαλαιοῦν means, 'to collect together again'. The two New Testament occurrences of the verb ἀνακεφαλαιώσασθαι are then discussed in the light of this. In Romans 13₉, 'and if there be any other commandment, it is summed up in this word (ἐν τῷ λόγῳ τούτῳ ἀνακεφαλαιοῦται), namely, Thou shalt love thy neighbour as thyself', S. Paul teaches that that which before was separated and in parts in the Law is now comprised in the commandment of love of Leviticus 19₁₈ (3). This is an example of ἀνακεφαλαίωσις. In

Ephesians 1₁₀, 'a dispensation of the fullness of the times, to
sum up all things in Christ (ἀνακεφαλαιώσασθαι τὰ πάντα), the
things in the heavens, and the things upon the earth', the
intention is that God in Christ joined again to Himself
those men who had been divided from Him in sin. Christ is
the κεφάλαιον of the communion of God and man. Relevant
passages in S. Irenaeus are then discussed (7–10). Recapitulation is the repetition by Christ of the actions of Adam, in
the same manner, or in reverse, that He may subject all
things to Himself (11).

This exposition may be compared with that given of the
verb ἀνακεφαλαιώσασθαι as it occurs in Ephesians 1₁₀, by
S. D. F. Salmond, in Volume III of the *Expositor's Greek
Testament* (London, 1903). In the classics it is used of
repeating summarily the points of a speech, gathering its
argument together in a summary form. 'The subsequent
specification of the objects of the ἀνακεφαλαιώσασθαι, however,
makes it plain that what is in view here is not a logical or
rhetorical, but a real and objective summing up. Further,
as the verb comes not from κεφαλή but from κεφάλαιον, it does
not refer to the summing up of things under a *head*, and the
point of view, therefore, is not that of the Headship of
Christ.' 'On the other hand it does not seem necessary to
limit the sense of the word to the idea of a *résumé* or *compendious presentation* of things in a single person.' The
force of the preposition ἀνα is then considered, and the view
preferred is that it does not add the idea of 'again' to the
compound verb. 'This "summing up" is not the recovery
of a broken pristine unity, but the gathering together of
objects now apart and unrelated into a final, perfect unity.
Nevertheless it may be said that the verb, if it does not itself
definitely express the idea of the restoration of a lost unity,
gets that idea from the context' (p. 261).

Many writers upon S. Irenaeus have essayed a definition
of the meaning of the word 'recapitulation' as used by him,
and with a perplexing variety of results. These results are
found to be variations upon several themes. 'Recapitulation'

is: 'to unite under a single head', or, 'to restore to the original', or, 'to make a new start', or, 'to bring to a climax', or, again, 'to go over the ground a second time'. Thus to Harnack it is the reunion of things unnaturally separated.[1] To Wendt the word unites the two meanings of restoration to the original and of collection of the separated.[2] Bonwetsch expounds it as leaning to Johannine conceptions. It is an all-collecting rehearsal which leads to perfection.[3] As there has been a Fall this necessarily works restoration to the original.[4] Seeberg finds that Recapitulation means collecting together, and not reiteration. It is a thought similar to the Johannine conception of the faithful as in Christ and the Father, perfected in unity.[5] To Vernet it denotes the work of reconstruction and restoration after the primitive plan of God.[6] Loofs states that Recapitulation is for Irenaeus first of all restoration.[7] The 'putting under one head' of Ephesians plays no part in S. Irenaeus. Alone, Loofs maintains that the Recapitulation of Irenaeus is not associated with Ephesians 1 10.[8] Werner finds it expressive of a Pauline idea, namely, that Christ is the mid-point of all history, the goal of all former development, and the initiator of new life.[9] Bousset gives an analysis which is at once most illuminating and a little too subtle. The idea of Recapitulation combines the thoughts of evolution and of supernatural intervention. It contains the idea of a long course of development, but not in a straight line. It is a development, which leads back to the beginning, and which yet finishes at a higher level. Recapitulation expresses the idea of a spiral climb.[10] Thus Bousset appears to find a combination of salvation by a natural process of education and of salvation by a birth to new life. The most comprehensive exposition is given by Beuzart. To him Recapitulation appears to be the restoration of humanity into the blessed state of collectivity by

---

[1] *H.D.* II.238.　　[2] *m.Vollkommenheit*, p. 26.　　[3] *Theologie d.I.* p. 98.
[4] ibid. p. 101.　　[5] *DG.* p. 325.　　[6] *Dictionnaire*, VII, cols. 2471-2.
[7] *Theophilus*, p. 370.　　[8] ibid. pp. 364, 368.　　[9] *Paulinismus*, p. 85.
[10] *Kyr.Ch.* p. 356.

Christ, the Second Adam.[1] To accomplish this Christ went through experiences parallel to those of Adam, but with the opposite outcome in each case.[2] Christ realizes for man the primitive destination of the race.[3] He shows the unity of the work of all those who have sown the Word, whether patriarch, prophet, or apostle. This is an example of Recapitulation.

For further clarification we must turn to the actual writings of S. Irenaeus, to find out the exact manner in which he explains the saving work of Christ. From this may be forthcoming a more precise exposition of the word ἀνακεφαλαίωσις, as it is used by him at least. It will be found that all the elements mentioned above have their place in the scheme of Irenaeus, though some are much more fundamental than others. The foundation of all would seem to be the conception of 'going over the ground again', rather than that of 'comprehension in unity', even though the latter springs so naturally from the derivation of the word. The fundamental fact in the work of Christ is that He went through all the experiences of Adam, but with the opposite result. The result of this process provides a secondary conception. The human race was given a new start. Last in the train of derived conceptions is that of collection under a single head, inasmuch as saved humanity is one in Christ.

'Ανακεφαλαίωσις is a Biblical word. The ultimate source of this term, so characteristic of S. Irenaeus, is doubtless Ephesians 1₁₀. We notice that he cites this text several times when writing of the *Recapitulation*.[4] A warning is necessary, however, that this connexion does not necessitate that Irenaeus used the word in the same sense as S. Paul. Irenaeus appears to have recognized the word as one used by S. Justin Martyr, for the celebrated quotation from Justin's lost work against Marcion[5] describes the incarnation in a phrase quite typical of Irenaeus: *suum plasma in semetipso recapitulans*, 'summing up His own handiwork in Himself'.[6]

---

[1] *Essai*, pp. 104–5.   [2] ibid. pp. 105–6.   [3] ibid. p. 108.
[4] I.**10**.1, i.42; III.**16**.6, i.330; *Dem.* 30.   [5] IV.**6**.2, i.390.
[6] Harvey, ii.159.

However, this takes the matter little farther, for the doctrine of *Recapitulation* is not a distinct part of Justin's theological system, and the use of the word here may be no more than a passing quotation of Scripture. Justin certainly sheds no light upon the doctrine found in Irenaeus. Bousset contends that only the first sentence of the passage in question goes back to S. Justin, and that the true quotation in Irenaeus is only the short form as it occurs in Eusebius, *H.E.*, IV. xviii. 9.[1] This would eliminate a mention of '*Recapitulation*' in Justin. This is not impossible, but is unlikely, for the first clauses of the second sentence return to a 'me', harking back to the 'I' with which the quotation starts. When S. Irenaeus speaks for himself, on the other hand, he writes impersonally, or as 'we'.

A detailed investigation of the teaching of S. Irenaeus regarding the work of Christ may well begin with the following most significant passage. 'He has therefore, in His work of recapitulation, summed up all things (*omnia ergo recapitulans recapitulatus est*),[2] both waging war against our enemy, and crushing him who at the beginning had led us away captive in Adam . . . in order that, as our species went down to death through a vanquished man, so we may ascend to life again through a victorious one.'[3] Jesus Christ went over the same ground as Adam, but in the reverse direction. He placed Himself in the same circumstances as Adam, and was confronted with the same choices.[4] At every point where Adam weakly yielded, slipping down to destruction, Christ heroically resisted, and at the cost of His agony retrieved the disaster. Thus was wrought out a decisive victory over the Adversary. The benefits of this victory can

---

[1] *Kyr.Ch.* p. 348, note 3.

[2] Harvey, ii.380. The sense of this important but rather difficult passage would seem to require that *recapitulari* be here regarded as deponent. *Recapitulari* is in the Latin version of Irenaeus sometimes deponent, e.g. III.23.3, Harvey, ii.123; V.20.2, Harvey, ii.380; though the usage is variable.

[3] V.21.1, ii.110–11.

[4] cf. Molvitz, *De Ἀνακεφαλαιώσεως in Irenaei Theologia Potestate*, pp. 11, 30–1.

pass to mankind, because Christ was acting as the Champion of humanity.[1] 'He was man contending for the fathers.'[2] The Incarnation was consequently the great climax of the history of the human race. The ground lost in the Fall was regained, and a new order of spiritual progress initiated. The essential conception of Irenaeus is admirably expressed in a fine sentence from his contemporary, Clement of Alexandria: καὶ σαρκὶ ἀναπλησάμενος τὸ σωτήριον δρᾶμα τῆς ἀνθρωπότητος ὑπεκρίνετο γνήσιος γὰρ ἦν ἀγωνιστὴς καὶ τοῦ πλάσματος συναγωνιστής.[3]

It is impossible to over-estimate the crucial importance of this matter in seeking an understanding of the thought of S. Irenaeus, and in estimating his great significance in the history of Christian thought. In his brief but momentous history of the doctrine of the Atonement,[4] Dr. Gustav Aulén does not hesitate to open his study with S. Irenaeus, as the Christian Father who gives the first thorough treatment of the Atonement, and who prefigures the Christian thought of a thousand years.[5] The clue to Irenaeus is to be found in the statement that Christ came down from heaven 'that He might kill sin, deprive death of its power, and give life to man': *ut occideret quidem peccatum, evacuaret autem mortem, et vivificaret hominem.*[6] Aulén continues: 'By the side of this pregnant saying we will set another, chosen from among many similar passages, which develops the dramatic idea in fuller detail: "Man had been created by God that he might

---

[1] It is a misfortune, when one comes to render into English the word ἀγωνιστής as it has been applied to the Redeemer, that the chivalric associations of 'champion' have been so largely displaced by those of the prize-ring. We keep the former associations in mind here. There is, of course, no assumption made here that Irenaeus himself used the word ἀγωνιστής.

[2] III.**18**.6, i.342; see also *Dem.* 31.

[3] *Exhortation*, X. 'Fashioning Himself in flesh He enacted the drama of human salvation: for He was a true champion and a fellow-champion with the creature.'

[4] *Den kristna försoningstanken* (Stockholm, 1930), translated under the title *Christus Victor* by A. G. Hebert (S.P.C.K. 1931).

[5] *Christus Victor*, pp. 32–3.

[6] III.**18**.7, i.344; Harvey, ii.102.

have life. If now, having lost life, and having been harmed by the serpent, he were not to return to life, but were to be wholly abandoned to death, then God would have been defeated, and the malice of the serpent would have overcome God's will. But since God is both invincible and magnanimous, He showed His magnanimity in correcting man, and in proving all men, as we have said; but through the Second Man He bound the strong one, and spoiled his goods, and annihilated death, bringing life to man who had become subject to death. For Adam had become the devil's possession, and the devil held him under his power, by having wrongfully practised deceit upon him, and by the offer of immortality made him subject to death. For by promising that they should be as gods, which did not lie in his power, he worked death in them. Wherefore he who had taken man captive was himself taken captive by God, and man who had been taken captive was set free from the bondage of condemnation" (III.23.1, i.363). . . . The main idea is clear. The work of Christ is first and foremost a victory over the powers that hold mankind in bondage: sin, death, and the devil. These may be said to be in a measure personified, but in any case they are objective powers; and the victory of Christ creates a new situation, bringing their rule to an end, and setting men free from their dominion.'[1]

In passages such as these there comes to view that which Aulén calls the 'classic' idea of the Atonement, namely, that God Himself, in the Person of His incarnate Son, entered the world of men, and on man's behalf victoriously contended with the foes of mankind.[2] This is the doctrine of an objective Saving Work wrought out through the 'drama' of Christ the Champion. In contrast to this 'dramatic' exposition there is another 'objective' view of the Atonement, which took its rise in the Latin Church, and which is first clearly seen in S. Anselm. This 'Latin' idea of the Atonement is essentially juridical in character. Man's relation to God is thought of throughout in terms of law.[3] The emphasis

---

[1] *Christus Victor*, pp. 35–6.   [2] ibid. pp. 20–3.   [3] ibid. pp. 106–7, 163.

falls not so much upon the breaking of the power of Satanic tyranny, but upon the release of man from the legal pains and penalties of sin.[1] This release was procured by the satisfaction offered to God the Father by His suffering incarnate Son.[2] The 'Latin' doctrine of the Atonement, stated in various forms during passing ages, is inferior to the 'Classic' idea, which it has almost entirely supplanted in the Western Church. The 'Classic' doctrine is that of the New Testament.[3] It moves at a higher level, and presupposes a more adequate conception of sin, than does the 'Latin' doctrine.[4] The 'Classic' doctrine, furthermore, speaks of a continuous divine activity: God Himself incarnate, at work in the world. The 'Latin' doctrine answers to a discontinuous divine activity; for while the work of Atonement takes its origin in the will of the Father, it is in itself that which is offered by Christ *as man* to God.[5] Aulén also notices a third type of doctrine, which took its origin in reaction to the deficiencies of the 'Latin' system. This is the 'Abelardian' or 'subjective' view of the Atonement.[6] This too is unsatisfactory, for it reduces the Saving Work of Christ to an act of revelation. Here is a masterly and illuminating, and in most respects also a convincing, survey of the history of the doctrine of the Atonement. It will be noticed that it gives to S. Irenaeus a most important place in the development of Christian thought, and that attention is focused upon this particular matter of the Championship of Christ. We will therefore do well to unfold the plot of 'the drama of salvation' in much greater detail than has been attempted in *Christus Victor*.

In detailing the career of the heavenly Champion of man most of the important things that S. Irenaeus has to say about the saving work of Christ fall into place. The more one looks into the detail the more convincing becomes the whole scheme. This circumstance substantiates the claim

---

[1] *Christus Victor*, p. 166. [2] ibid. pp. 105–6. [3] ibid. pp. 82–93.
[4] ibid. pp. 108, 164–6. [5] ibid. pp. 21–2, 102.
[6] ibid. pp. 112–13, 149–59, 163.

that it is this conception which is essentially represented by the word 'Recapitulation'. God 'sent His creative Word, who in coming to deliver us came to the very place and spot in which we lost life, and brake the bonds of our fetters'.[1] Satan was conquered 'by means of human nature'.[2] 'He, in the last times, was made a man among men; ... He ... destroyed and conquered the enemy of man, and gave to His own handiwork victory against the adversary.'[3] Christ bound Satan, the strong man, and spoiled him of the human race, his ill-gotten gains.[4] Those who were in the power of Satan were in the power of death, 'wherefore, when the foe was conquered in his turn, Adam received new life'.[5]

S. Irenaeus is seen at his best when he comes to detail how this victory was won by 'Christus Victor'. To encourage those who were suffering for their faith the writer to the Hebrews had dwelt upon the fact that the Lord Jesus went that way too. Because He had lived a life of sinless obedience to the calling of God, undeterred by persecution and grievous suffering, His life had proved adequate to pioneer the way of salvation. It was the way of God 'in bringing many sons to glory, to make the Pioneer of their salvation, ἀρχηγὸς τῆς σωτηρίας αὐτῶν, perfect through suffering' (Hebrews 2₁₀). In expounding his doctrine of Recapitulation S. Irenaeus follows this exactly. Christ was the victorious Champion of the human race through His obedience.

An example of this obedience is seen in the Matthean account of the Temptation of Christ.[6] As for Milton, this was the story of Paradise Regained. Christ fasted 'that His opponent might have an opportunity of attacking Him'.[7] He made Himself one with man to the extent of laying Himself open to real temptation, so that the moral conflict

---

[1] Dem. 38.   [2] V.24.4, ii.121; see also IV.33.4, ii.9; Dem. 31.
[3] IV.24.1, i.458.
[4] III.23.1, i.363; see also III.18.6, i.342; III.23.7, i.367; IV.24.1, i.458; IV.33.4, ii.9; V.19.1, ii.107; V.21.1-3, ii.110-14; V.24.4, ii.121.
[5] III.23.7, i.367; see also III.18.7, i.343-4; V.19.1, ii.107; V.21.1, ii.111; Dem. 31.
[6] V.21.2, ii.111-13.   [7] V.21.2, ii.111.

on behalf of man might take place under genuine human conditions.[1] In spite of all the temptations of the Devil, and under these conditions, Christ kept the commandments of the Law perfectly. Three times He vanquished Satan. As a consequence 'there was done away that infringement of God's commandment which had occurred in Adam'.[2] 'The apostate angel . . . is . . . vanquished by the Son of Man keeping the commandment of God.'[3] Irenaeus constantly emphasizes that it was this real and grim, yet completely victorious, moral struggle of the Incarnate Son that robbed Satan of his power, and saved man. Christ's obedience reversed the result of Adam's disobedience.[4] The climax of all this was His passion and death.[5] 'It is clear that the Lord suffered death, in obedience to His Father.'[6] 'And the trespass which came by the tree was undone by the tree of obedience, when, hearkening unto God, the Son of Man was nailed to the tree.'[7] It is thus no mere conventional formula when one reads that Christ saved man 'by His death'. 'But the Lord, our Christ, underwent a valid . . . passion', and 'established fallen man by His own strength'.[8] 'Jesus Christ . . . redeemed us from apostasy with His own blood.'[9] 'And truly the death of the Lord became healing and remission for sins.'[10] The death was 'a recapitulation . . . of the effusion of blood from the beginning', in the sense that it was the climax of all martyrdoms.[11]

The use of the conception of *obedience* as a clue to the meaning of the Cross is a piece of excellent New Testament theology, reflecting as it does both the mind of our Lord and the usage of all our main New Testament sources. 'And He began to teach them that the Son of Man *must* suffer many things' (Mark 8:31; cf. Mark 9:12, Matthew 16:21, Luke 9:22, Luke 17:25). This 'must' of divine constraint is illuminated by the cry in Gethsemane: 'Howbeit, not what I will, but

---

[1] III.**19**.3, i.346; V.**21**.2, ii.111–13.   [2] V.**21**.2, ii.113.   [3] V.**21**.3, ii.113.
[4] III.**18**.6, i.342; III.**18**.7, i.343–4; III.**21**.10, i.358; V.**17**.1, ii.100.
[5] cf. Hebrews 5:8–10.   [6] V.**23**.2, ii.118.
[7] *Dem*. 34; see also III.**18**.6, i.342; V.**16**.3, ii.99–100.   [8] II.**20**.3, i.191.
[9] III.**5**.3, i.268, etc.   [10] IV.**27**.2, i.468.   [11] V.**14**.1, ii.92.

what Thou wilt' (Mark 14₃₆; cf. Matthew 26₃₉, Luke 22₄₂). In line with this S. Paul writes: 'He humbled Himself, becoming obedient even unto death' (Philippians 2₈). So also 1 Peter 2₂₃ reads: 'Christ . . . when He suffered, threatened not, but committed Himself to Him that judgeth righteously': and similarly, Hebrews 5₇,₈: 'Who in the days of His flesh, having offered up prayers and supplications with strong crying and tears unto Him that was able to save Him from death, and having been heard for His godly fear, though He was a Son, yet learned obedience by the things which He suffered.' Akin is the Johannine exposition: 'For I am come down from heaven, not to do mine own will, but the will of Him that sent me' (John 6₃₈; cf. 4₃₄, 5₃₀).

The saving work of Christ by His 'Championship through obedience' is further illuminated in detail by a consideration of what S. Irenaeus calls the 'analogy'. Here the root idea of ἀνακεφαλαίωσις as 'going over the ground again' comes to view. By His obedience the Champion trod precisely the same path as Adam did in his disobedience, but in the reverse direction. Thus an analogy between the careers of Christ and Adam may be drawn. This is worked out to great elaboration in an endeavour to show that every circumstance in the career of Adam was duplicated in the career of Christ, and that at every point where the former made a wrong choice the latter made the counter-balancing right choice. In the first place, both were virgin-born. 'From this, then [i.e. the new-formed earth], whilst it was still virgin, God took dust of the earth and formed the man, the beginning of mankind. So then the Lord, summing up afresh this man, took the same dispensation of entry into flesh, being born from the Virgin by the Will and the Wisdom of God.'[1]

For S. Irenaeus this is the chief theological significance of the Virgin Birth, a doctrine to which he attaches great importance. 'If, then, the first Adam had a man for his father, and was born of human seed, it were reasonable to say that the

---

[1] *Dem.* 32; see also III.**18**.7, i.343–4; III.**21**.10, i.358–9.

second Adam was begotten of Joseph. But if the former was taken from the dust, and God was his maker, it was incumbent that the latter also, making a recapitulation in Himself, should be formed as man by God [i.e. not by Joseph] to have an analogy with the former as respects His origin.'[1] Furthermore, the disobedience of a woman provided the historical occasion of the Fall. In like manner, the obedience of a woman provided the occasion of the Incarnation of the One who recapitulated the Fall. 'Mary the Virgin is found obedient, saying: "Behold the handmaid of the Lord; be it unto me according to thy word." But Eve was disobedient: for she did not obey when as yet she was a virgin. And even as she, having indeed a husband, Adam, but being nevertheless as yet a virgin . . . having become disobedient, was made the cause of death, both to herself and to the entire human race; so also did Mary, having a man betrothed [to her], and being nevertheless a virgin, by yielding obedience, became the cause of salvation, both to herself and the whole human race. . . . And thus also it was that the knot of Eve's disobedience was loosed by the obedience of Mary. For what the virgin Eve had bound fast through unbelief, this did the Virgin Mary set free through faith . . . an inversion of the process by which these bonds of union had arisen.'[2]

The obedience of the Blessed Virgin Mary is in fact a subsidiary recapitulating action, exactly analogous to the obedience of Christ. She is a subsidiary Champion. 'Virginal disobedience having been balanced in the opposite scale by virginal obedience . . . that the Virgin Mary might become the patroness [advocata][3] of the virgin Eve.'[4] Mary's is thus 'that pure womb which regenerates men unto God'.[5] Vernet has recorded the views of Pusey, who limited this to the circumstance that Mary had given birth to the Redeemer, and of Newman, who in reply stated that the teaching of S. Irenaeus is that the Virgin is not merely a physical instrument, but a co-operator in redemp-

[1] III.21.10, i.358–9.   [2] III.22.4, i.361–2.   [3] Harvey, ii.376.
[4] V.19.1, ii.107; see also *Dem.* 33.   [5] IV.33.11, ii.14.

tion.[1] It is to be admitted that on the face of it the language used inclines one to the latter view. It should be noted, however, that the motive of these statements of Irenaeus is not to elevate the Blessed Virgin to a place of honour, but to trace out further details in the 'analogy'. He hereby gives recognition to the fact that Christ did not save the world automatically, but was dependent to a certain extent upon the moral goodness of the men and women who lived about Him. Our Lord lived as part of human society, not as an alien thrust in. There is thus a distinct value in the place given by Irenaeus to the Virgin in the scheme of salvation, nor need the honour be limited to her. There is, however, no evidence in *Adversus Haereses* to support Vernet's claim that it is reasonable to see in Mary as the *advocata* of Eve the power of the Virgin to intercede in heaven.[2] Nevertheless, we may certainly agree that S. Irenaeus is the first theologian of the Virgin Mary.[3] He clearly points the way for later developments.

The 'analogy' is further traced in Christ's own obedience. Regarding the Temptations Irenaeus writes: 'For as at the beginning it was by means of food that [the enemy] persuaded man, although not suffering hunger, to transgress God's commandments, so in the end he did not succeed in persuading Him that was an hungered to take the food that proceeded from God. . . . The corruption of man, therefore, which occurred in paradise by both [our first parents] eating, was done away with by [the Lord's] want of food in this world.'[4] So at the end, in 'doing away with that disobedience of man which had taken place at the beginning by the occasion of a tree, "He became obedient unto death, even the death of the cross"; rectifying that disobedience which had occurred by reason of a tree, through that obedience which was [wrought out] upon the tree'.[5]

---

[1] *Dictionnaire*, VII, cols. 2485–6.   [2] ibid. col. 2486.
[3] ibid. col. 2487.   [4] V.21.2, ii.111–2.
[5] V.16.3, ii.99–100; see also V.17.3–4, ii.102–3; V.19.1, ii.106–7; V.23.2, ii.118; *Dem.* 34.

Another way of expounding *Recapitulation* as 'going over
the ground again' was to show that Christ shared successively every part of human experience. So, His birth
'hallowed our birth'.[1] 'He passed through every stage of
life, restoring communion with God to all.'[2] 'For He came
to save all by means of Himself—all, I say . . . infants, and
children, and boys, and youths, and old men. He therefore
passed through every age, becoming an infant for infants,
thus sanctifying infants; a child for children, thus sanctifying
those who are of this age. . . . So likewise He was an old man
for old men, that He might be a perfect Master for all. . . .
Then at last He came on to death itself.'[3] The last human
experience shared by Jesus was His burial. 'For three days
He dwelt where the dead were,'[4] 'preaching His advent
there also, and the remission of sins received by those who
believe in Him.'[5] 'His descent into hell was the salvation of
them that had passed away.'[6]

One of the most valuable and pleasing things about
S. Irenaeus is the circumstance that the *Recapitulation*
provides a doctrinal system in which an adequate place is
found for the whole human career and the human character of
our Lord. It is obvious that at this point S. Irenaeus far excels
many of the most honoured Fathers of the Church. Maybe
at times the 'analogy' between Christ and Adam runs off
into unprofitable details, but underlying these comparisons,
however strained, there is a religious principle of paramount
importance. The plan of salvation is to be seen working
itself out not only in one or two great events like the
Incarnation and the Cross, but also in the events of Christ's
life in general. The Son of God became incarnate in order
that He might persevere from childhood to manhood in a
life of perfect moral obedience. He ran the whole gamut of
human experience. The value of this affirmation may be
made plain by a comparison with the work of S. Athanasius
on the Incarnation. In this he stands for many others. Like

---

[1] *Dem.* 38.   [2] III.18.7, i.343.   [3] II.22.4, i.200.
[4] V.31.1, ii.139.   [5] IV.27.2, i.467.   [6] *Dem.* 78; see also IV.22.1, i.454.

Irenaeus, Athanasius wrote to vindicate the Incarnation of God the Son as the necessary foundation for and central fact in a Gospel of Redemption. However, the sole reason he could find for the continuance of the Incarnate One upon earth for the course of a complete human life was the almost grotesque one that, if He had become incarnate and died and risen and ascended to heaven all in a single moment, then the human race would not have known that the Incarnation had happened.[1] The bare fact of the Incarnation was all that was necessary to work the salvation of man, presumably because the salvation of the world was conceived of as a semi-mechanical inoculation of humanity with the Divine. S. Irenaeus, on the other hand, had a good reason for the Saviour's continuing and complete human life. He was much more than the bearer to earth of a mysterious heavenly substance. He was above all a Champion, who wrought out human salvation by a life of active moral travail. As Schmidt observes, the Christian Confession is not confined to Christ's nature as the Word, but concerns also His life.[2] Vernet also notices that Irenaeus never speaks as if Christ's redeeming death were a mere appendage to the Incarnation. *Incarnatus* and *passus* are almost synonymous in such passages as I.9.3, i.39, and III.18.3, i.339.[3] Aall maintains that Athanasius follows Irenaeus in viewing Christ's life essentially as a drama of salvation, the entry of God into the world.[4] He does not, however, notice the great superiority of S. Irenaeus at this point.

It has already been observed that there is a two-sided doctrine of God in S. Irenaeus.[5] Characteristic of him is a robust Biblical doctrine of the Living God. The conception of the Holy Trinity is expressed in terms of '*The Two Hands of God*'. However, Irenaeus finds it quite natural also to express the conception of the Deity in the Greek terms of current culture, and to follow the Apologists in expounding

---

[1] *De Incarnatione*, XVI.4,5.   [2] *Kirche b.I.* p. 66.
[3] *Dictionnaire*, VII, col. 2473.   [4] *Logosidee*, p. 467.
[5] See pp. 122–5, 132–3 *supra*.

Christ in terms of the Logos.[1] The same double aspect is
worn by the doctrine of Salvation. Characteristic of S.
Irenaeus is a powerful doctrine of the Saving Work of
Christ as the Divine-human Champion of man, 'Christus
Victor'. This is most essentially associated with the idea of
Recapitulation. Here is a specifically Biblical element in the
theology of S. Irenaeus. He can, however, on occasion
speak of salvation in quite other terms, which are more
associated with the secular culture of his day. This aspect is
not to be admitted as so typical of S. Irenaeus as is the
'drama of salvation', nor is it so central in his system, but
an exposition of his doctrine of salvation would not be a
balanced one were not due account taken of it.

The dominating conception here is that man is to be
made god, or a son of God.[2] 'He who was the Son of God
became the Son of Man, that man ... might become the son
of God.'[3] This process of 'divinization' may be represented
in two ways. In the first place, S. Irenaeus may be found
teaching that man is to be divinized by beholding the Vision
of God in the Incarnate Son. A Biblical motif was ready to
hand as the medium of expression for this doctrine. The
Genesis Creation-story taught that man was made after the
image and likeness of God. In some passages Irenaeus
expresses the opinion that the 'image of God' in man had
been lost as the result of the Fall, though the subject is a
somewhat perplexed one.[4] Furthermore, the Incarnate Son
was God made visible to man. It followed that the work of
Christ could be represented as a restoration, from the
original Model, of the defaced or obliterated portrait of God
in man. The Beginning was used to reportray the end. Here
is *Recapitulation* translated into Greek terms, and defined as
'showing the image after which man was made'. So Irenaeus
writes: 'the Lord, summing up afresh this man, took the
same dispensation of entry into flesh ... that He also should
show forth the likeness of Adam's entry into flesh, and that

---

[1] See p. 135 *supra*.   [2] IV.33.4, ii.8; IV.38.4, ii.44; IV.39.2, ii.46.
[3] III.19.1, i.345; see also III.10.2, i.282.   [4] See p. 209 *infra*.

there should be that which was written in the beginning, man after the image and likeness of God.'[1] The sight of the Image of God restored to man the lost divine image. 'In times long past, it was *said* that man was created after the image of God, but it was not [actually] *shown*; for the Word was as yet invisible, after whose image man was created. Wherefore also he did easily lose the likeness. When, however, the Word of God became flesh, He confirmed both these: for He both showed forth the image; . . . and He re-established the likeness after a sure manner, by assimilating man to the invisible Father by means of the visible Word.'[2]

The process of divinization may also be spoken of almost in mechanical terms, as though it were a sort of spiritual inoculation. The conception plainly answers to the notion of the spiritual and the Divine as an ethereal substance, pure and incorruptible. The Incarnate Son is represented as the One who brought down to earth from heaven the metaphysical substance of Divinity, and united it to the substance of humanity. Thus man comes to share in the Divine Nature, and becomes 'incorruptible' and 'immortal'. This idea lies behind one of the most widely quoted sayings of S. Irenaeus: 'The Son of God became the Son of Man, that man . . . might become the son of God.'[3]

Under the heading of salvation as 'divinization' a variety of terms are worthy of note. The divine inoculation may be described in Biblical language as the gift of the Holy Spirit. 'But when the spirit here blended with the soul is united to [God's] handiwork, the man is rendered spiritual and perfect because of the outpouring of the Spirit.'[4] Irenaeus can write that the purpose of the Incarnation was that Christ might be the Mediator of communion between God and man. Sometimes it would seem that personal intercourse

[1] *Dem.* 32; see also V.**12**.4, ii.85; V.**21**.2, ii.111.
[2] V.**16**.2, ii.99; see also IV.**33**.4, ii.9; *Dem.* 22.   [3] III.**19**.1, i.345.
[4] V.**6**.1, ii.68; see also II.**19**.6, i.188; IV.**20**.4, i.442; IV.**28**.1,2, ii.42-3; V.**1**.1, ii.56; V.**6**.2, ii.69-70; V.**8**.1, ii.72-3; V.**8**.2, ii.73; V.**10**.2, ii.79-80; V.**11**.1, ii.81; V.**12**.2, ii.83-4; V.**20**.2, ii.110; *Dem.* 7, 97.

with God is in mind. This might be supported from: 'And therefore in the last times the Lord has restored us into friendship through His incarnation, having become "the Mediator between God and men"; propitiating indeed for us the Father against whom we had sinned, and cancelling our disobedience by His own obedience; conferring also upon us the gift of communion with, and subjection to, our Maker.'[1] Irenaeus then significantly goes on to deal with the forgiveness of sins. The same is probably true of one other passage,[2] but the general usage shows that 'communion' is in reality only another name for 'divinization-union'. Christ is the Mediator because His body was the initial contact of the human and the Divine, the vessel in which God was brought down to man, and the point of infection whence *divine-humanity* propagated itself through the race. The Incarnate One is the medium of an inoculation rather than a personal Mediator. The communion of God and man is the blending of God and man. The Incarnation was the means 'by which the blending and communion of God and man' took place,[3] *commixtio et communio Dei et hominis.*[4] Fellowship with God is defined as that which produces incorruption.[5] The vision of God makes one immortal.[6] Here is another aspect of the work of Christ as Mediator. He became incarnate 'that the paternal light might meet with and rest upon the flesh of our Lord, and come to us from His resplendent flesh, and that thus man might attain to immortality, having been invested with the paternal light'.[7] As the Virgin Mary was the means of the entry of the Divine into the human, hers was 'that pure womb which regenerates man unto God'.[8]

'Regeneration' and 'Adoption' are for S. Irenaeus names for the union of God and man. ἢ πῶς ἄνθρωπος χωρήσει εἰς Θεόν, εἰ μὴ ὁ Θεὸς ἐχωρήθη εἰς ἄνθρωπον; *Quemadmodum autem*

---

[1] V.17.1, ii.100.   [2] V.1.1, ii.55.

[3] IV.20.4, i.441; see also V.27.2, ii.129.   [4] Harvey, ii.215.

[5] *Dem.* 40; see also III.20.2, i.349; IV.20.5, i.443; V.2.1, ii.59; V.16.2, ii.99; *Dem.* 6, 31, 97.

[6] IV.20.5–6, i.442–3; see also IV.38.3, ii.44.

[7] IV.20.2, i.440; see also *Dem.* 31.   [8] IV.33.11, ii.14.

relinquet mortis generationem, si non[1] *in novam generationem
mire et inopinate a Deo, in signum autem salutis, datam, quae est
ex Virgine per fidem regenerationem? Vel quam adoptionem
accipient a Deo, permanentes in hac genesi, quae est secundum
hominem in hoc mundo?* 'Or how shall man pass into God,
unless God has [first] passed into man? And how shall he
escape from the generation subject to death, if not by means
of a new generation, given in a wonderful and unexpected
manner, but as a sign of salvation, by God—that regeneration which is from the Virgin through faith? Or how shall
they receive adoption from God if they remain in this
generation, which is naturally possessed by man in this
world?'[2] '*Regeneratio*' and '*adoptio*' are here equivalent terms,
representing divinization. Those who are joined to God are
also 'the perfect'[3] and 'the spiritual'.[4] They possess the
image and likeness of God.[5] Once it is said that the divinized
are rendered impassible.[6] However, by far and away the
most usual expressions to denote the effect of divinization
are 'incorruptibility', and 'immortality' or 'life'.[7] These
words appear constantly. An example or two will suffice to
show the way in which these various terms are used as
parallels and interchangeable equivalents. *Ignorantes autem
eum qui ex Virgine est Emmanuel, privantur munere eius, quod
est vita aeterna: non recipientes autem Verbum incorruptionis,
perseverant in carne mortali, et sunt debitores mortis, antidotum
vitae non accipientes. Ad quos Verbum ait* . . . Ταῦτα λέγει
πρὸς τοὺς μὴ δεξαμένους τὴν δωρεὰν τῆς υἱοθεσίας, ἀλλ᾽ ἀτιμάζοντας
τὴν σάρκωσιν τῆς καθαρᾶς γεννήσεως τοῦ λόγου τοῦ Θεοῦ,

---

[1] The loss of some words is suspected here.

[2] IV.**33**.4, ii.8–9; Harvey, ii.259.

[3] IV.**38**.2, ii.43; IV.**39**.2, ii.46–7; V.**36**.3, ii.157.

[4] V.**1**.3, ii.58; V.**6**.1, ii.68.

[5] III.**18**.1, i.338; IV.**38**.3–4, ii.44–5; V.**1**.3, ii.58; V.**2**.1, ii.58; V.**6**.1, ii.68;
V.**8**.1, ii.73; V.**12**.4, ii.85; V.**16**.2, ii.99; V.**21**.2, ii.111; V.**28**.4, ii.133; V.**36**.3,
ii.157; *Dem.* 32, 97.

[6] IV.**24**.2, i.458.

[7] With much justice Frick observes that Irenaeus conceives of salvation as
ζωή and ἀφθαρσία, and that these qualities are equated with personal
communion with God; *Reich-Gottes*, p. 59.

καὶ ἀποστεροῦντας τὸν ἄνθρωπον τῆς εἰς Θεὸν ἀνόδου, καὶ ἀχαριστοῦντας τῷ ὑπὲρ αὐτῶν σαρκωθέντι λόγῳ τοῦ Θεοῦ. Εἰς τοῦτο γὰρ ὁ λόγος ἄνθρωπος, ... ἵνα ὁ ἄνθρωπος τὸν λόγον χωρήσας, καὶ τὴν υἱοθεσίαν λαβὼν, υἱὸς γένηται Θεοῦ. Non enim poteramus aliter incorruptelam et immortalitatem percipere, nisi adunati fuissemus incorruptelae et immortalitati. 'But, being ignorant of Him who from the Virgin is Emmanuel, they are deprived of His gift, which is eternal life; and not receiving the incorruptible Word, they remain in mortal flesh, and are debtors to death, not obtaining the antidote of life. To whom the Word says ... He speaks undoubtedly these words to those who have not received the gift of adoption, but who despise the incarnation of the pure generation of the Word of God, defraud human nature of promotion into God, and prove themselves ungrateful to the Word of God, who became flesh for them. For it was for this end that the Word of God was made man ... that man, having been taken up into the Word, and receiving the adoption, might become the son of God. For by no other means could we have attained to incorruptibility and immortality, unless we had been united to incorruptibility and immortality.'[1] 'We have not been made gods from the beginning, but at first merely men, and then at length gods ... For it was necessary, at first ... that what was mortal should be conquered and swallowed up in immortality, and the corruptible by incorruptibility, and that man should be made after the image and likeness of God.'[2]

Many scholars have emphasized the connexion of this part of the theology of S. Irenaeus with the Johannine writings. Bousset is prominent in regarding Irenaeus as distinctively Johannine. He writes that, consciously or unconsciously, Irenaeus walks in the path of Johannine mysticism.[3] The most profound and beautiful chapter in which S. Irenaeus celebrates the self-revealing love of God (IV.20, i. 437–51) is with much justice hailed by Bousset as one

[1] III.19.1, i.344–5; Harvey, ii.102–3.   [2] IV.38.4, ii.44–5.
[3] Kyr.Ch. p. 338.

in which, as nowhere else, Irenaeus shows his personal piety.[1] Such phrases as: 'For as those who see the light are within the light, and partake of its brilliancy; even so, those who see God are in God, and receive of His splendour', and 'Fellowship with God is to know God'[2] are taken as illustrative of the theme that the mystical piety of divinization through the vision of God, which is to be constructed from separate fragments in the Johannine literature, is here met in a vigorous and convincing form.[3] This clear expression of the divinization ideal is a piece of Hellenistic piety, and when Irenaeus roundly says that men are to become gods one cannot deny the connexion with a piety rooted in polytheistic ground.[4]

It is apparent that Bousset's statement depends on certain assumptions about the Johannine literature that will not be accepted by all, namely, that the Fourth Gospel itself faces decisively toward Hellenistic piety. So Bousset introduces his statement by drawing a sharp distinction between Pauline and Johannine Christianity. He states that Irenaeus took over only the words of S. Paul's cross-mysticism, of dying and rising with Christ. He did not take the actual thought. The conceptions of sin, guilt, and forgiveness recede into the background in S. Irenaeus, as in the Johannine writings.[5] We may rightly demur here. To assume thus that Paul speaks of release from sin, and John of attainment to divine life, is to make the matter much too simple, and the division between the two much too great. Alongside the doctrines of 'light' and of 'eternal life' there is in the Johannine writings a clear witness that man is to be released from the deep guilt and from the enslaving power of sin, and that the saved are to experience a change of moral will. Furthermore, salvation is wrought out through the death of the Lord.[6] The truth of the matter is that the Fourth Evangelist preaches a Gospel of

---

[1] *Kyr.Ch.* p. 339.   [2] IV.20.5, i.442–3.   [3] *Kyr.Ch.* p. 338.
[4] ibid. p. 342.   [5] ibid. p. 337.
[6] cf. John 1₂₉; 8₂₁,₃₄,₄₄; 9₄₁; 10₁₅; 12₃₅; 14₁₅,₂₁; 15₁₀-₁₇,₂₄; 16₈-₁₁; 20₂₃; 1 John 1₈-₁₀; 2₁-₆,₁₂; 3₄-₅,₈-₉; 5₁₈.

real ethical redemption by the power of the Living God, and is not confined to Hellenistic 'divinization'. At the same time, a Greek air undoubtedly blows through his Gospel. Brunner is right in his observation that in Irenaeus is united the whole New Testament witness, the Johannine and the Pauline.[1] The two are not so opposed that they cannot truly be held together. Finally, perhaps the thing in which the Fourth Gospel is most typical of later Greek Christianity is that the primitive eschatology is almost completely spiritualized away. S. Irenaeus does not follow in this. He is in a sense therefore more 'primitive' than the Johannine literature.

The characteristic emphasis of the Fourth Gospel upon 'Truth' and 'Light' as leading men to 'Eternal Life' brings to our notice that which, for lack of a better term, may be described as the philosophical or intellectual aspect of Christian salvation. A very important part of the human personality is the mind, with its faculty of reason. As in the sphere of the moral will and affections salvation is principally through 'the faith that works by love', and 'the expulsive power of a new affection', so in the sphere of mental life salvation is principally through the knowledge of the truth. One would say 'principally' in each case, for it is unsound to speak as though human personality functions in water-tight compartments. A movement of the will and affections commonly arises as the response to knowledge which has been presented to the mind. The movement of heart and will always needs to be disciplined by knowledge if it is to result in rightful activity. Conversely, the mind will often refuse whole-heartedly to accept manifest truth presented to it, particularly if that truth be painful, unless some stimulus first move the will and affections. Nevertheless, it remains that attainment to knowledge of the truth is a distinct aspect of Christian salvation, even as the mind is a part of the man. The work of Christ as the supreme revelation of God

[1] *Der Mittler*, p. 219.

answers to this aspect. Such may be described as the philosophical or intellectual aspect of salvation, inasmuch as it denotes the Gospel as it meets the specific needs of the reasoning mind. It is the Gospel as it appeals to the intellectual man in his search for knowledge, and to the philosopher as he seeks to arrange all truth in a coherent whole. It is but natural that wherever the attempt is made to present the Gospel to that part of mankind which cherishes these intellectual interests, the corresponding aspect of salvation will be emphasized. It is also natural that as modes of intellectual activity change in succeeding ages, the intellectual aspect of salvation will be restated to correspond to these modes.

It is clear that, among other elements of value, the Johannine literature enshrines a first essay in the philosophical or intellectual aspect of Christian salvation. The Fourth Gospel is the Gospel of the meditative man for meditative men. Evidence of this is the presence of a Logos-prologue, which is best viewed as an attempt, by the use of a familiar term of current thought, to give the Gospel an introduction likely to be attractive to the man of culture. Further evidence is the re-casting of the teaching of Jesus into academic dialogues. In line with this we find that Christ is preached as bringing light into darkness, and as setting men free by the truth. The One who does this is the climax of revelation. The Logos is God revealed, so that he who has seen Him has seen the Father. This is salvation stated in intellectual terms. There is also a certain contrast here to the work of S. Paul, though this contrast should not be over-stressed.[1] Paul was certainly an intellectual giant, yet he was a prophet rather than a meditative man. He had real contact with the Greek culture of the world of his day, but the world of Judaism was his true background. He had little use for intellectual curiosity as such, and could almost exult that 'not many wise after the flesh are called'. He thought of salvation mainly in terms of moral will, and of

[1] See pp. 160–1 *supra*.

love dwelling in the heart. There is little sign in his writings that he deliberately sought to present the Gospel in such a way as to attract the cultured and thoughtful world. Pauline Christianity is in this nearer to the 'primitive' than is Johannine.

The relation of S. Irenaeus to the Pauline and to the Johannine expressions of the Gospel is surely correctly described by Brunner, who claims that in Irenaeus is united the whole New Testament witness, the Johannine and the Pauline.[1] In his two-sided expression of the doctrine of God, and of the way of salvation, S. Irenaeus treads in the same path as the Fourth Evangelist. In each the two-sidedness is due to the employment of the terminology of Greek thought as the vehicle for Christian truth. The Fourth Gospel and Irenaeus are alike in that the Greek air blows through both. However, development has also taken place. The whole conception of *divinization by the vision of the Divine*', with its allied notions, occurs in a far more emphatic and systematic form in the writings of Irenaeus. One might say that he is more avowedly part of the Gentile world than is any New Testament writer. To this extent Bousset is justified in his claim that that which is to be constructed from separate fragments in the Johannine literature is in Irenaeus to be met with in a vigorous and convincing form.[2] At the same time, this development is amply complemented by the doctrine of *Christus Victor*, which is so largely a development from Pauline origins, and which has roots in the teaching of our Lord Himself. Thus although S. Irenaeus moves with confidence in the Greek-speaking world, and also firmly holds on to the heritage of the Apologists, he is by no means prevented thereby from a full appreciation of those parts of the New Testament where the Greek wind does not blow (e.g. he is a Millenarian). This is a singular mark of the versatility of his spirit, and of the value of the tradition for which he speaks.

A word must be said regarding the spiritual evaluation of

[1] *Der Mittler*, p. 219.　　　[2] See pp. 159–60 *supra*.

this Greek side to S. Irenaeus. We can never afford to forget
the greatness of the task that was performed by the early
Church in transplanting the Christian Faith out of the seed-
bed of Judaism into the vast and unsheltered Gentile world.
This was an absolutely necessary task if the Church was to
fulfil her mission. The concrete and relatively unspeculative
modes of thought characteristic of the Hebrew Bible are
admirably suited to safeguard specifically religious values.
However, it could not be that the whole Gentile world
should become Jewish, and, discarding the ethical and
intellectual values of Greek thought, become content to
nourish her religion exclusively upon the Bible. This would
be to cast away some of the greatest works of the human
mind and spirit. Therefore the only way in which a universal
mission could be carried on was to attempt to embody the
unique religious values of primitive Christianity in the
terms of current secular thought, and to unite the Gospel
with the heritage of Greek philosophy. Thus was combined
the best of both Jewish and Gentile worlds. In this process
there was an inherent danger that the religious values of
essential Christianity should be compromised with pagan
elements. The rise in due course of unsatisfactory doctrinal
formulations, and of definite heresies, is the mark that this
danger was not invariably circumvented. It would be unworthy, however, on this account to regret the necessary
means employed in the necessary task. Hence the experiments of the Fourth Evangelist, and after him of the Apologists, are spiritually justified. The double-sidedness of S.
Irenaeus is a token that he is farther along the course of
these experiments. That he preserves so many vital Biblical
elements is a mark that the tradition for which he speaks had
not compromised the Faith with pagan thought. There is a
Christian Hellenism which is the combination of the primitive Christian faith with the best elements of Greek thought,
and which constitutes a mode of expression for the essential
Christian faith. This is legitimate Christian Hellenism.
There is also a religious Hellenism which goes beyond this,

and which admits into the very substance of its creed
fundamentally pagan notions of God and of the religious
life. Such is illegitimate Hellenism, e.g. Gnosticism, Arianism. Inasmuch as legitimate Hellenism is found in germ in
the Johannine literature it may be acknowledged as Biblical
Hellenism. The position of S. Irenaeus is that of a notable
example of the progress of this legitimate and Biblical
Hellenism. It would perhaps not be too much to claim that
in him the scales are weighted in favour of the Hebraic
interest. He is definitely Greek, but he is eminently Biblical.

Though this be the essential truth about S. Irenaeus there
is one proviso to be allowed. If consideration be given again
to the Greek side of the doctrine of salvation in Irenaeus it
will be seen that a prominent element in it is the conception
of ἀφθαρσία, 'incorruptibility'. It must be admitted that one is
less happy about this than about other aspects of the
divinization doctrine. To teach that man is saved by
becoming a 'partaker of the divine nature' (2 Peter 1₄) is a
legitimate expression, so long as pagan pantheism is firmly
excluded by a sound Biblical doctrine of God. The *general*
proposition of 'divinization' is not to be rejected. Divinization by 'beholding the vision of God', by 'seeing the Image
of God' in Christ, and by enjoying 'the paternal light', etc.,
are not in themselves objectionable phrases, provided that
it be borne in mind that they describe only a single aspect of
salvation, i.e. the intellectual. This much is not more than a
development of what is to be found in the Johannine literature. It is perhaps otherwise with divinization expounded as
'the blending of God and man', the inoculation of humanity
with the substance of Divinity through the medium of the
Incarnation, so as to produce ἀφθαρσία. Here is an Hellenistic modification of the notion of salvation of a much more
far-reaching character, savouring as it does more of the
pagan 'Mysteries'. It does not, indeed, necessarily and
inevitably involve conceptions of God and of salvation
opposed to Biblical teaching, but it requires careful statement if this is to be avoided. So we find that S. Paul himself

can occasionally use the doctrine of ἀφθαρσία. Thus Romans
1₂₃ describes God as 'the incorruptible God'. Ἤλλαξαν τὴν
δόξαν τοῦ ἀφθάρτου Θεοῦ ἐν ὁμοιώματι εἰκόνος φθαρτοῦ ἀνθρώπου.
For the word ἄφθαρτος see also 1 Corinthians 9₂₅ and 15₅₂;
also 1 Timothy 1₁₇ and 1 Peter 1₄,₂₃. Ἀφθαρσία as an attribute
of the saved occurs in Ephesians 6₂₄: ἡ χάρις μετὰ πάντων
τῶν ἀγαπώντων τὸν Κύριον ἡμῶν Ἰησοῦν Χριστὸν ἐν ἀφθαρσίᾳ;
'Grace be with all them that love our Lord Jesus Christ in
uncorruptness' (R.V.), and as a description of the resurrection body in 1 Corinthians 15₄₂,₅₀,₅₃. Here ἀφθαρσία is used
as the counterpart of φθορά. Σπείρεται ἐν φθορᾷ, ἐγείρεται ἐν
ἀφθαρσίᾳ, 'It is sown in corruption; it is raised in incorruption' (verse 42); δεῖ γὰρ τὸ φθαρτὸν τοῦτο ἐνδύσασθαι ἀφθαρσίαν,
'For this corruptible must put on incorruption' (verse 53).[1]

Here is indeed a Greek element in S. Paul, but it does not
follow that it is a case of direct borrowing from the Gentile
world. It is not unlikely that it is Hellenization at second-
hand, through the medium of the Greek Old Testament. In
two notable passages in the Wisdom of Solomon the
ἀφθαρσία granted to man is connected with the ἀφθαρσία of
God's own nature—2₂₃-₄: Ὅτι ὁ Θεός ἔκτισεν τὸν ἄνθρωπον
ἐπ᾽ ἀφθαρσίᾳ, καὶ εἰκόνα τῆς ἰδίας ἰδιότητος ἐποίησεν αὐτόν: 'Because God created man for incorruption, and made him an
image of his own proper being'; and 6₁₈-₁₉ runs: 'And love
[of Wisdom] is observance of her laws, and to give heed to
her laws confirmeth incorruption; and incorruption bringeth
near unto God.'[2] In this circumstance there is a salutary
warning against over-simplification of the New Testament.
In combating the erroneous proposition that S. Paul con-
structed his theology by inserting borrowings from pagan
mystery-cults into the Christian Faith, and in vindicating his
essential Judaism, it is easy to go too far. Thus too great a
division has sometimes been made between the Johannine
literature, where the Greek wind is allowed to blow, and the

---

[1] For the word ἀφθαρσία see also Romans 2₇; and also 2 Timothy 1₁₀.

[2] ἀφθαρσία occurs also in 4 Maccabees 9₂₂, 17₁₂; used of those who attain to
immortal life. The word ἄφθαρτος occurs in Wisdom 12₁, 18₄.

Pauline, where it is excluded. Here we see S. Paul using typically 'Greek' language, such as one might be tempted to assign to the 'non-Biblical side' were it found in S. Irenaeus. On the other hand, we are warned by the example of S. Paul that the use of such expressions as ἀφθαρσία does not of itself involve the certainty that the underlying thought is radically Gentile.

Salvation by change of metaphysical substance does not, however, *necessarily* carry with it an adequate emphasis that the saved man *must* experience a radical change of moral will, of affections, and of mind. This is a serious weakness. Religion which is not firmly anchored to the ethical and the rational easily and naturally slips into magic. This is what has actually happened all too often when Christianity of this genius has been preached among uninstructed people. Wherever Christianity has passed over the great divide which separates healthy sacramental religion from degrading superstition the inoculation-theory is to be suspected as at the root of the error. S. Irenaeus does not enter into this danger, for his Greek aspect is complemented by the doctrine of salvation through the moral triumph of 'Christus Victor'. Recapitulation has a necessary ethical and rational connotation. There are, however, certain statements in Irenaeus which taken in isolation might lead to the dangers of the inoculation-theory.

In view of this double aspect worn by S. Irenaeus it is not surprising that many have tried to expound him as a Christian Gnostic. For example Bousset writes: 'This earthly Jesus is for him the divine announcer of the secrets of the heavenly world. He is the great Mystagogue, who initiates us into the divine secrets.' The Mystagogue is also referred to as the Master. 'It is true that the mysticism evolved by Irenaeus can easily pass into a definite rationalism: the Gnosis resting on the vision of God can take on an intellectual character; the character of Mystagogue who initiates into the heavenly secrets can flow over into that of Teacher. But in general one is right in conceiving of

Irenaeus as on the mystical side.'[1] The error in this is not that passages cannot be found to substantiate it. It is rather in a lack of balance so serious as to amount to misrepresentation. In saying that Irenaeus regards our Lord as the great Mystagogue attention is fixed exclusively upon one side of the case, and this one side is stated in a form far too extreme.

The doctrine of the saving activity of God in Christ Jesus is a Biblical one in S. Irenaeus. As the conception of God is rooted in the Old Testament, so this is grounded firmly upon the New. The establishment of this proposition is of the greatest possible importance in coming to an understanding and evaluation of Irenaeus, the more so as his work has been so widely represented as a stage in the departure of the Catholic Church and theology from primitive and Biblical Christianity. The investigation raises two questions, a wrong answer to either of which will confuse the issue. They are: 'What is the New Testament doctrine of the Saving Work of Christ?' and 'What is the teaching of S. Irenaeus?' The doctrine of 'Christus Victor', the Divine Champion of humanity through obedience, is not indeed the whole of the teaching of Irenaeus upon salvation, but it is the most vital and constructive element.[2] This doctrine has now been described in detail, and the one question has been answered. It is therefore necessary to proceed to the other. It will not be possible here to give a detailed discussion of so vast a subject as the New Testament theology of the Atonement, but a summary may be given of the findings of some of the best modern work. This will perhaps suffice for the basis of a comparison with S. Irenaeus.

Aulén claims that the 'classic' idea of the Atonement is rooted in the teaching of our Lord Himself, inasmuch as Christ viewed His function as that of the Adversary of the Satanic powers.[3] This important point is, however, passed over with but slender treatment. By contrast, in *Jesus and*

---

[1] *Kyr.Ch.* p. 340.   [2] See pp. 144–5, 147–9, 152–3, 155 *supra.*
[3] *Christus Victor*, pp. 92–3.

His Sacrifice (London, 1937), Dr. Vincent Taylor discusses the Passion-Sayings of our Lord in a wealth of erudite detail. His striking results form a most valuable contribution to the study of the Atonement. They are the more striking because the author's powerful plea is that the Passion and Death of the Lord are to be viewed as a sacrifice offered to God, provided that this conception be framed in ethically satisfying terms. Subjective 'Abelardian' or 'moral influence' theories of the Atonement are to be regarded as inadequate to the mind of Christ. Dr. Taylor's work may usefully be reviewed here, inasmuch as it is a representative and able modern example of the defence of a theology of the Atonement which is divergent from the doctrine of S. Irenaeus. The doctrinal findings of a careful scientific discussion of the authenticity and interpretation of all the Passion-Sayings are as follows: (i) Our Lord believed that the Passion was no mere tragic stroke of fate. Its purpose lay deep in the providence of God (pp. 255–6). (ii) In His sufferings He was perfectly at one in spirit with the Father. Thus the prayer of the Passion is: 'Not what I will, but what thou wilt' (256–7). This principle excludes every Atonement theory which represents Christ as suffering vindictive punishment as a substitute for man (276), though the conclusion of an able and beautiful discussion of Mark 15₃₄ is that the Cry of Dereliction upon the Cross is to be taken seriously. 'Jesus so closely identified Himself with sinners, and experienced the horror of sin to such a degree, that for a time the closeness of His communion with the Father was broken' (157–63). (iii) 'Jesus interpreted His suffering, death, and resurrection positively, as active elements in His Messianic vocation. He did not speak of His Passion as a revelation ... but rather as a task laid upon Him' (257–8). (iv) Our Lord thought of the Messianic vocation of suffering as necessary to the full establishment of the Kingly Rule of God (258–9). (v) He looked upon His death as a victorious struggle with the forces of evil (260–1). (vi) He believed His Messianic suffering to be representative and vicarious (261–2). (vii) He felt Himself to be identified with sinners, even to an agony of spirit (262–5). (viii) He called on men to identify themselves with Him in His sufferings, so that they may make His self-offering their sacrifice, and share in its power (265–8). (ix) Thus men were to reproduce His vocation (268–9).

One of these conclusions merits some critical attention, in view of the present discussion. This is number (vi). Dr. Taylor will not allow that it is enough to say that Christ regarded His sufferings as vicarious only in the limited sense that what One suffered was destined to turn to the blessing of many (261). In discussion of the 'Ransom' passage, Mark 10₄₅, it is observed that our Lord taught that He came 'to give His life a ransom for many', ἀντὶ πολλῶν, and that the use of the rarer preposition ἀντὶ instead of the more colourless ὑπέρ indicates that ἀντὶ is here to be given its commonest meaning of 'instead of', rather than the weaker 'on behalf of' (103). Be this as it may, the main weight of the argument that Christ conceived of His death as *representative* and vicarious is the plea that He identified Himself with the Suffering Servant of Isaiah 53. The evidence adduced for this identification is as follows: (i) The sayings on the coming suffering and rejection of the Son of Man (Mark 8₃₁, 9₃₁, 10₃₃f., with parallels) are coloured from the picture of the Suffering Servant of God, though only by way of dark allusion (87–90). (ii) The 'Ransom' passage (Mark 10₄₅, Matthew 20₂₈) is of primary importance. The thought of the Suffering Servant is implied in the declaration of the context that 'the Son of man came . . . to *serve*'. The phrase '*for many*' is suggested by Isaiah 53₁₁,₁₂, where the word '*many*' occurs three times (101–2). (iii) Mark 14₂₄ (cf. Matthew 26₂₈): 'This is my blood of the covenant, which is shed for many' has the same suggestion (127). (iv) There is an express citation of Isaiah 53₁₂ in Luke 22₃₇: 'For I say unto you, that this which is written must be fulfilled in me, And he was reckoned with transgressors' (192–4). (v) The words placed by the Evangelist in the mouth of John the Baptist: 'Behold, the Lamb of God, which taketh away the sin of the world' (John 1₂₉, and also 1₃₆), are perhaps an allusion to Isaiah 53₇,₁₂ (226-7).

Regarding this evidence we may say that it is clear that our Lord was impressed by the portrait of the 'Suffering Servant', and, in view of Luke 22₃₇, that He applied this portrait to Himself. It is somewhat less clear that this application was a *dominant* element in His thinking, for only one of the supporting sayings goes beyond a possible allusion. What is not at all clear is the proposition that the self-identification of our Lord with the Servant of Jehovah involves the idea that He regarded His Messianic sufferings as a sacrifice *representative* for humanity. Had this been a vital idea to Him He would hardly have repeatedly alluded to Isaiah 53, and yet avoided the very verses which would have served to bring the conception clearly to view (e.g. verses 4, 6). It is equally hard to believe, in view of the use made by the Church of Isaiah 53 from the earliest times (cf. Acts 8₃₂-₅), that in the period before the compilation of our Gospels the Church would have allowed to slip out of the tradition any other of our Lord's citations of Isaiah 53, had they been of a character more explicit than that one actually preserved. An application to Himself of 'Surely he hath borne our griefs', 'But he was wounded for our transgressions', 'the Lord hath laid on him the iniquity of us all', etc., would hardly have been passed over and forgotten as of no interest to the primitive community. The argument from silence does not, of course, prove that Jesus never applied these sayings to Himself, but it does go far to prove that there was no knowledge of this in the primitive Church. We may conclude with some safety that our Lord read Isaiah 53 as a poignant picture of the evil fate of the righteous, that He saw that the suffering of the good can work the blessing of the sinner, and that He applied this to Himself. It is somewhat precarious to go beyond this, and to affirm that He definitely connected this chapter with the idea of representative suffering. Our Lord may have done so, but it would appear to be going beyond the recorded facts to

expound the representative sufferings of the Servant of
Jehovah as a dominant element in Christ's view of His own
mission. It is dangerous to treat this as a great fixed principle
in the Gospel tradition, something which may be used to
give a positive interpretation to other merely allusive or
ambiguous passages. As Dr. Taylor himself observes:
'Although there is little doubt that Jesus interpreted His
suffering and death in the light of the Servant-conception,
we cannot infer the substance of His interpretation directly
from His reported sayings' (281). There is an interesting
parallel here to the exegesis of S. Irenaeus. He can show
great interest in the Song of the Suffering Servant as a
prophecy of the Passion, and yet pointedly fail to draw
from it the conception of substitutionary or representative
suffering.[1]

By contrast, there is most certain evidence that one
interpretation by our Lord of His Messianic work was in
terms of the conquest in the world of the powers of evil.
There is Christ's own story of the Temptation (Matthew
4_{1-11}, Luke 4_{1-13}). The whole great mission of exorcism and
healing is the token of the overthrow of the kingdom of
Satan, now fallen as lightning from heaven (Matthew 11_{2-6},
Mark 3_{22-30}, Luke 7_{18-23}, Luke 10_{17-24}). Furthermore, Christ
has bound the strong man, Satan (Matthew 12_{27-9}, Mark 3_{27},
Luke 11_{21-2}). Upon the dark betrayal night our Lord speaks
of a conflict with evil men, and with 'the power of darkness'
(Luke 22_{53}). In light of this it is a little difficult to give assent
to Dr. Taylor's proposition that 'the belief of Jesus that His
Messianic suffering is representative and vicarious' is 'more
central' than 'His belief that His death is a victorious struggle
with the powers of evil' (260–1). It is 'Christus Victor' that
is the certain and undoubted feature of the Gospels. The
'Servant of Jehovah' is by no means excluded from the picture,
but the outline of this figure is not very clear.

In the reconstruction of the New Testament doctrine of
the Atonement the exposition of S. Paul is next in importance

[1] See p. 63 supra.

to the consideration of the teaching of our Lord Himself. A representative and very convincing treatment of the objective Saving Work of Christ is that given by Dr. C. A. Anderson Scott in *Christianity According to St. Paul* (Second Edition, Cambridge, 1932). It is first observed that in the Bible there is a strong tendency to lift the emphasis off the idea of 'price paid' in the use of λύτρον, '*ransom*', ἀπολύτρωσις, '*redemption*', etc. This leaves the generalized idea of deliverance or emancipation (pp. 27–8).[1] Dr. Scott then proceeds: 'The first form of servitude from which Paul believed that Christ had delivered men was servitude to spirit-forces of evil, demons, or the Evil One' (28). These are described as 'the elements of this world', 'the prince of this world', 'principalities and powers', etc. If it be asked: 'How has Christ delivered us out of the power of darkness, and translated us into the kingdom of the Son of his love?' (Colossians 1₁₃); 'How will he reign till he hath put all his enemies under his feet?' (1 Corinthians 15₂₅), the crucial passage for an answer is to be found in Colossians 2₁₅: 'Having put off from himself the principalities and the powers, he made a show of them openly, triumphing over them in (the cross)'. Having clothed Himself in σάρξ, '*physical constitution, flesh*', the Divine Son 'came into relation, hostile relation, with these spirit-forces of evil which hold the world in fee' (35). Thus it came to pass that 'the rulers of this world, which are coming to nought', overreached themselves, in that they 'crucified the Lord of glory' (1 Corinthians 2₆,₈). The apparent defeat of the Cross was in reality a victory, because 'in the act of dying He divested Himself of that flesh, the medium through which He had become involved in the human experience of the hostility of evil Potentates and

---

[1] We observe, however, that in discussing the Greek word λύτρον and the Hebrew equivalent *Kopher*, Dr. Vincent Taylor writes: 'Both the Greek and the Hebrew words describe something which is counted as an equivalent for purposes of deliverance or redemption. There is thus a definitely substitutionary idea in the terminology, although, of course, not one that is necessarily mechanical, or which demands a theory of vicarious punishment' (*Jesus and His Sacrifice*, p. 103).

Powers, the spirit-forces which had usurped authority over men' (35). This is the intention of the apparently perplexing phrase 'he stripped off from himself, ἀπεκδυσάμενος (*med.*), the Principalities and Powers' (Colossians 2₁₅) (34).

A second form of servitude from which Christ had delivered man was bondage to the Mosaic Law. To S. Paul as a Pharisee the Law had been the glory of Israel, and the means of salvation. To S. Paul as a Christian, in light of his painful realization that man cannot keep the commandments of God, the Law was seen as nothing other than the means by which disobedient man was visited with the curse of Deuteronomy 27₂₆. Our Lord was born a Jew, and so identified Himself with the Jewish race that He also was involved in bondage to the Law (39). 'He suffered the extreme consequence of being under the Law, namely, the death *of the cross,* which according to the Old Testament involved the victim in a curse. He was identified with His race as it lay under the judgement of a broken Law.' 'But once more His triumph over that death which spelled curse, meant triumph over the Law which imposed the curse and the deliverance of His people from its yoke' (40). Thus 'Christ redeemed us from the curse of the Law, having become a curse for us' (Galatians 3₁₃). The 'stumbling-block' to the Jew was the inconceivable and hideous paradox that the One who was hailed as Messiah by the Christians had suffered the death which God's Law pronounced accursed. One way to solve the paradox was to reject Christ as discredited. The Christian, who knew that his Lord had been vindicated after death by the Resurrection, was bold to solve the paradox in the alternative way. It was the Law which was discredited. It was no longer to be regarded as God's last word to the world, and His appointed path to Himself. Thus 'Christ is the end of law unto righteousness to every one that believeth' (Romans 10₄). It is to be observed that S. Paul assumes a distinction between the Law as a system by which man could be justified in the sight of God, and the contents of the Law as a moral standard. The

former is cancelled, while the latter continues (Romans 3₃₁)
(41–6).

Christ also delivered man from servitude to sin, the most
universal of all forms of bondage (46–52). S. Paul taught
that this redeeming act, like the two former, depended on
the fact of the Incarnation. The Divine Son took upon
Himself that human nature which was helplessly enslaved
to sin, and to death the consequence of sin (Romans 5₁₂;
1 Corinthians 15₅₆, etc.). Christ was born 'in the likeness of
the flesh which belonged to sin' (Romans 8₃). So complete
was this self-identification that the Apostle can write: 'Him
who knew no sin God made to be sin on our behalf' (2
Corinthians 5₂₁) (52). On the Cross our Lord 'died unto sin
once for all': τῇ ἁμαρτίᾳ ἀπέθανεν ἐφάπαξ (Romans 6₁₀).
'Christ at that moment divested Himself of the Flesh, and
thereby died out from under the condition of Servitude in
which He was involved by the Incarnation. . . . His triumph
over death is a triumph over Sin together with all the other
spirit-forces of Evil' (52–3).

We have also briefly observed that the writer to the
Hebrews taught an essentially similar doctrine.[1] The scope
of the redeeming act is indeed of narrower compass than in
the Pauline Epistles, but we have the advantage that we
have it before us worked out in a systematic form. The Lord
was One who came from God and made Himself one with
man (Hebrews 1₂₋₄, 2₉₋₁₀). As man he wrestled with sins
and doubts and fears, and wrestled to the last extremity (5₇).
Throughout He remained without sin (4₁₅). Thus Satan and
Death were vanquished (2₁₄₋₁₅). Aulén, indeed, speaking of
the 'classic' idea of the Atonement, claims that Hebrews 2₁₄
is perhaps more quoted by the Fathers than any other New
Testament text: 'Since then the children are sharers in flesh
and blood, He also Himself in like manner partook of the
same: that through death He might bring to nought him that
had the power of death, that is, the devil, and deliver them
who through fear of death were all their lifetime subject to

[1] See p. 148 *supra.*

bondage.'[1] When the Son went back in triumph to be with
the Father, this life of sinless obedience, and of constant moral
triumph within the sphere of human affairs through faith in
God, was the true and spiritual sacrifice of the great High
Priest (9_{11-15}). Those men who by the same faith tread the path
blazed by their Pioneer will be received into the same Holy
Place above (4_{14-16}, 10_{19-23}). In both Paul and Hebrews the
vital conception is that God as man faced man's foe, and
as man prevailed. The same thing in embryo may perhaps
be seen in the early speeches of Acts. There Christ is
preached as the One who faced death, and could not be
holden of it (Acts 2_{23-4}). His Resurrection, the pledge of the
reality of that victory over death, was likewise the pledge
that despite the shame and the curse the Crucified was
nevertheless the Messiah of God (2_{33}, $_{36}$).

The Fourth Gospel is a great and mysterious book. It is
great in spiritual beauty and in the mark it has made upon
the life of the Church, mysterious in that it is a blend
of undoubted historical reminiscence and of undeniable
interpretation. The Johannine Gospel and Epistles show
the first signs of the development within the Church of an
alternative exposition of the way of salvation. This is the
theme that in the Incarnate Son man sees the light and
truth of God, and receives thereby the gift of eternal life and
communion with God.[2] In its maturer form, particularly,
this doctrine contrasts strongly with the conception of
Christus Victor, though there is no necessary contradiction
between the two. The theology of *Christus Victor* is realistic
and dramatic. Deliverance is from evil conceived of as an
external compulsive power which holds man in bondage.
The Gospel that man becomes the son of God through the
Vision of God in the Incarnate Son is a translation into
abstract and philosophical terms. Evil is then conceived of
as wholly internal to man, and indeed, as an impoverishment of the human substance. It is largely a defect of
intellect, rather than of moral will and action. The two

---

[1] *Christus Victor*, p. 90.   [2] See pp. 161-2 *supra*.

theologies can be held together in the same Church, or even as diverse interests of the same individual. The realistic and dramatic theology belongs to the life of practical piety and moral resolve. It makes its main appeal to the 'simple believer', and so can maintain its position in the life of the Church even alongside an alien system of formal theology.[1] On the other hand, the abstract and philosophical theology essentially belongs to the academic life of the Church. Its main use is in the attempt to expound the Christian Faith as an integral part of a coherent philosophy of life.

This two-fold interest is found in a rudimentary state of development in the Johannine literature. So we catch glimpses of 'Christus Victor' moving in the background, behind the typical 'Johannine' mystical theology. Christ is represented as cleansing the Temple, and as promising to raise the temple of His body in three days (John 2₁₃-₂₂). This is a two-fold triumphant challenge to the power of evil. He preaches openly in the Temple in the presence of His enemies, and overawes those sent to arrest Him (7₂₅-₅₂). He has power to lay down His life for the sheep, and to take it again. No one has power to snatch His sheep from out of His hand (10₁₈,₂₈). A voice from the Father signifies the conquest of Satan. 'Now is the judgement of this world: now shall the prince of this world be cast out' (12₃₁). 'The prince of this world hath been judged' (16₁₁). When the enemies of Christ have their will, His disciples will be scattered, but He will remain in the Father. 'These things have I spoken unto you, that in me ye may have peace. In the world ye have tribulation; but be of good cheer; I have overcome the world' (16₃₃). In the Garden of betrayal the guards fall backward before His majesty (18₆). This element comes to more explicit expression in 1 John: 'the whole world lieth in the evil one' (5₁₉). The men of this world are subject to Antichrist (2₁₈,₂₂, 4₃). Nevertheless, 'greater is he that is in you than he that is in the world' (4₄; cf. 2₁₃,₁₄, 5₁₈). The purpose of Christ's coming is thus summed up in 1 John 3₈:

---

[1] *Christus Victor*, pp. 115–16.

'To this end was the Son of God manifested, that He might destroy the works of the devil.'

It will be asked by some: 'But where in this construction of the New Testament doctrine of the Saving Work of Christ is room found for the most essential element of all, that of sacrifice, of *propitiation*?' This is a question that plainly requires a careful answer if any accurate comparison is to be made between S. Irenaeus and the New Testament. The origin of the institution of Sacrifice is a vast and obscure subject. Even upon the narrower issue of the meaning of Sacrifice in the Old Testament, and in the mind of first-century Judaism, there have been very diverse opinions. In his able chapter on Sacrifice Dr. Vincent Taylor opens by noticing the contrasting views of Robertson Smith and of G. B. Gray. In *The Religion of the Semites* (pp. 224, 6 f.) the former holds that predominantly sacrifice is 'an act of social fellowship between the deity and his worshippers'; it is 'an act of communion, in which the god and his worshippers unite by partaking together of the flesh and blood of a sacred victim'. On the other hand, in *Sacrifice in the Old Testament* (p. 20) the latter writes: 'Wherever in later times the Jew sacrificed, he was consciously intending his sacrifice to be a gift to God.'[1] It is then observed by Dr. Taylor that it is not typical of Old Testament Sacrifice that a propitiatory offering is intended to appease the anger of Jehovah.[2] The idea of sacrifice is not to be linked to the mere destruction of a victim.[3] The spiritual value of the sacrificial system of historic Jewish religion is then estimated.[4] Despite defects, it held out to the worshipper a real possibility of spiritual fellowship with God. It is, however, admitted that the general tendency was to take the institution for granted as a divine ordinance.[5] The ways of God were inscrutable, and so men were not encouraged to reflect upon the wherefore of the traditional rites.[6] The attitude of Jesus to the Temple-sacrifices is then discussed.[7] 'The conclusion must be drawn

---

[1] cf. *Jesus and His Sacrifice*, p. 49.   [2] ibid. p. 50.   [3] ibid. pp. 54–5.
[4] ibid. pp. 55–67.   [5] ibid. p. 49.   [6] ibid. p. 59.   [7] ibid. pp. 67–75.

that, in relation to the sacrificial system, the attitude of Jesus was not that of an iconoclast, but rather that of one who, while alive to its limitations, recognized its place in the religious life of the nation.'[1] Our Lord looked upon the Temple with affection, yet from the independent critical standpoint of a reformer. That He thought of His death in terms of sacrifice may be supported from two passages: the '*Ransom*' passage (Mark 10₄₅), provided that this reflects the influence of Isaiah 53, and with certainty, 'This is my blood of the covenant' (Mark 14₂₄).[2]

In light of the above construction we must first observe that caution is necessary in deducing the manner in which our Lord regarded His death from the circumstance that He is found to speak of it as a sacrifice. In the first place, an element in Christ's teaching which finds its main support from two passages only is hardly an element of central importance. In the second place, if it be true that the Jew did not reflect upon the Temple-ritual, but took it for granted as the divinely-ordained and traditional mode of worship, a limitation is placed upon what we may regard as involved by the use of the term 'sacrifice'. We may imagine the less thoughtful type of Jew as content to say: 'This is the divinely-appointed way of purchasing God's favour by offering Him a gift.' A nobler type would perhaps say: 'This is the divinely-appointed way of giving myself to God in penitence and adoration, and of enjoying sweet communion with Him.' In neither case would the question necessarily be raised: 'Why does this ritual accomplish this end?' We cannot exclude the possibility that this is how our Lord felt, and that He is to be regarded as the supreme example of the second class. When He spoke of His death as a sacrifice He may have meant no more than that it was to be the supreme means by which man was to be joined in communion to God. He may have intended more than this, and thought of Himself as a representative offering to God, but the evidence hardly exists upon which a secure judgement might be made.

---

[1] *Jesus and His Sacrifice*, p. 70.   [2] ibid. p. 74.

One thing is certain: if the appeasement of an angry God by a gift is below the higher levels of Old Testament sacrificial doctrine it is incredible that One who always selected the noblest themes of the Hebrew Scriptures could ever have entertained the idea of appeasement. This particular notion of 'sacrifice', at least, is to be rejected. Thus more generally we may say that while the idea of Sacrifice is not to be excluded from our Lord's teaching, it is by no means a dominant conception of clear and certain content to us.

It is now necessary to consider the teaching of S. Paul on this issue. That the Apostle could speak of the death of his Lord as a sacrifice is evidenced first by the frequent connexion of salvation with 'the blood of Christ'.[1] There are also two passages where the death of Christ is definitely connected with sacrificial language, Ephesians 5₂ and 1 Corinthians 5₇. Upon the former, 'Christ also loved you, and gave himself up for us, an offering and a sacrifice (θυσία) to God for a sweet-smelling savour', Dr. C. A. A. Scott observes that S. Paul elsewhere uses the words 'offering' and 'sacrifice' to describe human acts of devotion and self-surrender (Romans 12₁, 15₁₆), while 'for a sweet-smelling savour' is once connected with the preaching of the Gospel (2 Corinthians 2₁₄) and once with the gifts of the Philippians (Philippians 4₁₈). Ephesians 5₂ should therefore not be pressed too strongly to a doctrinal use.[2] 1 Corinthians 5₇, 'for our passover has been sacrificed, even Christ', has a somewhat attenuated sacrificial connotation, inasmuch as in contemporary Judaism the Passover was a common sacred meal far more than a blood-sacrifice.[3] Taken by themselves, and read with no presuppositions in mind, the passages mentioned above are of a general kind. They do not give any definite information about S. Paul's theology of sacrifice. They do not therefore positively demand more than the sense that the death of Christ is the divinely-appointed means for man to have communion with God. There remains,

---

[1] e.g. Romans 5₉, Ephesians 1₇, 2₁₃, Colossians 1₂₀.
[2] *Christianity according to S. Paul*, pp. 90-1.   [3] ibid. p. 91.

then, the one crucial passage, Romans 3₂₄₋₆: 'Christ Jesus, whom God set forth *to be* a propitiation, through faith, by his blood, because of the passing over of the sins done aforetime, in the forbearance of God; for the shewing, *I say*, of his righteousness at this present season; that he might himself be just, and the justifier of him that hath faith in Jesus' (R.V.). For centuries it has seemed obvious to commentators that this text speaks of penal sufferings borne by Christ as a substitute for man, so as to enable a righteous God to forgive. It has, indeed, been the historic sheet-anchor of the 'Latin' theory of the Atonement. If this exegesis be justified, S. Paul has indeed declared his theology of sacrifice in definitely substitutionary terms. This conclusion would justify reading a definite content into the relatively numerous generalized sacrificial passages already referred to, and this in turn would suffice to make substitutionary sacrifice a weighty element in S. Paul's theology of the Atonement.

Much sound modern scholarship is, however, not satisfied with the traditional exegesis of Romans 3₂₄₋₆. An admirable treatment is that of Dr. C. H. Dodd, in his volume on 'Romans' in the *Moffatt New Testament Commentary* (London, 1932).[1] First to be considered is the phrase 'Being justified (δικαιούμενοι) freely by his grace'. Dodd observes that δικαιόω, 'to justify', means in Greek writers 'to account or pronounce right', 'to acquit', or 'to treat justly'. The usage of this Greek verb is, however, coloured by a Hebrew background. The Old Testament *Righteousness of God* is 'an act by which a wronged person is given his rights, is vindicated, delivered from oppression' (pp. 9–13). In the Septuagint this conception is expressed by the word δικαιοσύνη. Thus, when S. Paul says 'they are justified freely by his grace' 'the idea uppermost in his mind is that of deliverance. But as he is stating it in legal, forensic terms, deliverance takes the form of an acquittal in court' (pp. 51–2). The next phrase is: 'through the redemption (or 'ransom') διὰ τῆς ἀπολυτρώσεως that is in Christ Jesus.' Dodd observes that the term

[1] cf. also C. A. A. Scott, *Christianity according to S. Paul*, pp. 59–74.

ἀπολύτρωσις is not concrete (= 'the sum of money paid to redeem a prisoner') but abstract (= 'the act of redeeming'). The word can be used without any explicit reference to payment of money, as a simple equivalent of 'emancipation'. This Dodd claims to be the basis of S. Paul's usage (pp. 53–4). The critical phrase in the passage is: 'Whom God set forth to be a propitiation' (or, 'as propitiatory') ὃν προέθετο ὁ Θεὸς ἱλαστήριον. While a very common meaning of the corresponding verb ἱλάσκεσθαι in pagan Greek writers is 'to placate' a man or a god, the alternative meaning of 'to expiate' a sin, i.e. *to perform an act by which its guilt is annulled*, is the normal Septuagint usage of the word. 'But, as (Hebrew) religious thought advanced, it came to be felt that, where the defilement was moral, God alone could annul it; and so the verb is used with God as subject in the sense of "to forgive".'[1]

It is claimed by Dodd that this usage is determinative for S. Paul. 'The rendering "propitiation" is therefore misleading, for it suggests the placating of an angry God, and although this would be in accord with pagan usage, it is foreign to Biblical usage. In the present passage it is God who puts forward the means whereby the guilt of sin is removed, by sending Christ. The sending of Christ, therefore, is the divine method of forgiveness' (55). We then turn to v. 26 : 'For the shewing, I say, of his righteousness (τῆς δικαιοσύνης) at this present season: that he might himself be just (δίκαιον), and the justifier (δικαιοῦντα) of him that hath faith in Jesus.' Chiefly to be observed in reading this is that 'righteousness', 'just', and 'justifier' are all cognate words. Bearing in mind what has already been said regarding the *Righteousness of God*, this text can be rendered: 'It was to demonstrate His righteousness (i.e. deliverance) at the present epoch, showing that God is just Himself, and that He vindicates (or delivers) man.' To cite further from Dodd: 'There is no suggestion that a device has been found by which the justice of God can be satisfied (by the

[1] p. 55. See also *Journal of Theological Studies*, Vol. XXXII, pp. 352–60.

vicarious punishment of sin, for example), while at the same time His mercy is exerted to save the sinner. No such antithesis between justice and mercy was in Paul's mind' (59). Finally we have: 'because of the passing over of the sins done aforetime.' The mere passing over of man's sin carried with it the danger that man might come to think that God was indulgent to sin. It was therefore merely 'a provisional measure, suitable to the age in which God's decisive action regarding sin was still awaited' (60). The tremendous significance of this exegesis is apparent. One does not presume that it will be accepted by all competent scholars, but if upheld it goes far to evacuate S. Paul's theology of the conception of substitutionary sacrifice. As has been seen above, the remaining sacrificial passages are of a general nature only.

If the foregoing exegesis be allowed one may perhaps be permitted to suggest that New Testament language concerning sacrifice is best understood as a metaphor used to present the Saving Work of Christ, rather than as a rationale of the actual Work. What the Divine Son did in point of fact was to unite Himself with human nature to become a real man. In the conditions of human life He faced all those things which enchain and darken the spirit of man—the spiritual dullness of men and their tardiness in response to the appeal of the good, envy at pure goodness, fear of the bold reformer, compromise or wickedness entrenched in high places, corruption in religious systems, the loneliness of a spirit nobler than all companions, the keen tooth of ingratitude, sore temptation, and the last dread mystery of death. In the power of God the Incarnate Son sustained a human life of sinless moral triumph in face of all these foes. He never failed to pour Himself out in loving friendship to man, in hatred of wrong, in reverent devotion to His Heavenly Father. The Cross was the climax of the trial. The Empty Tomb and the glorious Resurrection Body were the supreme pledges of final victory. This is no 'modernization' of the Synoptic Gospels, but a statement of the empirical facts therein recorded, apart from elements of interpretation. Here is the hard kernel of the conception of 'Christus Victor'. S. Paul's doctrine is a statement of these empirical facts in the manner natural to one who thought of man's bondage principally in terms of the spirit-forces of evil, the Law with its curse, and of sin and death.

The effect of the triumphant Divine-human life was that God had provided the perfect and all-sufficient means by which man might be cleansed from the defilement of sin and released from its power, and by which he might hold lasting communion with God. To men brought up upon Scriptures which spoke of sacrifices as the divinely-ordained means of cleansing and communion, and who enjoyed the Temple sacrifices as one of their most venerated modes of worship, a most expressive metaphor for this would be that Christ was a *Sacrifice*. We may even dare to say that this would represent the mind of our Lord Himself, as He contemplated His mission, His sufferings, and the spiritual results that would follow. We may well imagine that the language of Scripture would count more with Him than the somewhat compromised ritual at Jerusalem. It may with some reason be claimed that such an exposition does justice to all that the New Testament says regarding the atoning death of Christ as a Sacrifice. We have seen that there is a wide consensus of opinion, including that of some who would emphasize representative sacrifice as a central element in the teaching of Jesus, that the use of this metaphor of Sacrifice does not necessarily involve the conceptions of penal substitution and divine appeasement. We affirm that the doctrine of the Sacramental hymn:

> The Bread dried up and burnt with fire
> Presents the Father's vengeful ire
>   Which my Redeemer bore:
> Into His bones the fire He sent,
> Till all the flaming darts were spent,
>   And Justice ask'd no more,

is to be resolutely dismissed as unscriptural doctrine. We

have also seen that it is a defensible position that the use of the metaphor of Sacrifice does not involve any particular theory of Sacrifice. Sacrifice may quite well be 'taken for granted' simply as the traditional and well-loved means of communion, though one would hardly care definitely to state that our Lord could not have seen more than this when He viewed His death as a sacrifice. There will always be room for reverent reserve when we speak of the mind of Jesus.

A word of caution is necessary, lest this position be misunderstood. It should not be assumed that an attempt is here being made to depreciate the sacrificial language of our Lord, or of S. Paul, as 'a mere metaphor'. The greatest work of the human mind is indeed to discover a truth, but second only to this is the discovery of a way in which the truth may effectually be declared. Any teacher will agree that how one says a thing is next in importance to the rightness of what one says, for a distasteful presentation of the truth is one of the surest ways to lead most men into error. In a day and generation when men's minds will kindle to the thought of 'Sacrifice' there is the amplest justification for using this conception as a means of preaching the essential work of Christ. This would appear to be what is found in the New Testament. The matter may be illustrated from present-day religious experience. In point of historical fact the words 'a full, perfect, and sufficient sacrifice, oblation, and satisfaction' owe their place in the Communion Office to the theology of Sacrifice held by the Church. From the point of view of practical piety, however, the position is reversed. One who through long usage of these and kindred words is accustomed to describe as a *Sacrifice* the central act of his devotional life, whereby he lays hold of the Real Presence of his Lord, will naturally find that his heart and mind kindle to the thought of 'Sacrifice'. The word will call up every hallowed and helpful association. Thus it is the Christian who lays most store by Eucharistic worship who most loves to speak of the death of Christ as a *Sacrifice*. This can hold good quite apart from any specific theory of the Atonement, or of the

nature of the Eucharist, for this is a matter far more of 'association' than of reasoned theological principle. The New
Testament writers were in just this position, having before
them the Jewish sacrifices. The case in point is surely the writer
to the Hebrews. When he speaks of the *actual work* of the historic Christ it is in terms of the victorious Champion, who
endured even unto 'strong crying and tears', and who brought
to nought 'him that had the power of death, even the devil'
(Hebrews 2₉-10, 14-15, 414-16, 57-10). He then proceeds to *apply*
this Gospel to the hearts and minds of his readers through the
medium of a sustained and splendid *metaphor* of Sacrifice. The
intention of the sacrificial language of Hebrews is therefore
the enforcement of the surpassing worth of the work of
'*Christus Victor*', by an illustrative comparison based on
Platonic theory. The New Testament language of Sacrifice
is a metaphor indeed, but it is most out of place to describe
it as a '*mere*' metaphor. This mode of preaching the facts
about Christ is a matter of the greatest possible value and
significance.

If the foregoing representation of New Testament doctrine
be justified it is apparent that in his doctrine of the Saving
Work of Christ by *Recapitulation* S. Irenaeus is a sound
Biblicist. A glance at the objections which have been raised
on this score will suffice to demonstrate this. Werner, for
example, says that there is present in Irenaeus only a putative
Paulinism, in that he indeed emphasized the value of the
death of Christ, but did not succeed in finding a distinct
place in his scheme for the sufferings and death of the Lord,
as the saving work was substantially complete in the mere
occurrence of the Incarnation.[1] Likewise, Loofs claims that
the much-boasted Recapitulation-doctrine is 'a playful thing',
and that the apparent Paulinism of Irenaeus springs from
the mere unthinking reproduction of sources.[2] Seeberg has
an interesting statement which shows the mind which
appears to lie beneath many of the common assertions that

---

[1] *Paulinismus*, p. 157.   [2] *Theophilus*, p. 434.

S. Irenaeus has diluted S. Paul. We learn that the Cross had
not the significance for Irenaeus that it had for Paul because,
while the death of Christ is proved a necessary part of the
Recapitulation, the forgiveness of sins is not particularly
connected with the Cross.[1] The death of Christ has no more
connexion with salvation than His resistance to temptation.[2]
This seems to reflect an assumption by Seeberg that S. Paul
looked upon the Cross as something separate from the life
of Christ, and connected the forgiveness of sins only with
His death. This assumption is part of a wider one, namely,
that the Pauline doctrine of the Cross is some form of substitutionary theory, in which the actual dying of Jesus is the
one thing of real moment for the forgiveness of man. So
Harnack, in claiming that there is only a rudimentary conception of reconciliation in Irenaeus, states that he does not
teach the vicarious suffering of Christ, and seldom speaks of
God as offended through Adam's sin.[3] Beuzart expresses
this assumption still more plainly. He produces the following facts as evidence for the proposition that Irenaeus used
Pauline language about the expiatory and reconciling death
without sharing the Pauline thought: Christ's death was for
obedience, parallel to Adam; the death was no more than
part of Christ's humiliation; Christ's death was an event
in His earthly career, not *the* event.[4,5] This is followed by the
statement that the element of expiation was not present in
the doctrine of the Lord's death, and this is a token that sin
had not the gravity for Irenaeus that it had for S. Paul.[6] In
reply we may say that S. Irenaeus was nearer to an under-

---

[1] *DG.* p. 330.   [2] ibid. p. 332.   [3] *H.D.* II.291–2.

[4] *Essai*, p. 112. See also Bonwetsch, *Theologie d.I.* p. 113, Werner, *Paulinismus*, p. 97.

[5] We observe that the grand movement of thought in Philippians 2₅-₁₁ is
precisely that for which S. Irenaeus is blamed. Here the Cross is the climax
of self-humiliation. The climax is indeed such a stupendous one that the
process tends to fade from view, and the Apostle speaks of salvation by the
death of Christ. Yet the death remains the culmination of a process. It is
always the surpassingly important event of the earthly career of Jesus. It
is never *the* event.

[6] See also pp. 214–15, 223–4 *infra*.

standing of S. Paul's estimate of Christ's death than were
many later Latin and Reformation theologians.

We may safely affirm that Recapitulation as expounded on
pp. 144–5, 147–9, 150, and 152–3 is, in the light of Christ's
sayings regarding the conquest of evil and the Evil One,[1] a
legitimate interpretation of some very important elements in
our Lord's own attitude to His Messianic career and the
Kingdom of God. There is, furthermore, the closest parallel
between the work of Christ as interpreted by S. Paul and by
S. Irenaeus. The Apostle preached that the power of a
manifold bondage to the Satanic powers and demons, to the
Law with its curse, and to Sin and Death, had been broken
by the victorious Championship of the Incarnate Son of God,
in His life of sinless obedience.[2] The essence of the doctrine
of *Recapitulation* in Irenaeus is just this, with the significant
exception that the Law with its curse no longer figures as
part of the bondage. The reason for this is not far to seek.
S. Irenaeus, and the Gentile Church for which he speaks,
had not been through the bitter experience reflected in
Romans 7 7-25. Unlike S. Paul, he had not been brought up to
accept it as a cherished religious tradition that the way to
God was to attempt 'the righteousness of the Law'. He had
never arrived at the desolating realization that this was for
him the way of spiritual death. Irenaeus did not vehemently
rebel against the Mosaic Law. On the contrary, his spiritual
adversaries were Gnostics, who would cut the Church and
her theology completely adrift from the Hebrew religion of
the Old Testament. It was therefore a powerful polemic
interest with him to assert the continuity of the Law and the
Gospel. It would therefore have been most surprising had
we found S. Irenaeus sharing S. Paul's severe view of the
Law. We must admit that there is a certain toning down of
S. Paul at this point. However, the *essence* of the Apostle's
cardinal doctrine of '*Justification by Faith, and not by the
Works of the Law*' is the simple and vital principle that man
is no longer to cling to an utterly vain hope of making him-

---

[1] See p. 172 *supra*.   [2] See pp. 173–5 *supra*.

self into a good man, well-pleasing to God, by the sterling worth of his own moral efforts. He is to put all his trust in a miraculous redeeming work of God in Christ. The hostile attitude toward the Law, which occurs in some passages of Paul, though by no means generally,[1] is as it were the psychological accident to the Apostle's doctrine, rather than the doctrine itself. S. Irenaeus is hardly to be attacked as seriously un-Pauline because he does not follow S. Paul in this particular feature. He does follow in the essence of the doctrine, in that he most adequately emphasizes that for salvation man is to trust not in himself, but in a great objective Divine redeeming work.[2] That the conception of substitutionary sacrifice or Divine appeasement forms little or no part of the theology of Irenaeus in no way mars this Pauline parallel, for the same may be claimed to be the case with S. Paul.

Before we leave the present discussion one proviso is due. The vindication of the substantial fidelity of S. Irenaeus to the New Testament in his doctrine of the Atonement is a matter of great moment. This vindication has been made upon the basis of a certain exegesis of the New Testament itself. To this end a survey, and perforce a brief survey, has been made of a large number of points of Biblical scholarship. One cannot but be aware that some of these points are subjects of great intricacy, and of frequent controversy. A summary is bound to present the appearance, at times, of rushing in where angels fear to tread. A careful reading of the evidence for the results in question appears convincing to the present writer, but it would be an excess of dogmatism to assume that this will be so in the case of all competent scholars. Those who remain convinced that the death of our Lord is properly a sacrifice *offered to God* on behalf of man, and the occasion of *substitutionary* punishment for man's sin, and that here are vital and precious elements of Christian doctrine, will certainly maintain that S. Irenaeus moves at a lower spiritual level than the New Testament.

[1] See pp. 174–5 *supra*.   [2] See pp. 239–40 *infra*.

The present section may profitably be concluded by a
consideration of the adequacy of the doctrine of *Recapitulation* as a basis for the Christian Gospel. It may be said that
sinful man is separated from God by two things. The first is
the load of a guilty conscience. A sensitive man feels that he
has done wrong in the sight of the Holy God, and is utterly
unworthy to appear before Him. He has a deep and dis-
heartening conviction that he is not the man to aspire after
holy things. The second thing that separates man from God
is his stubborn disbelief in himself, born of long unhappy
experience of strong moral resolves weakly broken. It has
become impossible to imagine that he can ever become
radically better than at present. To be adequate to the Gospel
any exposition of Christ's saving work must therefore safeguard two elements. It must convincingly demonstrate that
God has now actually done all that needs to be done, if His
prodigal child is to return. It must move the believer's heart
through penitence to love, so that he dare look up to his
Father and be forgiven. The Satisfaction and Penal Substitution theories of the Atonement have sufficed for precisely
this need. Hence, these theories have for so long held an
honoured place in Christian theology, despite the ethically
questionable picture of God which they imply. On the other
hand, man must be moved to hope and confidence as well as
to love. Solid ground must be provided for supposing that
God can indeed overcome the lower side of human nature,
and in particular, that He can do it for *me*, and even in *my*
circumstances. It will be found that S. Irenaeus admirably
suffices on both scores, though some criticisms have to be
met.

As to the first: in advancing the theme that Irenaeus used
Pauline language about the death of Christ without sharing
Pauline thought, Beuzart states that Christ's death was
explained as occurring merely for the sake of obedience,
parallel to Adam's disobedience, and that it did not move
Irenaeus to love, as in Western piety.[1] This charge, if

---

[1] *Essai*, p. 112.

substantiated, would reveal a grave failing indeed. However, Beuzart is surely guilty of a serious overstatement of the case. It is to be admitted that *Adversus Haereses* does not display much rapture when the Lord's death is contemplated. There is little sense of:

> The o'erwhelming power of saving grace,
> The sight that veils the seraph's face;
> The speechless awe that dares not move,
> And all the silent heaven of love.

He would be a bold man, however, who would state that S. Irenaeus shows himself incapable of such feelings. His surviving work is exclusively polemic and instructional, not devotional. It is therefore bound to move at a lower level of feeling. Hence it is most significant that even at this lower level there are to be found many moving testimonies to the love of God as revealed in Christ's self-sacrifice, and as demanding a response in man's love. If not rapturous, they are at least profound and beautiful. So God's 'pre-eminent goodness',[1] and perpetual good-will,[2] are shown in the fact that He 'has called us to the knowledge of Himself'.[3] That man should know God is a mark of God's great favour toward man.[4] The graciousness of God is further seen in that 'God manifested long-suffering in regard to the apostasy'.[5] He is 'the Father of our Lord . . . who does indeed through His infinite kindness call the unworthy'.[6] 'Man, who had been led captive in times past, was rescued from the grasp of his possessor, according to the tender mercy of God the Father.'[7] All this beneficent activity is prompted by nothing less than love, for its aim is to win love in return. God has saved man that he 'may always live in a state of gratitude to the Lord'. He has brought him to immortality so 'that he might love Him the more'.[8] Such is the quality of God's love that it is right and necessary that those who look

[1] II.25.3, i.214. [2] IV.37.1, ii.36. [3] III.9.1, i.278. [4] III.6.4, i.271.
[5] I.10.3, i.44; III.23.1, i.363. [6] IV.36.6, ii.33; *Dem.* 41.
[7] V.21.3, ii.114; see also III.20.1, i.347–8; III.23.6, i.367; III.25.3, i.372; *Dem.* 60.
[8] III.20.2, i.348.

into the ways of God 'should increase in the love of Him who
has done, and still does, so great things for us'.[1] When, in
response to the love of God, in the heart of man 'love
toward God increases, He bestows more and greater' gifts.[2]
God 'is always willing to confer a greater grace upon the
human race',[3] 'for the love of God, being rich and ungrudg-
ing, confers upon the suppliant more than he can ask from
it'.[4] The self-sacrifice of the Incarnation is the most sublime
motion of divine grace. The Son, 'because of His surpassing
love towards His creation, condescended to be born of the
Virgin'.[5] In particular this is seen in Christ's sufferings as
the Champion. 'He fought and conquered, for He was man
contending for the fathers. . . . For He is a most holy and
merciful Lord, and loves the human race.'[6] Finally, S. Irenaeus was by no means a stranger to 'the faith that works by
love'.[7]

Irenaeus was also conscious that the Christian is a forgiven
man, who has been restored by grace to friendship with God.
References are not so numerous or so emphatic as some could
wish, but the theme is present. 'And therefore in the last
times the Lord has restored us into friendship through His
incarnation, having become "the Mediator between God and
men"; . . . conferring also upon us the gift of communion
with, and subjection to, our Maker. For this reason also He
has taught us to say in prayer, "And forgive us our debts";
since indeed He is our Father, whose debtors we were. . . .
Rightly then does His Word say to man, "Thy sins are
forgiven thee"; He, the same against whom we had sinned
in the beginning, grants forgiveness of sins in the end.'[8]
Most usually the word 'communion' has a meaning less
rich than that of 'personal friendship with God',[9] though
this sense appears to be present in the passage V.1.1, ii.55-6.
Bonwetsch, however, goes a little too far in saying that there

[1] II.28.1, i.219.   [2] IV.9.2, i.401; see also IV.11.3, i.407; V.3.1, ii.62.
[3] IV.9.3, i.402.   [4] III.Pref., i.257.
[5] III.4.2, i.264; see also III.20.4, i.350; V.Pref., ii.55.
[6] III.18.6, i.342; see also V.2.1, ii.59; *Dem.* 88.
[7] See pp. 242-3 *infra*.   [8] V.17.1, ii.100-1.   [9] See pp. 156-7 *supra*.

is no idea in Irenaeus of a forgiveness of sins that opens the way to communion with God of a personal nature.[1]

S. Irenaeus apparently knows nothing of any theology of Penal Substitution, of Divine Appeasement, or of Satisfaction. The one passage which may be read to indicate the contrary is: 'And therefore in the last times the Lord has restored us into friendship through His incarnation, having become "the Mediator between God and men"; propitiating indeed for us the Father against whom we had sinned, and cancelling our disobedience by His own obedience.' *Et propter hoc in novissimis temporibus, in amicitiam restituit nos Dominus per suam incarnationem, 'mediator Dei et hominum' factus; propitians quidem pro nobis Patrem, in quem peccaveramus, et nostram inobedientiam per suam obedientiam consolatus.*[2] We have no external evidence which would serve to interpret what is intended by *propitians* save, on the one hand, that it has *Patrem* as the object, which reads like Divine Appeasement, and, on the other hand, that on at least one occasion Irenaeus very pointedly fails to speak of Divine Appeasement,[3] and that this and allied conceptions have no part in the doctrine of *Recapitulation*. We cannot exclude the thought that S. Irenaeus was sufficiently near to the New Testament to give '*Propitiation*' its Biblical sense, in which the notion of the appeasement of an angry God is probably absent.[4] Vernet is therefore probably incorrect in his statement that Irenaeus teaches that Christ made a satisfaction for the debt of man, though without using the word.[5] In the sense that there is no doctrine of Substitution Harnack is right in his observation that Irenaeus does not teach the vicarious suffering of Christ.[6] There is, however, a real doctrine of vicarious suffering. Our Lord underwent His Passion for the express purpose that His sufferings might work our blessing. 'Despise Him not because of the sufferings which for thy sake He of purpose endured.'[7] 'It is manifest therefore that

---

[1] *Theologie d.I.* p. 143.   [2] V.17.1, ii.100; Harvey, ii.369.

[3] See p. 63 *supra*.   [4] See pp. 182–3 *supra*.

[5] *Dictionnaire*, VII, cols. 2475–6.   [6] *H.D.* II.291.   [7] *Dem.* 70.

by the will of the Father these things occurred to Him for the sake of our salvation.'[1] Christ saved men 'by His death'.[2] This was a token of God's complete good-will toward erring man. Our Lord lived a martyred life of self-humiliation and self-sacrifice in striving with man's foe. This happened according to the will of God, and God made the supreme revelation of Himself in that life. The pledge that the way is open for the prodigal child of God, being penitent, to return to His Father and be forgiven, rests upon the simple ground that Christ was prepared so to suffer. Mature Christian thought will surely allow this simple ground to be a sufficient one. S. Irenaeus is adequate to the Gospel under this first head.

Whatever doubts sensitive souls may have regarding the possibility of forgiveness for sin, for the mass of men the difficulty is to imagine that God is able to do anything that will 'make a difference'. The spirit of man has been enchained by despair of good more than by anything else. Belief in malignant Fate has been a more dread foe than guilty fear. In any exposition of the Saving Work of Christ the objective side is therefore of at least as great moment as the subjective. The deep question of the soul is: 'Am I provided with a solid and intelligible ground for a confident assurance that God has made the world around me a different and a better place, in which I may hope to be a different and a better man?' We turn therefore to this other side of the Gospel. It will be found that S. Irenaeus does himself ample justice.

The doctrine of the conquest of Satan, and of the analogy of the New and old Adam, has been described as mythological. To Bousset it is the ancient song of the return of the primitive Golden Age, and a conception of world-history as a drama played between the devil and man.[3] The idea of the two acts of the race, in Adam and in Christ, certainly has a mythological colour,[4] as has the conquest of Satan.[5] It must be borne in mind, however, that the mythology is a Biblical

---

[1] *Dem.* 69. [2] See p. 149 *supra*. [3] *Kyr.Ch.* p. 351.
[4] So Beuzart, *Essai*, p. 118. [5] ibid. p. 122.

and not a classical one. To S. Irenaeus the Golden Age was not the *past* one of the wistful pagan. It was the Golden Age, always a *future* Golden Age, of the hopeful Hebrew prophets and apocalyptists. Though he may at times speak as though human salvation were exhausted in the restoration of fallen man to his original condition, his fullest thought is that the restoration is but the beginning of a course of endless progress which shall end in carrying man to spiritual attainments far beyond his first endowment.[1] However, an age which took mythology seriously was bound to have a mythological theology of redemption, nor was it necessarily the worse for that. If, for example, a man feels himself to be in bondage to the *Evil One*, rather than to abstract evil existing in the marred heritage of the race, or in his own perverse will, he is bound to conceive of his rescue as a drama of supernatural *personages*. As he conceives his enemy, so he conceives the work of his Saviour. Yet all the while the essential and valuable element is that he does actually know himself to have been rescued. S. Irenaeus shared with S. Paul, and with the African convert of the present day, the joyous sense that Christ had faced and quelled the demonic powers. The only thing that has robbed such exposition of its value to the modern mind is that imaginative supernaturalism has evaporated before the fire of natural science. There is now insufficient background in a vivid sense of the actual existence of personal entities, invisible and other than human, of higher or of lower station. Today the release that Christ works is more naturally and convincingly expounded in psychological terms. The mythological element in the doctrine of *Recapitulation*, however, in no way impugns its historic value as a basis for preaching a Gospel of real redemption.

Bousset rightly observes that though S. Irenaeus loves the thought of evolution he nowhere draws the consequence that Jesus is simply the crown of human development, the perfect man in whom the Logos was fully revealed. Jesus

[1] See pp. 211–12 *infra*.

remains the Divine Logos incarnate. Grace coming from
above speaks the last word in development, so that at the
crucial point a full supernaturalism is safeguarded.[1] Loofs
on the other hand quotes V.18.3, ii.105–6: 'For the Creator
of the world is truly the Word of God: and this is our
Lord . . . who in an invisible manner contains all things
created, and is inherent in the entire creation; . . . and therefore He came to His own in a visible manner, and was made
flesh, and hung upon the tree.' This is claimed as an example
of Christology where the Incarnation is only inspiration.[2] We
admit that so long as he moves within the ambit of the
divinization-theology Irenaeus shares a weakness against
which that theology has constantly to be guarded, namely,
that the union of Divine and human in Christ is so easily
represented as the full and perfect example of that which
occurs in part in the spiritual man. However, when we turn
to the *Recapitulation* S. Irenaeus is seen to escape from this
snare. The elements of development and of divine inter-
position are admirably united in the following significant
passage. 'You will find that the whole conduct, and all the
doctrine, and all the sufferings of our Lord, were predicted
through [the prophets]. . . . What then did the Lord bring to
us by His advent?—know ye that He brought all novelty,
by bringing Himself who had been announced.'[3] The
typical Logos-theology so easily represented the significance
of the Incarnation as the means of revelation of a final and
perfect doctrine. This confusion is avoided here, for the
distinction between perfect knowledge of the nature and
doctrine of Christ, and the concrete historic Saving Work
of Christ, is clearly preserved. S. Irenaeus can well imagine
the entire Christian doctrine to have been *declared* by mere
prophets, yet there was still the place for the Redeemer to
come to *perform* the work itself. This is a token that Christ
came not only to teach something, but above all to *do*
something. The Incarnation is therefore certainly not inspiration to S. Irenaeus.

[1] *Kyr.Ch.* pp. 355, 361.   [2] *Studium DG.* p. 150.   [3] IV.34.1, ii.18.

Loofs maintains that the theological elements in Irenaeus derived from Theophilus of Antioch are richer and deeper than the recapitulation-doctrine. Theophilus had a systematic scheme of the progressive revelation of an almighty God, which is also the actualizing of the destiny of man: in prophecy and law as preparatory, in Christ as the invisible God made visible.[1] An example of this as reflected in Irenaeus is: 'God . . . having been seen at that time indeed prophetically through the Spirit, and seen, too, adoptively through the Son, . . . shall also be seen paternally in the kingdom of heaven.'[2] This interpretation is to be rejected, for the principle for which Loofs pleads is the seed of all Arianism and Unitarianism, while the virtue of S. Irenaeus is that he has so much to add to this. As Bousset truly remarks: 'The future belongs to the simple and complete redemption-supernaturalism of Irenaeus.'[3]

In conclusion some brief mention must be made of a kindred theme. It has frequently been held that S. Irenaeus is the father of the theory of a ransom paid to the Devil. Certain passages have been cited to illustrate the idea that the Devil has acquired 'rights' over man, which God in justice had to recognize. Such are: 'The Word of God, powerful in all things, and not defective with regard to His own justice, did righteously turn against that apostasy, and redeem from it His own property, not by violent means . . . but by means of persuasion';[4] and, 'For indeed the enemy would not have been fairly vanquished, unless it had been a man (born) of woman who conquered him. For it was by means of a woman that he got the advantage over man at first.'[5] However, 'For we were debtors to none other but to Him whose commandment we had transgressed'[6] has been taken as excluding the idea of a just debt to Satan. Vernet records the views of a number of writers, and concludes that Irenaeus would allow some right to the Devil, as he is to be treated according

---

[1] *Theophilus*, p. 441.   [3] *Kyr.Ch.* p. 361.   [5] V.21.1, ii.111.
[2] IV.20.5, i.442.   [4] V.1.1, ii.56.   [6] V.16.3, ii.100.

to the rules of justice, but that he does not fall into the gross
error of supposing that the blood of Christ was handed over
as a ransom. There is no question of strict legal rights.[1]
An examination of the context of the first of the above
passages plainly shows that the *'justice'* is done not to Satan,
but to God Himself as good. He redeemed us 'by means of
persuasion, as became a God of counsel, who does not use
violent means to obtain what He desires; so that neither
should justice be infringed upon, nor the ancient handiwork
of God go to destruction'. As also we read in another place:
'For there is no coercion with God, but a good will is
present with Him continually.'[2] The *'persuasion'* of 5.1.1
clearly represents the fact that in delivering man God exclusively employed rightful means. The Devil had snatched
man away. God will not beat him at his own game, and
rescue man by the *fiat* of omnipotence. Instead, He sent a
Champion who earned the moral right to be a Champion
by a life of moral obedience in the face of Satan's temptations.[3] As a result, 'justly indeed is he led captive, who
led man unjustly into bondage'.[4] God's justice is not a
concession to the Devil, nor even to His own reputation.
It is a definition of the means taken to defeat Satan.
'Vanquishing Satan' and the *'persuasion'* are really the same
thing. Vernet rightly observes that when Irenaeus uses
the verb *'to ransom'* it is in the simple Biblical sense of *'to
deliver'*, a natural usage in days of slavery. The question of
payment either to Satan or to God does not arise.[5]

[1] *Dictionnaire*, VII, col. 2480.   [2] IV.**37**.1, ii.36.
[3] So G. Molvitz, *De* Ἀνακεφαλαιώσεως *in Irenaei Theologia Potestate*,
pp. 18–19.
[4] V.**21**.3, ii.114; see also III.**18**.7, i.343.   [5] *Dictionnaire*, VII, col. 2479.

Chapter Twelve

THE LIFE OF MAN AND THE LIFE OF FAITH

MAN IS THE OBJECT of God's self-revelation, and of His redeeming act in Christ. S. Irenaeus has a wide variety of most important statements regarding the nature of man, and the manner in which he may receive what God offers. The aspects of the work of Irenaeus which are due for consideration at this point are of an importance second to none, and for several reasons. In the first place, our judgement regarding the standing of S. Irenaeus as a competent guide to the spiritual life, as distinct from a teacher of sound theology, will be largely decided by our findings. Furthermore, Irenaeus has left some of the issues very confused, with the result that there have been conflicting opinions about him. Finally, previous work on at least some of these points has commonly been somewhat inadequate. We have, then, to turn to what S. Irenaeus has to say concerning the original nature of man as created by God, concerning the Fall, the present nature of man, the doctrine of sin, man's need of grace for salvation, and concerning the act of faith whereby man appropriates the Saving Work of Christ. These topics have to be treated together because they are mutually related at several points.

It has already been observed that much of this ground has been traversed by Duncker.[1] To our consideration of him must be added some notice of the important work of Ernst Klebba, *Die Anthropologie des Hl. Irenaeus* (Münster, 1894). Klebba here states that the anthropology of Irenaeus is founded upon Scripture. Irenaeus begins with Genesis 1₂₆ (p. 15). Man was framed by the creative Hands of God, not, as in Gnostic theory, by angels (15–17). Man was created from dust, which to Irenaeus means real material earth, as

[1] See pp. 8–10 *supra*.

opposed to the Valentinian conception of an invisible ideal
'earth'. The breath of life, which makes man a reasonable
being, was breathed in by God. Man is dependent on God
for life (18–19). The world was created for man, that he
might come to God, and all creation springs from divine
love (20–1). Klebba then proceeds to investigate what
meaning S. Irenaeus attached to the divine word of Genesis
1₂₆: 'Let us make man in our image, after our likeness.'
The views of Duncker, who sees the *imago*, εἰκών, as part of
man's original nature, the *similitudo*, ὁμοίωσις, as a later goal
of perfection to be realized, and by contrast, of Zeigler, who
interprets the *similitudo* as not more than human reason and
free-will, are noticed (22). The terms 'image' and 'likeness'
are somewhat fluid. It has not always been remembered that
Irenaeus can use them of Adam both before and after the
Fall. The doctrine of the primitive condition of man is to be
established from those passages which refer to the former
state (23).

In Tatian the 'Image of God', εἰκών, and the 'Likeness of
God', ὁμοίωσις, are identical.[1] According to the record of
Irenaeus the Valentinians distinguished the two terms.
The passage in question (I.5.5, Harvey, i.49) runs as
follows: Δημιουργήσαντα δὴ τὸν κόσμον, πεποιηκέναι καὶ τὸν
ἄνθρωπον τὸν χοϊκόν· οὐκ ἀπὸ ταύτης δὲ τῆς ξηρᾶς γῆς, ἀλλ' ἀπὸ
τῆς ἀοράτου οὐσίας, ἀπὸ τοῦ κεχυμένου καὶ ῥευστοῦ τῆς ὕλης
λαβόντα· καὶ εἰς τοῦτον ἐμφυσῆσαι τὸν ψυχικὸν διορίζονται. Καὶ
τοῦτον εἶναι τὸν κατ' εἰκόνα καὶ ὁμοίωσιν γεγονότα· κατ' εἰκόνα
μὲν τὸν ὑλικὸν ὑπάρχειν, παραπλήσιον μὲν, ἀλλ' οὐχ ὁμοούσιον τῷ
Θεῷ· καθ' ὁμοίωσιν δὲ τὸν ψυχικὸν, ὅθεν καὶ πνεῦμα ζωῆς τὴν
οὐσίαν αὐτοῦ εἰρῆσθαι, ἐκ πνευματικῆς ἀποῤῥοίας οὖσαν.[2] Here the

---

[1] *Or.ad.Gr.*, 7.

[2] 'Having thus formed the world, he (the Demiurge) also created the
earthy (part of) man, not taking him from this dry earth, but from an
invisible substance consisting of fusible and fluid matter, and then afterwards,
as they define the process, breathed into him the animal part of his nature.
It was this latter which was created after his image and likeness. The material
part, indeed, was very near to God, so far as the image went, but not of the
same substance with him. The animal, on the other hand, was so in respect

εἰκών is the 'hylic' part of man, the ὁμοίωσις the higher and 'psychic'. S. Clement of Rome had already clearly described the formation of man as the impress of the divine image.[1] The expression also occurs in the *Epistle to Diognetus*[2] (23–4). In *Adv.Haer.* V.6.1, where Irenaeus treats of the perfect condition of man, he distinguishes between the *anima assumens spiritum Patris* and the *caro*,[3] the latter being formed after the Image of God. He subsequently speaks of the distinction between the *imago* and the *similitudo: Si autem defuerit animae Spiritus, animalis est vere, qui est talis, et carnalis derelictus imperfectus erit: imaginem quidem haben; in plasmate, similitudinem vero non assumens per Spiritum sicut autem hic imperfectus est* (V.6.1, Harvey, ii.334).[4] There is, furthermore, the important passage V.16.2, Harvey, ii.368: Ἐν τοῖς πρόσθεν χρόνοις ἐλέγετο μὲν κατ' εἰκόνα Θεοῦ γεγονέναι τὸν ἄνθρωπον, οὐκ ἐδείκνυτο δέ· ἔτι γὰρ ἀόρατος ἦν ὁ Λόγος, οὗ κατ' εἰκόνα ὁ ἄνθρωπος ἐγεγόνει· διὰ τοῦτο δὴ καὶ τὴν ὁμοίωσιν ῥᾳδίως ἀπέβαλεν. Ὁπότε δὲ σὰρξ ἐγένετο ὁ Λόγος τοῦ Θεοῦ, τὰ ἀμφότερα ἐπεκύρωσε· καὶ γὰρ καὶ τὴν εἰκόνα ἔδειξεν ἀληθῶς, αὐτὸς τοῦτο γενόμενος ὅπερ ἦν ἡ εἰκὼν αὐτοῦ· καὶ τὴν ὁμοίωσιν βεβαίως κατέστησε, συνεξομοιώσας τὸν ἄνθρωπον τῷ ἀοράτῳ πατρί . . . *per visibile Verbum*.[5] Here the εἰκών includes the whole of human nature, because it is stated that the Logos, in

[1] I Clem. xxxiii.4.   [2] X.2.

[3] *Perfectus autem homo commixtio et adunitio est plasmata animae assumentis spiritum Patris, et admixta ei carni, quae est plasmata secundum imaginem Dei* (V.6.1, Harvey, ii.333).

[4] 'But if the Spirit be wanting to the soul, he who is such is indeed of an animal nature, and being left carnal, shall be an imperfect being, possessing indeed the image in his formation, but not receiving the similitude through the Spirit; and thus is this being imperfect' (V.6.1, ii.68).

[5] 'For in times long past, it was *said* that man was created after the image of God, but it was not (actually) *shown*; for the Word was as yet invisible, after whose image man was created. Wherefore also he did easily lose the similitude. When, however, the Word of God became flesh, He confirmed both these; for He both showed forth the image truly, since He became Himself what was His image; and he re-established the similitude after a sure manner, by assimilating man to the invisible Father by means of the visible Word' (V.16.2, ii.99).

to likeness; and hence his substance was called the spirit of life, because it took its rise from a spiritual outflowing' (I.5.5, i.23).

becoming incarnate, became that which was His image. The εἰκών is the whole bodily and spiritual nature of man, without any added supernatural gift (24–6). Of the ὁμοίωσις in Adam, on the other hand, we read of a loss at the Fall. 'Αποβαλεῖν definitely answers to *loss*, not to mere diminution. The ὁμοίωσις, *similitudo Dei*, in original man was hence an accident, i.e. not an element necessary to human nature, but that which could be lost. It is this divine quality which the Logos restores (26). In this sense also is to be understood III.**18**.1, i.337–8. Klebba concludes that Irenaeus sees the following propositions as involved in *Faciamus hominem*:—The first man was sinless; He was a child in knowledge (knowledge not being necessary to please God); A relative perfection is not denied to Adam, but he was not the Ideal Man; The first man was without trouble, he was bodily immortal, and the lord of Creation (27–9).

Regarding the supernatural gift in Adam, Irenaeus only says that our first parents were like what the perfected believer will be, i.e. possessed of the Divine Spirit (29). Klebba discusses the passage V.**12**.2,[1] and concludes that Irenaeus clearly distinguishes the Breath of Life in Adam from the supernatural life-principle (29–31). Adam was hence perfect, in the sense that the believer who possesses the life-giving Spirit may be called perfect, human perfection consisting in ability to progress through the Spirit. He was not perfect as is the uncreated God, or as are the Blessed (31–2). In III.**23**.5, i.366, S. Irenaeus likens Adam's righteousness to a robe, *stola*, a most apt expression to denote the conception

---

[1] 'For the breath of life (πνοὴ ζωῆς, *afflatus vitae*, Harvey, ii.350), which also rendered man an animated being, is one thing, and the vivifying Spirit another, which also caused him to become spiritual. . . . The breath, then, is temporal, but the Spirit eternal. . . . For there had been a necessity that, in the first place, a human being should be fashioned, and that what was fashioned should receive the soul (*anima*); afterwards that it should thus receive the communion of the Spirit. . . . As, then, he who was made a living soul forfeited life when he turned aside to what was evil, so, on the other hand, the same individual, when he reverts to what is good, and receives the quickening Spirit, shall find life' (ii.83–4).

of a *donum superadditum* (33).[1] Here is a relative perfection in Adam, which is not of the nature of Adam. Many
modern theologians have maintained that Irenaeus here
and there denies this original perfection, but Klebba cannot admit that a complete contradiction is present (34).
One position fundamental to Irenaeus is that man should
come to moral good by the action of his own moral will,
and not spontaneously and by nature. This requires moral
development in man, from the natural to the spiritual (35,
37). However, we cannot rightly apply this 'imperfection'
to Adam, for it is also a plain apologetic and moral interest
that man should be expounded so far as possible as having
come perfect from his Maker (38). Irenaeus has not con-
tradicted himself, so much as failed to make clear two trains
of thought regarding man's development. Furthermore, the
conception of Recapitulation presupposes the restoration
of something lost (39). Adam was perfect, in the sense that
the Holy Spirit dwelt in him (40). In physical condition
Adam was a child. This 'childhood' was conceived of mainly
as of the disposition and understanding, though bodily
maturity was not entire (41–2). The result of this discussion is an affirmation that S. Irenaeus taught that our first
parents were perfect in respect of free will and eternal
destiny, and in spiritual equipment for that destiny, but that
there was room for spiritual advance through man's own
action (43–4).

Concerning the Fall, in opposition to the Gnostics,
Irenaeus kept to the Genesis story, literally understood
(45–7). The source of sin is not in creation, but is spiritual,
i.e. Satan's envy of man (48–50). Irenaeus is both the
accuser and apologist of Adam, emphasizing both that he
was truly guilty, and also that his sin was due to overmastering temptation, and that he was penitent (53–5).
God's purpose in punishing Adam was the beneficent one
of turning evil to greater good (57–9). The curse was

[1] *Quoniam, inquit, eam quam habui a Spiritu sanctitatis stolam amisi per
inobedientiam.* (III.23.5, Harvey, ii.128.)

turned on the Serpent and also upon the soil, not on man
(60–1). As a result of the Fall man's whole nature was
disordered, and he fell into wrongful but actual slavery to
Satan (64–5). However, human nature was not entirely
incapable of good, for Adam repented, and was rewarded
by God for this (65–6, 68). Death is the collective expression
for all the consequences of sin (71–2). That which Adam
lost is the *stola* of the supernatural, that indwelling by God
which produces holiness of heart (72). In conclusion,
Klebba observes that the teaching of Irenaeus agrees with
the later dogmatic definition, namely, that Adam was
vulneratus in naturalibus, spoliatus in gratuitis (74).

The basis of Original Sin is common descent from Adam.
Each individual has forfeited life without his own co-
operation (77–8). The ground of Original Sin is not a
natural condition of concupiscence, nor is the sin of Adam
merely imputed to us. Adam sinned for us in a manner
parallel to that in which Christ suffered for us. Actual sin is
not absolutely necessary in the life of each individual,
though every man's flesh is now the σάρξ ἁμαρτίας, for sin
dwells there. Man cannot save himself, though Irenaeus does
not emphasize this (79, 82–3). The great interest in the
work of S. Irenaeus on this point is in the contrast he presents to the Apologists, to whom it sufficed to speak of the
actual sins of the heathen, not of Original Sin. It is remarkable that Irenaeus, based upon S. Paul, should have made
so complete a first essay that his successors have added
hardly anything to it (86–7).

With the treatment in Klebba may be compared the
modern work of Emil Brunner in *Man in Revolt*.[1] Irenaeus,
the first great theologian of the early Catholic Church, outlined the path of later times by distinguishing a double
element in man; the Image of God, which is freedom and
rationality; and the Likeness of God, which is his self-
determination according to divine destiny, a special divine
gift of supernatural communion with God. The effect of sin

[1] English translation by Olive Wyon (London, 1939).

is seen as the destruction of the Likeness of God. Here is a simple and brilliant solution of the central problem of anthropology.[1] Luther recognized the Hebrew parallelism of the phrase: 'Let us make man in our image, after our likeness' (Genesis 1₂₆), and maintained the unity of human nature. Through sin man has not lost a super-nature, but has become de-natured. The *Imago Dei* has been destroyed also, leaving only a relic of itself in man's rationality.[2] Brunner gives a valuable appendix (I), '*The Image of God in the Teaching of the Bible and the Church*'. The doctrine of the *Imago Dei* is not important in the Bible. Whatever it is in Genesis 1₂₆, etc., it is referred to man as he now is. The Bible is against Catholic dogma, though this dogma is a natural development from a starting-point in the Johannine idea of 'being like God' as the summit of perfection (1 John 3₂, etc.).[3] Brunner then notices the work of Strucker: *Die Gottebenbildlichkeit des Menschen in der urchristlichen Literatur der ersten zwei Jahrhunderte* (1913). The concept of the *Imago Dei* had no place in the body of primitive Christian doctrine as a whole. The usage is almost exclusively *Imago = humanum* (reason, freedom, speech, special position in nature, etc.). Diognetus is at the other extreme: *Imago Dei = Self-imparting love of God*.[4] Brunner then follows Klebba, that the distinction of *Imago* and *Similitudo* appears in Irenaeus, having sprung from the Valentinians, but being otherwise interpreted by Irenaeus. The anthropology of Irenaeus is Gnostic, but purified by Scripture, and with an element of Greek philosophy. The *Imago Dei* is Reason, for God is Reason. S. Irenaeus was, however, too Biblical and Christian to be content with this. He combines this result with the distorted reading of Genesis 1₂₆. The *Similitudo Dei*, over against that *Imago Dei* which man cannot lose, consists in man's relation to God. That the *Similitudo* emerges in Christ, not in Adam, is shown in V.**16**.2, ii.99. Hence original man is not conceived of as

---

[1] *Man in Revolt*, p. 93.   [2] ibid. pp. 94–5.
[3] ibid. pp. 499–500.   [4] ibid. pp. 503–4.

almost perfect. However, if Adam is a big child, it is hard to see what was lost at the Fall. He could not lose the *Imago*, which was his nature as man, while the *Similitudo* was present only in germ, a future promise rather than a present reality.[1] Finally, S. Augustine took over the distinction of the *Imago* and the *Similitudo Dei*, but departed from S. Irenaeus by teaching that the original state of man was a definite spiritual perfection.[2]

With this introduction we may now proceed to a further examination of the statements of S. Irenaeus upon these various issues. In the first place, he generally speaks of the natural man as two-fold. There is the body of flesh, and the soul (ψυχή, *anima*, 'animal soul'). Men 'are compound by nature, and consist of a body and a soul'.[3] The soul is the principle of animation and growth.[4] It is also the intellect.[5] Presumably the faculty of moral experience and discrimination is a function of the soul. It is something which, like the soul, and unlike the indwelling Spirit, is found in every man, for without it a man would not be a man.[6] The body is the somewhat unhandy tool of the soul. 'For the body may be compared to an instrument; but the soul is possessed of the reason of an artist. As, therefore, the artist finds the idea of a work to spring up rapidly in his mind, but can only carry it out slowly by means of an instrument, owing to the want of perfect pliability in the matter acted upon, and thus the rapidity of his mental operation, being blended with the slow action of the instrument, gives rise to a moderate kind of movement; so also the soul, by being mixed up with the body belonging to it, is in a certain measure impeded, its rapidity being blended with the body's slowness.'[7] It must not be forgotten, however, that Irenaeus constantly insists, against the Gnostics, that the body is not the sinful element

---

[1] *Man in Revolt*, pp. 504–5.   [2] ibid. p. 506.
[3] II.13.3, i.154; see also IV. **Pref.** 4, i.377; *Dem.* 2.
[4] II.33.4, i.249.   [5] II.29.3, i.230–1.   [6] IV.39.1, ii.46.
[7] II.33.4, i.249–50; see also II.28.4, i.223–4.

in man.[1] The body 'has fellowship with the soul'.[2] The
blood is 'the bond of union between the soul and body'.[3]
S. Irenaeus does not teach that the soul (as opposed to the
body) is 'the real man', but follows Scripture in affirming
that a man without a body is not a man: 'for if anyone
take away the substance of flesh . . . such then would not
be a spiritual man, but would be the spirit of a man.'[4]

In the Christian believer there is a third element, the
indwelling Spirit of God. This divine principle is not part of
man's nature, but is a supernatural gift of God. Without it,
the man of body and soul, that is, the bodily, nervous,
sensible, and intelligent natural man, is to be classed as
'animal'. 'But if the Spirit be wanting to the soul, he who is
such is indeed of an animal nature.'[5] This 'animal man' is
essentially man as originally created by God, 'God having
predestined that the first man should be of an animal nature'.[6]
This goes far to dispose of the first item on Bousset's list of
differences between Irenaeus and Paul, namely, that Irenaeus taught that the first man was a noble god-like being,
but that Paul made him only an earthly ψυχὴ ζῶσα (1 Corinthians 15₄₅).[7] S. Irenaeus appears to follow the Apostle
closely. This does not, however, preclude him from teaching
that original man was immortal.[8] Man as made by God was
certainly not evil. 'And Adam and Eve . . . "were naked,
and were not ashamed"; for there was in them an innocent
and childlike mind, and it was not possible for them to
conceive and understand anything of this which by wickedness through lusts and shameful desires is born in the soul.
. . . And therefore they were not ashamed, kissing and em-
bracing each other in purity after the manner of children.'[9]
However, original man was not in that state of grace enjoyed
by the perfected Christian believer. Adam was created a
child, whose destiny was to develop to maturity. 'For he was
a child; and it was necessary that he should grow, and so

---

[1] e.g. V.13.3, ii.88. [2] II.34.4, i.253. [3] V.3.2, ii.63.
[4] V.6.1, ii.68. [5] V.6.1, ii.68. [6] III.22.3, i.361.
[7] Kyr.Ch. p. 356. [8] Dem. 15; see also p. 216 infra. [9] Dem. 14.

come to perfection.'[1] It is doubtful whether Vernet is correct
in stating that this was mainly a spiritual infancy.[2] 'In
paradise "they were both naked, and were not ashamed",
inasmuch as they, having been created a short time previously,
had no understanding of the procreation of children.'[3] It is
interesting to notice that this conception of the childhood of
Adam is also found in Theophilus of Antioch.[4]

The 'breath of life' that God breathed into Adam cannot
then have been the indwelling Holy Spirit, bringing equipment of supernatural grace. It was rather the agency by
which the body was animated. The 'breath of life' in man is
the soul. 'For the breath of life, which also rendered man an
animated being, is one thing, and the vivifying Spirit
another, which also caused him to become spiritual. . . .
Breath is indeed given in common to all people upon earth,
but the Spirit is theirs alone who tread down earthly desires.'[5]
In property the 'breath of life', the animating soul of man,
is a form of tenuous matter. The soul is in a sense corporeal.
'Souls themselves possess the figure of the body in which
they dwell, . . . just as water when poured into a vessel takes
the form of that vessel.'[6] However, 'souls are incorporeal
when put in comparison with mortal bodies'.[7] The soul is
not susceptible, as is the body, to dissolution by death. 'And
certainly they cannot maintain that the very breath of life is
mortal. . . . For this (the body) it is which dies and is
decomposed, but not the soul or the spirit.'[8] Irenaeus implies
a denial of the natural immortality of the soul, following
Justin Martyr.[9] 'For life does not arise from us, nor from
our own nature; but it is bestowed according to the grace of
God.'[10] Incorruptibility is not natural to man.[11] It is the soul
which receives the indwelling Holy Spirit.[12] 'So the soul

---

[1] *Dem.* 12; see also IV.38.1, ii.42.   [2] *Dictionnaire*, VII, col. 2456.
[3] III.22.4, i.361.
[4] *ad Autolycum*, II.25; see also Loofs, *Theophilus*, pp. 60–1.
[5] V.12.2, ii.83; see also V.7.1, ii.71.
[6] II.19.6, i.187; see also II.34.1, i.251.
[7] V.7.1, ii.70.   [8] V.7.1, ii.71.   [9] *Dial.* VI.
[10] II.34.3, i.252.   [11] III.20.1, i.348.   [12] III.22.1, i.359.

herself is not life, but partakes in that life bestowed upon her by God.'[1] Consequently, in the Christian the Spirit and the body are united in that each has communion with the animal soul.[2]

Klebba's effort to demonstrate that there is no real self-contradiction in S. Irenaeus upon the subject of the condition of original man[3] will have prepared the reader for the discovery that there is in Irenaeus a second theory of human nature, alongside the foregoing developed system. One exposition of the *Recapitulation* is that the Incarnation was the exhibition of the Image in which man was originally made. Connected with the conception of evil as an impoverishment of metaphysical substance, and of salvation as divinization, is the theory that man is saved by a transformation of substance that comes of beholding the vision of God. On his Greek side Irenaeus takes up this theory of salvation.[4] Between the Saving Work of Christ as '*the exhibition of the original image*', and salvation as '*beholding the vision*', there is a certain obvious analogy. It is therefore not surprising to find that the two ideas have fused, and that Irenaeus can at times speak of Christian salvation as the restoration to humanity of a divine image which was possessed at the beginning, and which was lost at the Fall. The Saving Work of the incarnate Son is to show forth that image in which man was created. This goes far toward involving the assumption that original man was created in that spiritual condition which is the hope and goal of the perfected believer. Irenaeus can thus on occasion give the appearance of denying his doctrine of '*the childhood of Adam*'.

This second exposition has some weight attached to it by a consideration arising from the letter, though not from the spirit, of the Genesis Creation-story. This had it that 'God said, Let us make man in our image, after our likeness' (Genesis 1.26). The 'image and likeness of God' could conveniently be equated with that 'image of God' which is

---

[1] II.34.4, i.253.		[2] V.9.1, ii.75.		[3] *Anthropologie d.H.I.* p. 34, etc.
[4] See pp. 155–7 *supra*.

the divinizing principle in man. So S. Irenaeus writes: Christ 'recapitulated in Himself the long line of human beings, and furnished us, in a brief, comprehensive manner, with salvation; so that what we had lost in Adam, namely, to be according to the image and likeness of God, that we might recover in Christ Jesus.' *Longam hominum expositionem in seipso recapitulavit, in compendio nobis salutem praestans, ut quod perdideramus in Adam, id est, secundum imaginem et similitudinem esse Dei, hoc in Christo Jesu reciperemus.*[1]

The phrase 'the image and likeness of God' does not, however, invariably involve the idea of Adam's 'original righteousness'. One passage which serves as good evidence for the doctrine of *'the childhood of Adam'* speaks of the human race as 'not gods from the beginning, but at first merely men, then at length gods'. This 'divinity' is described in various terms, among which is the phrase, 'the image and likeness of God'. *Irrationabiles igitur omni modo, qui non exspectant tempus augmenti, et suae naturae infirmitatem adscribunt Deo. . . . Nos enim imputamus ei, quoniam non ab initio dii facti sumus, sed primo quidem homines, tunc demum dii. . . . 'Ego', inquit, 'dixi, dii estis, et filii Excelsi omnes'; nobis autem potestatem divinitatis baiulare non sustinentibus, 'Vos autem,' inquit, 'velut homines moriemini'; utraque referens, et illud quod est benignum suae donationis, et infirmitatem nostram, et quod essemus nostrae potestatis. Secundum enim benignitatem suam bene dedit bonum, et similes sibi suae potestatis homines fecit. . . . Oportuerat autem primo naturam apparere, post deinde vinci et absorbi mortale ab immortalitate, et corruptibile ab incorruptibilitate, et fieri hominem secundum imaginem et similitudiem Dei, agnitione accepta boni et mali.*[2] Here, at least, 'the image and likeness of God' is hardly an original possession of man. Again, the *imago et similitudo Dei* may be described as a possession original to Adam, but defined in such a way as to preclude it from being regarded as representing the con-

---

[1] III.**18**.1, i.238; Harvey, ii.95; see also V.**2**.1, ii.58; V.**6**.1, ii.68; V.**12**.4, ii.85; V.**16**.2, ii.99; *Dem.* 32.
[2] IV.**38**.4, ii.44–5; Harvey, ii.297.

dition of perfected man. Man is 'in the likeness of God' because he has reason and free will, gifts which are natural to all men, unfallen, fallen, and perfected. So, 'man is possessed of free will from the beginning, and God is possessed of free will, in whose likeness man was created': *cuius ad similitudinem factus est.*[1] Man is 'endowed with reason, and in this respect like to God': *similis Deo.*[2] The natural man of body and animal soul is after the likeness of God. 'Now man is a mixed organization of soul and flesh, who was formed after the likeness of God.'[3] The 'image and likeness of God' is something that has been retained throughout the whole six thousand years of the world's history. 'Throughout all time, man, having been moulded at the beginning by the hands of God . . . is made after the image and likeness of God.'[4] Finally, other passages refer to salvation as attainment to the image and likeness of God without any associated statement for or against the doctrine of '*the childhood of Adam*'.[5] As Vernet admits, the *imago et similitudo Dei* sometimes designates the natural gifts of man, and sometimes the supernatural.[6]

In attempting to resolve these apparent contradictions regarding the original state of man the first thing to observe is that since Klebba wrote his very careful work the *Demonstration* has come to light, and that this writing contains two of the three main 'proof-texts' for the doctrine of '*the childhood of Adam*'.[7] Klebba has noticed IV.**38**.1, ii.42 as a 'difficult' passage.[8] The difficulty is increased when two more of a similar sense are to be added to it. However, the method used to resolve this difficulty remains to be upheld today. Klebba judges that there is present in Irenaeus not so much a self-contradiction as a failure to make clear two separate trains of thought regarding man's necessary development.[9]

[1] IV.**37**.4, ii.39; Harvey, ii.289.   [2] IV.**4**.3, i.385; Harvey, ii.154.
[3] IV.**Pref**.4, i.377.   [4] V.**28**.4, ii.132–3.
[5] IV.**38**.3, ii.44; V.**1**.3, ii.58; V.**8**.1, ii.73; V.**21**.2, ii.111; V.**36**.3, ii.157; *Dem.* 97.
[6] *Dictionnaire*, VII, col. 2453.   [7] *Dem.* 12, 14.
[8] *Anthropologie d.H.I.* p. 35.   [9] ibid. p. 39.

The obscurity is, in fact, due to lack of complete systematiza-tion. How true this is is demonstrated when it is observed that two of the passages which speak of Adam as a child[1] occur in a context where Irenaeus is expressly expounding the nature of man, while the other[2] occurs in a passage which is concerned with the allied theme that sin is not due to man's inborn nature, but to his own moral choice. On the other hand, the passages commonly cited as presupposing an original perfection in Adam are almost without exception drawn from contexts dealing with the Saving Work of Christ. It is clear that S. Irenaeus is powerfully prompted to speak of salvation as the *restoration* of something lost in the Fall. How deep-seated is this instinct is seen in the later history of Christian thought. However, it is no less clear that when he *expressly* turns his mind to *the doctrine of man* he tends to speak of '*the childhood of Adam*'. Particularly is it to be observed that in the passage *Demonstration*, 11–17, where as nowhere else in his writings, Irenaeus gives continuous and detailed exposition of the Genesis story, the childhood of Adam comes to view. On account of this evidence which has come to light since Klebba, such a change of emphasis is justified as to claim that here is the essential doctrine of man for Irenaeus. It is the conception of original perfection which has to take second place as not more than the con-comitant of the doctrine of the Saving Work of Christ. The confusion is due to the circumstance that, as so often, S. Irenaeus is not careful to reduce his every diverse state-ment to formal consistency.

For the sake of comparison we may notice that Duncker is on similar ground, though he classifies in a different way the divergent interests lying beneath the divergent state-ments in Irenaeus.[3] He expounds this point as follows. The anthropological conception of man proceeds from the self-consciousness of the Christian, in emphasis of the antithesis of the old life and the new life in grace. This speaks of man

---

[1] *Dem.* 12, 14.   [2] IV.38.1, ii.42.
[3] *Irenaeus Christologie*, pp. 99-101.

as ruined by sin, and of Christ as a restorer. Proceeding from God-consciousness, and from faith in His love, there is the theological conception. This emphasizes the thought of the world as the self-revelation of God. Here Christ is the One who carried man on to his destined perfection. To the former corresponds the idea of man as originally perfect, to the latter the thought of him as a child.[1] It may be claimed, however, that the present classification is more accurate. 'The childhood of Adam' is connected with the anthropological interest. We may further record that Wendt, who observes the contradiction, gives it as his opinion that original perfection is really alien to the system of S. Irenaeus.[2]

The general impression one gets is that S. Irenaeus looked upon Adam and Eve as entirely clean and wholesome, filled with every spiritual promise, and worthy of the God who had created them. They were in a state of salvation, and we can hardly imagine Irenaeus denying that the Holy Spirit rested upon them. In this sense they were 'perfect'. It may therefore be said that the saved Christian is but restored to the condition in which humanity originally was. At the same time, the first pair were emphatically not the Adam and Eve of much traditional theology. S. Irenaeus did not regard them as possessed of all fullness of intellectual insight and moral experience. These things could only be attained by gradual and, as it actually turned out, by painful growth. Irenaeus does not indeed explicitly say that there is one perfection of the infant, innocent, and complete in every faculty appropriate to infancy, and another perfection, which is the crown of the saint who has contended with sin and triumphed. This vital distinction is, however, not far from being implied by what is said of Adam as on the one hand perfect, and on the other hand, as possessed only of the destiny and equipment to perfection. This distinction, if brought to the study of S. Irenaeus, certainly lights up his work.

[1] *Irenaeus Christologie*, pp. 158–9. [2] *m.Vollkommenheit*, pp. 23–4, 27–8.

214 THE BIBLICAL THEOLOGY OF SAINT IRENAEUS

Akin to the doctrine of man's original state, but of still greater practical importance to the consideration of the way of salvation, is the doctrine of man's present state. When he came from '*the Hands of God*' man was good, though a child. To S. Irenaeus it was a matter of present sad experience that mankind is no longer like this. Man is morally an infirm being,[1] 'a fugitive from and a transgressor of the law, an apostate also from God'.[2] Such is the power of sin that it drives man to 'such a pitch of fury as even to look upon his brother as his enemy'.[3] Irrational conduct such as this makes man as the beasts.[4] The full tragedy of man's plight is not merely that he actually commits evil deeds, as that sin has very seriously impaired his power to choose the right. 'Now we were the vessels and the house of this (strong man, Satan) when we were in a state of apostasy; for he put us to whatever use he pleased, and the unclean spirit dwelt within us.'[5] Sin and the Devil tyrannize over the human race.[6] It is indeed God and not Satan who rules over the world, but Satan has power 'to deceive and lead astray the mind of man into disobeying the commandments of God, and gradually to darken the hearts of those who would endeavour to serve Him'.[7] It is the sad truth that man cannot pick himself out of the mire. 'It was not possible that the man who had once for all been conquered . . . could re-form himself, and obtain the prize of victory.'[8]

In the light of this Beuzart is hardly justified in his claim that sin had not the gravity for S. Irenaeus that it had for S. Paul.[9] The reason given by Beuzart for this judgement is that the thought of expiation is not present. This mode of argument gives another illustration of the mental process that lies behind much denial of kinship between Irenaeus and the Apostle, particularly in the writings of Continental Protestantism.[10] A rigid substitutionary theology is first read

---

[1] III.20.3, i.348; V.3.1, ii.61.   [2] V.21.3, ii.114.   [3] V.24.2, ii.119.
[4] V.8.2–3, ii.73–4.   [5] III.8.2, i.276.   [6] V.1.1, ii.56; *Dem.* 37.
[7] V.24.3, ii.120–1.   [8] III.18.2, i.338.   [9] *Essai*, p. 116.
[10] See also pp. 186–7 *supra*.

into Paul on traditional lines. When this is not found in Irenaeus it is assumed that he has departed from the teaching of the Apostle. Werner falls into the same trap when he writes that Irenaeus does not understand sin in the full Christian sense, involving personal guilt and alienation from God, for man is in no way shut out from the love of God by the Fall.[1] So also Harnack, in claiming that there is only a rudimentary conception of reconciliation in Irenaeus, states that he does not teach the vicarious suffering of Christ, and seldom speaks of God as offended through Adam's sin.[2] This would presuppose that the Pauline '*Wrath of God*' is

'The Father's vengeful ire,
Which our Redeemer bore'.

It is God's own action, and His attitude to man. Actually we prefer to expound '*the Wrath*' as the self-acting Nemesis that sin brings upon the sinner, and from which it is God's proper activity to rescue man.

This enslavement of the human race had its historical beginning in the sin of Adam and Eve. 'By means of our first [parents] we were all brought into bondage.'[3] Adam was conquered,[4] and was the first to go into captivity.[5] By his disobedience all were made sinners.[6] Irenaeus never tried to explain why the defeat of Adam brought bondage to all, further than to follow S. Paul in the exposition of Adam and the Second Adam as the two collective heads of the race. This most clearly comes to view in the strong insistence upon the salvation of Adam, which had been denied by Tatian.[7] 'When therefore the Lord vivifies man, that is Adam, death is at the same time destroyed. All therefore speak falsely who disallow his salvation . . . in that they do not believe that the sheep which had perished has been found. For if it has not been found, the whole human race is still held in a state of perdition.'[8] Adam is here practically

---

[1] *Paulinismus*, p. 135. [2] *H.D.* II.291-2. [3] IV.22.1, i.454.
[4] III.23.7, i.367. [5] III.23.2, i.363. [6] III.18.7, i.344.
[7] I.28.1, i.100-1. [8] III.23.7-8, i.368; see also III.23.1-2, i.362-4.

identified with the human race, though this theme is not worked out into a system.

The punishment of sin was toilsome labour for man, and the pain of childbirth and subjection to man for woman.[1] The first consequence of sin was expulsion from the Garden of Eden into this world, 'because Paradise receiveth not the sinful'.[2] The major consequence of sin was death, 'for death is next neighbour to him who has fallen'.[3] Furthermore, those who have sinned have made themselves children of the Devil. Such are disinherited, and are no longer children of God. Only those who repent and are converted are the sons of God.[4] Adam and Eve 'became forfeit to death . . . for along with the fruit they did also fall under the power of death, because they did eat in disobedience; and disobedience to God entails death'.[5] Consequently, just as man became sinful in Adam, so death was 'inflicted at the beginning upon disobedient man in Adam'.[6] Man has lost the breath of life.[7] 'Man, who had been disobedient to God', had thereby been 'cast off from immortality',[8] and is now 'under the power of death'.[9] It is worthy of note that when Irenaeus wishes to denote man's disabled condition he speaks of liability to death far more than of bondage to sin. The predominance of this Greek usage is perhaps largely due to the associations of the Fall story, with its doom, 'in the day that thou eatest thou shalt surely die'.

S. Irenaeus did not therefore believe in Original Sin in the proper sense of the word. The inherited defect of the human race is represented as a grievous disability, but not as involving man in guilt or constituting him the object of God's wrath. It is true that Irenaeus writes, 'by transgressing (God's) commandment we became His enemies'.[10] However, one is compelled here to side with Beuzart,[11] and against Vernet.[12] The evidence advanced by Vernet is

---

[1] IV.23.3, i.364; see also *Dem.* 17.   [2] *Dem.* 16.   [3] V.22.2, ii.116.
[4] IV.41.3, ii.52–3.   [5] V.23.1, ii.117; see also V.12.2, ii.84; V.23.2, ii.117.
[6] V.34.2, ii.149; see also III.23.7, i.367; *Dem.* 31, 33.   [7] V.12.3, ii.84.
[8] III.20.2, i.349.   [9] III.18.7, i.343.   [10] V.17.1, ii.100.
[11] *Essai*, p. 71.   [12] *Dictionnaire*, VII, col. 2459.

decisive proof that Adam, by his sin, 'has transfused death and pains of the body into the whole human race',[1] but it does not go any farther than this. There is nothing to clear Irenaeus of the anathema laid upon him who holds that there is transfused from Adam 'death and pains' only, 'but not sin also, which is the death of the soul'. Man is indeed 'born in sinfulness',[2] and infants come within the scope of Christ's saving work.[3] However, this need suppose no more than that the baby brings into the world a liability to yield to temptation, and that consequently the grace of God in Christ is required even at the earliest stages of life. To make it mean that new-born infants are burdened with a load of guilt is hardly in keeping with the general attitude of Irenaeus toward sin.[4] There is, furthermore, this statement to cite: 'Again, who are they that have been saved, and received the inheritance? Those, doubtless, who do believe God, and who have continued in His love; ... and innocent children, who have no sense of evil.'[5] The salvation of these children is not connected in any way with a Baptism that has washed away the guilt of Original Sin, but with the fact that they are not old enough to have attained to moral responsibility.

We can therefore hardly follow Duncker in saying that S. Irenaeus, in what he wrote of Original Sin, laid the foundation for S. Augustine.[6] Rather may we agree with Bonwetsch, that he says little of Adam's race as guilty.[7] In line with this is the reduced estimate of the seriousness of Adam's sin. The first transgression is represented as the disastrous yet understandable error of an inexperienced and easily beguiled child. It is not a considered and high-handed breach of the known law of God, done in full knowledge of the consequence and with no excuse of weakness, and as such, a crime of inconceivable heinousness. 'Man was a child, not yet having his understanding perfected; where-

---

[1] *Conc.Trid.* V.2.   [2] *Dem.* 37.   [3] II.22.4, i.200.
[4] See pp. 221-2 *infra.*   [5] IV.28.3, i.474.
[6] *Irenaeus Christologie*, pp. 140-2, 144.   [7] *Theologie d.I.* p. 81.

fore also he was easily led astray by the deceiver.'[1] S. Irenaeus seems to have had the spiritual insight to see how
incredible it is that one having an adequate knowledge of
good and evil joined to as complete freedom to do right as to
do wrong should ever come to choose evil. Man sinned:
therefore he was either not truly free, or he did not really
know. Irenaeus was firmly committed to the position that
Adam's sin was due to the action of his own free will, for the
doctrine that he was created morally imperfect was a part
of dualist heresy. Therefore it had to be maintained that
Adam sinned largely through moral inexperience. Thus
Irenaeus was forced to teach the childhood of Adam and
Eve. Experience brought deeper moral responsibility, and
therefore Cain was more guilty than Adam.[2]

A further circumstance in extenuation of Adam's sin was
his horror when he realized what he had done. In heartfelt
penitence he mortified his flesh in self-humiliation, with the
consequence that a gracious God was pleased to forgive.[3]
The curse, furthermore, was not placed upon Adam and
Eve, but 'God did . . . transfer the curse to the earth, that it
might not remain in man'. For his part, man received a
toilsome lot, and for woman, subjection to man and the pains
of childbirth, 'so that they should neither perish altogether
when cursed by God, nor, by remaining unreprimanded,
should be led to despise God'.[4] Even the loss of Paradise was
for man's good.[5] The curse was placed on Satan.[6] Irenaeus
does not entirely absolve Adam from blame, however. He
sinned 'through want of care no doubt, but still wickedly'.[7]
It is pleasing to notice how S. Irenaeus moves throughout
at such a high ethical level.

We must now turn to consider how far this doctrine of
man may be reconciled with the Bible, and in particular, with
S. Paul. The poetical and intellectual magnificence of
Paradise Lost is a lasting monument to the spaciousness of
that system of thought which has so often been erected by

[1] *Dem.* 12; see also III.23.3,5, i.364, 366.   [2] *Dem.* 17.   [3] III.23.5, i.366.
[4] III.23.3, i.364.   [5] III.23.6, i.367.   [6] III.23.5, i.366.   [7] IV.40.3, ii.50.

Christian theologians upon the foundation of the Genesis Fall-story. However, it is clear that the system has actually been an erection upon, and by no means a growth out of, the Bible. It is a momentous example of something read into Scripture. A dispassionate reading of Genesis 2 and 3 will reveal a picture of man coming from the hand of his Maker pure and lovely indeed, but inexperienced and painfully easy to deceive. Furthermore, cruel awakening to the inescapable and dire consequences of wrong-doing works not sinful rebellion, but penitence, while that penitence is met not by divine wrath but with consolation and remedy. We may candidly agree that S. Irenaeus tended to stress those elements in the story which serve to extenuate Adam's sin, while the bulk of traditional theologians have strongly emphasized those which condemn. They have blackened the Fall into a crime of such inconceivable heinousness as to merit and justify the inconceivably severe punishment of the damnation of the race. However, in the doctrine of '*the childhood of Adam*' Irenaeus was certainly far closer to the spirit of the story than was an Augustine or a Calvin.

Again, it is by no means clear that the doctrine outlined diverges in any important respect from the doctrine of S. Paul. References in the canonical Old Testament to the Genesis story are very few,[1] and none is relevant to the idea of Original Sin. The Old Testament, however, certainly teaches inborn depravity as a dreadful yet unexplained fact,[2] and also that sin is a universal human experience. For S. Paul the Adamic origin of sin would probably be not so much an important part of religious tradition, but rather by way of an innovation, for the first mention of the Fall of Adam and Eve as the historical starting-point of human sin is not found until Ecclesiasticus 25₂₄ (as late as about 180 B.C.), while the first establishment of a causal connexion between Adam's sin and inherited depravity has

---

[1] Job 31₃₃; Isaiah 43₂₇; Ezekiel 28₁₃; Hosea 6₇.
[2] Genesis 6₅, 8₂₁; Job 15₁₄f.; Psalm 51₅; Jeremiah 17₉.

to wait until 2 Esdras 7₁₁₈ (first century A.D.). It is significant that Paul does not press forward positively upon this
road, and is less definite than the writer of 2 Esdras. He
doubtless accepted the idea that the Genesis story implied
that physical death came into this world through the sin of
Adam, but the interest is nowhere in the inheritance of sin
or of guilt by all the sons of Adam. In both Romans 5₁₂₋₂₁
and 1 Corinthians 15₂₀₋₂,₄₅, the emphasis is clearly upon
the doctrine of '*the two Federal Heads*' of the human race. In
the acts of both the whole human race took a collective action,
in the first to damnation, and in the second to salvation.
There is a sense, therefore, in which each individual is
affected by the simple fact of membership of the race, for all
have taken part in a collective action through the Representative Head. So through Christ's victory an objective
difference has been made to the world. However, this does
not preclude the necessity for each individual man also to
appropriate by faith the fruits of the victory, if he personally
is to be saved. The same thing surely applies to the Fall in
Adam. S. Paul would have maintained that each man has by
his own sin to appropriate for himself that one sin which has
constituted an objective moral blight upon the world. This
is hardly to be described as a doctrine of inherited sin or
guilt. It is rather that each individual of a sinful race has inherited a tendency to sin. In the light of Romans 7₇₋₂₅, this
would perhaps appear to be regarded as an irresistible tendency,
yet it is noteworthy that throughout the argument S. Paul
confines himself to the facts of his own experience, and has
no thought of attempting an explanation in principle of why
his nature should have been so. That S. Paul goes no farther
than this in the case of so outspoken and searching a treatment of the dread mystery of the impotence of the human
will to do good hardly leaves the impression that the Adamic
origin of the moral frailty of the individual man was for the
Apostle a live or central element in theology. We conclude
that the tendency to sin, though in fact universal and overmastering, is not represented as more than a tendency.

There is little evidence for the conception of imputed guilt in S. Paul's writings. The nearest approach is perhaps Romans 5₁₆: 'the judgement came of one unto condemnation.' However, the context is here referring to 'sin' not as a guilty action, but as an objective state of 'falling short of the glory of God'. The race shares this condition through its collective act in Adam, but this condition does not of itself bring guilt, for S. Paul has just said: 'sin is not imputed where there is no law.' Only a wilful violation of known law is guilty sin. The general sense of S. Irenaeus is not therefore so far from that of the Apostle.

In approaching the discussion of the crucial problem of the nature and adequacy of the conception of saving Faith in the teaching of S. Irenaeus it is profitable next to proceed to the examination of his conception of sin. The scattered hints are most interesting and important, because this is a subject on which he showed real religious insight. Irenaeus starts from the fundamental principle that sin is a matter of moral choice, not of inborn nature. Moral responsibility presupposes a measure of free action.[1] Exposure to temptation, of such strength that to resist is the grimmest of struggles, is not the mark of a sinful condition, but rather the reverse, 'for there is nothing evil in learning one's infirmities by endurance'.[2] Conversely, a beautiful character that is the result of a fortunate inborn constitution is not rightly to be described as morally good. 'It would come to pass, that their being good would be of no consequence, because they were so by nature rather than by will. . . . What . . . crown is it to those who have not followed in pursuit of it, like those victorious in the contest?'[3] Neither is an unconscious lapse from ethical perfection rightly to be described as sin, because it carries no consent of the will. So Irenaeus writes of the incestuous intercourse of Lot, made drunken by his daughters, that he was 'not acting under the impulse of his

---

[1] IV.37.2, ii.37.　　　[2] V.3.1, ii.61.
[3] IV.37.6, ii.40; see also IV.37.2, ii.37.

own will, nor at the prompting of carnal concupiscence,
nor having any knowledge or thought of anything of the
kind'. Because 'Lot knew not', he was not 'a slave to lust'.[1]
It is even admitted that the apparent necessity of the case
excused Lot's daughters for the action. This is a more
dubious position.[2] In particular, the moral standard for the
race is progressively raised as moral experience deepens.
S. Irenaeus rightly insists that the Christian man, because
he has had the light of Christ, is to judge himself by a
standard more strict than that which is to be applied to the
worthies of the Old Testament.[3]

It is significant that S. Irenaeus takes such care to see
that the word 'sin' has the full content of 'wrong moral choice
by a responsible agent'. Sin is wrong moral choice and not
inborn defect of nature. Temptation is not sin. 'Sin in
ignorance' is a contradiction in terms. The moral standard
by which men are judged by God is progressive and
relative. Such teaching as this suffices to undermine the false
positions that have been so commonly taken up around that
true but misleading phrase, 'Original Sin'. It is a pity that
Irenaeus did not give a more systematic and careful treatment of the problem of sin. If the second century had
called forth a telling witness to the truth that a defect
original and *in-born* in man, even though infinitely grievous
in sinful consequence, cannot *of itself* be accounted as sin
guilty in the sight of God, then the malign shadow of an
undue ascetic fear of 'the flesh' might not have fallen across
the Church in later ages.

There is, however, one passage which seems to teach
another view of sin. That God denied access to the tree of
life was an act of mercy toward Adam, lest man, living for
ever, 'should continue a sinner for ever', and 'that the sin
which surrounded him should be immortal, and evil inter-
minable and irremediable. But He set a bound to his sin, by
interposing death, and thus causing sin to cease, putting an

---

[1] IV.31.1, ii.2.   [2] IV.31.2, ii.2.
[3] IV.27.2, i.468; IV.28.1,2, ii.471–2; IV.36.4, ii.30; *Dem.* 56.

end to it by the dissolution of the flesh.'[1] It is to be admitted
that this appears like an approach to the dualist view
that sin is bound up with bodily existence. Some allowance
must be made for the circumstance that in this context
Irenaeus is arguing against Tatian for the salvation of Adam,
and is trying to explain away difficulties in the Genesis story.
The real intention of S. Irenaeus is no more than that the
exclusion from Paradise was not a mark of God's anger.
Furthermore, in other places he plainly witnesses that the
Pauline 'sinful flesh' is not identical with the body.[2]

The religious adequacy of this doctrine as a background
for the Gospel has been challenged by some writers. The
main ground for this is a certain number of passages which
appear to minimize the need for grace. Vernet has to admit
that some of the language has a Pelagian sound.[3] The reason
is that S. Irenaeus was under a strong controversial necessity
to assert man's free will. The Gnostics taught that the
different levels of moral attainment in man were due to
inborn constitution. Against this Irenaeus argued that 'man
. . . is himself the cause to himself, that sometimes he
becomes wheat, and sometimes chaff'.[4] Against that dualism
which made the Creator the cause of moral evil he maintained that man was created good,[5] and is himself 'the cause
to himself of his own imperfection'.[6] Furthermore, moral
responsibility involves a measure of free action, and therefore the will of man must be free.[7] It is in the course of
asserting this freedom of the will that Irenaeus makes
Pelagian-sounding statements, such as: those who do evil
'shall receive the just judgement of God, because they did
not work good when they had it in their power so to do',[8]
and, 'not merely in works, but also in faith, has God preserved the will of man free and under his own control'.[9]

[1] III.23.6, i.367.   [2] V.10.2, ii.80; V.12.3, ii.84.
[3] *Dictionnaire*, VII, col. 2460.   [4] IV.4.3, i.385.
[5] See pp. 207–8, 213 *supra*.   [6] IV.39.3, ii.47; see also IV.39.4, ii.48.
[7] IV.37.3, ii.38; IV.37.5, ii.39; V.29.1, ii.133.
[8] IV.37.1, ii.37; see also IV.37.2, ii.37; IV.41.3, ii.52.
[9] IV.37.5, ii.39.

The context shows that the latter does not mean that man
has it entirely within his own power to turn to God. The
sense is but little more than that 'if anyone is unwilling to
follow the Gospel itself, it is in his power' to reject it.[1] In
short, Irenaeus has to maintain the goodness of God as
Creator, the moral responsibility of man, and the need of
grace for salvation, and so he adopts the 'common sense'
attitude that the free will of man was grievously attenuated
by the Fall, but by no means formally annihilated. It is most
unfair to accuse him of Pelagianism on account of this.
Brunner shows admirable insight in writing that Harnack is
wrong in saying that S. Irenaeus has not an estimate of sin
sufficient for a doctrine of Atonement. He observes that the
emphasis given to the fact of man's original free will, which
Harnack describes as moralistic rationalism, is for the
purpose of exhibiting man's sin as disobedience, and not as
a mere matter of fate.[2] Irenaeus was not a philosopher, and
did not see the difficulty in accounting for the universality
of sin and guilt, if the will be genuinely free (which difficulty
remains). He could, therefore, easily unite the two sides of
the truth in a single passage. God 'made men like to
Himself, in their own power; while at the same time . . .
He knew the infirmity of human beings'.[3]

The strongest criticism of S. Irenaeus upon this point
comes from Werner, who strongly maintains that the
Pauline Gospel has been completely compromised. It is
claimed that the use of Paul to prove man's free will to do
right is not consistent with an understanding of Romans 9,
and also that Irenaeus does not come to the full religious
position because the deprivation of man is not from all good,
but only from the possibility of realizing the likeness of
God.[4] Bousset likewise observes that Irenaeus sees a freedom
remaining in man, while Paul proclaims the absolute weakness of the flesh.[5] So also Beuzart states that Irenaeus quotes

[1] IV.37.4, ii.38.
[2] *Der Mittler*, p. 227; see also Bonwetsch, *Theologie d.I.* p. 138.
[3] IV.38.4, ii.45.   [4] *Paulinismus*, p. 131.   [5] *Kyr.Ch.* p. 357.

Paul much, but without understanding him, for his teaching on liberty verges on Pelagianism.[1] The proof advanced for Werner's former proposition is the passage IV.**37**.1,4,5,7, ii. 36-41, which furnishes a considerable proportion of the 'Pelagian-sounding' passages noted above. The theme, eloquently advanced against the Gnostic divisions of the human species, is that the Lord 'set forth the ancient law of human liberty, because God made man a free (agent) from the beginning, possessing his own power, even as he does his own soul, to obey the behests of God voluntarily, and not by compulsion of God'.[2] One line of argument to support this is to cite a number of texts from the Pauline Epistles, each sounding the note of strong ethical exhortation.[3] Irenaeus points out that such exhortation presupposes the possibility of real moral choice in the hearers. For example: 'And again he says . . . "For ye were sometimes darkness, but now ye are light in the Lord; walk honestly as children of the light, not in rioting and drunkenness, not in chambering and wantonness, not in anger and jealousy. And such were some of you; but ye have been washed, but ye have been sanctified in the name of our Lord." If then it were not in our power to do or not to do these things, what reason had the apostle, and much more the Lord Himself, to give us counsel to do some things, and to abstain from others?'[4] We must, however, insist that this is quite a fair use of S. Paul, and not in any way contrary to the intention of Romans 9. Werner sees a contradiction where none is because, in line with one great historical tradition of Christianity, he interprets the latter chapter in a particular way. Theology has been too ready to see the Jacob and Esau of Romans 9 as personal Patriarchs rather than as representative heads of nations. The chapter has thus been read as referring almost exclusively to God's dealing with the individual soul, when actually the real interest is with divine destiny for the different historical

---

[1] *Essai*, p. 171.   [2] IV.**37**.1, ii.36.

[3] Romans 2₄₋₅, 13₁₃; 1 Corinthians 6₁₁, 9₂₄₋₂₇; Ephesians 4₂₅,₂₉.

[4] Romans 13₁₃ and 1 Corinthians 6₁₁ in IV.**37**.4, ii.38-9.

peoples. S. Paul is not writing about the problem of man's
theoretical free will to turn to God, but is concerned to trace
out the meaning of what God has actually done in history.
We may cordially agree with the Apostle that there is in
history a mysterious divine predestination for the nations.
Each is allotted its peculiar characteristics and abilities, and
in its own time, as opportunity offers, each is called to play
its own role in God's plan for the world. Being a collection
of free individuals a nation can refuse this destiny, and
prostitute its gifts. History shows that some have actually
done this, and that none have been entirely faithful. When,
however, the positive contributions of the nations to the life
and culture of the world are considered, it must be admitted
that these have come about fundamentally through divine
endowment, and not merely through the will of man. This
destiny, therefore, whether more or less honourable, whether
to succeed or to suffer, must be accepted. It cannot be made
by man. It by no means follows from this, however, that free
moral choice for the individual is excluded, though that choice
always has to be exercised within the circumstances of time
and national destiny. The main theme of Romans 9, etc.,
which may be regarded as part of S. Paul's serious thought
of lasting value, in no way provides ground for an assumption
that had he ever turned his mind to the speculative issue of
human free will he would have so circumscribed its scope as
to infringe upon man's full moral responsibility. Against that
assumption stands the frequent and urgent note of ethical
exhortation. Upon this S. Irenaeus rightly fixes.

We must admit that there is in the chapter a secondary
and less happy theme, where in passing S. Paul seeks to
apply the principle of predestination to the individual. The
process of thought may be seen in the passage Romans 9 14-21.
God's action in choosing the Hebrews and passing over the
Edomites is there justified by the consideration that He can
rightly have mercy upon whom He will. Divine mercy, and
not his own effort, is man's sole title to the blessing (14—16).
The Apostle in his argument then unfortunately yields to

the natural impulse to draw the converse. The inability of primitive Hebrew thought to express the conception of secondary causation provided him with a tempting text to quote. From the statement that God hardened Pharaoh's heart, i.e. that his heart became hardened, is drawn the consequence that 'whom He will He hardeneth' (17–18). This is a position utterly at variance with the great foundation of S. Paul's Gospel, namely, the free and universal saving grace of God, a thought to which he inevitably returns within the space of a few verses. Paul is the first to see the inevitable objection to what he has just laid down (19), and in seeking to defend the indefensible produces an argument that has rightly been described as the weakest point in the whole Epistle. 'Hath not the potter a right over the clay?' (21). 'Shall the thing formed say to him that formed it, Why didst thou make me thus?' (20). Man is not clay. God has made man so that this is just the question that he will for ever ask, and has thereby morally bound Himself to give an answer. This isolated, single, momentary, and relatively unimportant lapse is not to be described as 'Paulinism'. It is the place where the Apostle proves false to all he has stood by elsewhere. That S. Irenaeus did not follow S. Paul into the lapse is not to be held out as evidence that he was lacking in understanding of the message of the Epistles, or that he has in any way compromised the authentic Christian Gospel.

Werner's further charge is that S. Irenaeus came short of the full religious position because he did not teach that man is deprived of all good by the Fall. It is to be admitted that he did not take this extreme view of human depravity. However, it is by no means clear that S. Paul did either. The primary evidence is that moving chapter of idealized autobiography, Romans 7 7-25. It is very dangerous, however, to deduce from this any speculative doctrine of the utter impotence of man's will to accomplish any motion of good whatsoever. Before his conversion Paul clearly found himself in a state of agonized bondage to sin and the lower nature, which experience left him certain that man cannot be saved except by the sheer miracle of God's grace. Yet the fact that the bondage was an *agonized* one is a sure token that here was a soul striving with singular devotion to find God, and to live an upright life. That Paul could see God's law so plainly, and know it to be good, and be pained at his inability to do it, is itself a confession that he was not deprived of *all* good. We can hardly imagine one so zealous for God assenting to the proposition that unregenerate man is so sinful that there is no significant moral difference in the sight of God between the noblest attainments of those who strive to justify themselves and the open lapses of the careless. By way of example: to S. Paul the civic power of his day, the Roman Empire, was certainly no part of God's covenant of saving grace. It was, however, like the Law of Moses among the Hebrews, ordained by God as a temporary discipline to restrain overflowing wickedness, and to act as a healthful discipline until Christ should come (Romans 13₄). One who could argue thus would certainly not be found dismissing the accepted virtues of the natural man as 'splendid vices', in the manner of some supposed 'Paulinists'. This is just the position correctly attributed by Werner to Irenaeus. The natural man is not utterly devoid of good, but he cannot of himself attain to the likeness of God, i.e. save himself.

In turning, therefore, to what S. Irenaeus has to say about the need for grace, we need not hesitate to disregard the charges of Pelagianism. We give full value to his statements. He takes a grave view of sin,[1] and strongly emphasizes man's utter need of grace if he is to be saved. 'For as it was not possible that the man who had once for all been conquered . . . could re-form himself, and obtain the prize of victory; and as it was also impossible that he could attain to salvation who had fallen under the power of sin, the Son effected both these things.'[2] Consequently, salvation is a work of grace.

[1] See p. 214 *supra*.

[2] III.18.2, i.338; see also III.18.7, i.343; III.20.1-3, i.347-350; IV.27.2, i.468; IV.33.4, ii.8-9; V.3.1, ii.61; *Dem.* 97.

'For life does not arise from us, nor from our own nature; but it is bestowed according to the grace of God',[1] *secundum gratiam Dei.*[2] The vision of God is a gift of grace, 'for man does not see God by his own powers, but when He pleases He is seen by men'.[3] So is communion with God,[4] and knowledge of the things of God.[5] The new covenant of liberty is a work of grace,[6] and so is salvation at the Last Day. The Lord will come in order that He 'may, in the exercise of His grace, confer immortality on the righteous and holy, and those who have kept His commandments',[7] ἵνα . . . ζωὴν χαρισάμεος ἀφθαρσίαν δωρήσηται.[8]

A further aspect of the doctrine of man regarding which S. Irenaeus has been charged with departure from S. Paul is the conception of 'the flesh'. Most notably, Bousset submits that the section of *Adversus Haereses* (V.9–14, ii.73–94) which Irenaeus devotes to rebutting the Gnostic use of 1 Corinthians 15 50, 'flesh and blood cannot inherit the kingdom of God', shows a complete distortion of S. Paul's thought. The strong insistence on the salvation of the flesh is non-Pauline. Bousset maintains that Irenaeus merely borrows Paul's words without reproducing their meaning. A case in point is that Paul would not with Irenaeus have been able to say of the σάρξ: *quae est plasmata secundum imaginem Dei.* The rugged antithesis 'flesh-spirit' is toned down, and an exegetically moderated Paulinism is conveniently admitted into the Church. He has torn away from the system of Paulinism all those statements from which the Gnostics had drawn consequences. Gone is the pessimistic view which heightened the disharmony in man, which divided mankind into 'pneumatic' and 'psychic', which overemphasized the

[1] II.34.3, i.252; see also II.25.3, i.214; III.19.1, i.344–5; III.21.6, i.356; V.2.3, ii.60; V.9.4, ii.77; V.21.3, ii.114.
[2] Harvey, i.382.   [3] IV.20.5, i.442.
[4] IV.14.2, i.417; V.2.1, ii.59.   [5] II.28.3, i.221; II.28.7, i.226.
[6] IV.9.1, i.400.   [7] I.10.1, i.42–3.
[8] Harvey, i.91; see also Werner, *Paulinismus*, p. 209; Schmidt, *Kirche b.I.* p. 159; Vernet, *Dictionnaire*, VII, cols. 2487–8.

new in Christian redemption, and which yearned for another
spiritual world. This was a master-stroke which prevented
the annexation of S. Paul to Gnostic dualism, with its world-
denying salvation.[1]

There is an element of truth in this ingenious construction. Paul was a prophet, a man of fiery temperament and
outspoken speech. Irenaeus was a pastor who was accustomed
to measure his words. There is therefore naturally between
the two a certain difference in temperature, and rightly so.
It by no means follows from this that S. Irenaeus kindled a
strange fire. There are to be found in Paul extreme statements and rugged antitheses. If these be isolated from the
remainder of the Apostle's teaching, and extreme implications be drawn from them, the picture of Paul painted by
Bousset can be substantiated. This is exactly what Marcion
did. However, Irenaeus was aware that the general drift of
Paul's message was quite otherwise, for he had many other
things to say, of which the heretic took no account. Thus
S. Irenaeus was not removing things from S. Paul, but
balancing them one against another. Bousset writes that
what remained in Irenaeus was a Paulinism useful to the
Church. 'The volcano has burned out, and its glowing
masses of lava turned into the nourishing fruitful earth of a
new world.'[2] We assent to this picture. Yet the 'Paulinism
useful to the Church' was no dilute or corrupt Paulinism, as
the critic would suggest. It was the true Paulinism, the
exposition that would give due but not undue weight, not
merely to some but to all the elements of the diverse mind of
the Apostle. This was Catholicism as distinguished from
heresy.

A detailed examination of some of Bousset's points will
confirm the judgement that he goes astray. In the first place,
he states that Paul compromised his position in 1 Corinthians 15 50 by admitting the resurrection of the body, albeit
of a new and glorious body.[3] This doctrine, which has
become traditional in the Church, may be regarded as a

---

[1] *Kyr.Ch.* pp. 359–61.   [2] ibid. p. 360.   [3] ibid. p. 359.

compromise with or modification of the more material type of Jewish hope, which Paul had perhaps learned as a Pharisee. However, it is hard on Paul to describe it as a compromise with himself. He continued in that Hebrew mode of thought which did not divide man into separate elements of body and soul, and in which the phrase 'resurrection of the body' consequently conveyed the sense of *victory of the whole man over death*', as opposed to the *mere survival* of a disembodied shade of the departed. This Hebraic tradition, however, had been both confirmed and modified for S. Paul by the experience of our Lord's Resurrection. The flesh arose on the third day, in token of which the tomb was empty. Yet the Risen Lord was transfigured in glory. The hope of the Christian was naturally and rightly moulded by these circumstances, and the result was the doctrine of a real bodily resurrection for man, though of a transfigured body. Bousset errs in saying that S. Irenaeus makes 'dexterous use' of this chapter, with the implication that he is ingenious in explaining away the plain sense of a Pauline text that happens not to fit in with the interests of dogma. Irenaeus is simply insisting in taking that chapter in S. Paul's own sense, and in denying a one-sided construction upon it.

Bousset is also somewhat unfortunate in his argument for rejecting as un-Pauline the exposition of 'flesh and blood' as 'fleshly deeds'. The exegesis of Irenaeus may indeed be criticized as mistaken, but not on the grounds advanced by Bousset. The Gnostic had quoted 'flesh and blood cannot inherit the Kingdom of God' in a dualist sense, denying the resurrection of the body. Irenaeus sought to avoid this construction by maintaining that the phrase referred to fleshly lusts, which the saved are to put off.[1] In proof of this he cited a number of passages where Paul spoke of 'the flesh', in the sense of fleshly lusts, as a definition of that which cannot inherit the Kingdom.[2] This shows that Irenaeus had not

[1] V.11.1, ii.81; V.12.3–4, ii.84–5; V.13.3, ii.88; V.14.4, ii.94.
[2] 1 Corinthians 15₅₀; Romans 8₈,₉,₁₃, in V.10.2, ii.80; Galatians 5₁₉–₂₁, in V.11.1, ii.81.

grasped the fact that there is a certain distinction in connotation between the word 'flesh' in 1 Corinthians 15₅₀ and in the
typical Pauline phrase 'the flesh'. The general concept of
'the flesh' refers to man's nature, both bodily and mental, in
so far as it is in rebellion against God's will.[1] On the other
hand, the 'flesh and blood' which will not inherit the Kingdom appears to be man's present animal body, as distinct
from the glorious resurrection body, no question being raised
as to whether this present body is obedient or disobedient to
God. Confusion between these two terms has landed
Irenaeus into the necessity of making an unfortunate attempt
to explain away the clear meaning of 1 Corinthians 15₅₀.
Bousset, however, criticizes the treatment on quite other and
erroneous grounds. It is represented as un-Pauline because
it is part of an effort by Irenaeus to find in Paul the doctrine
of the resurrection of the body.[2] As has been observed, the text
in question is actually completely consistent with this doctrine.
In passing it is to be noticed that the exposition of the
passages mentioned above, referring to 'the flesh', is an
outstanding example in Irenaeus of insight as an exegete.
He firmly grasps the truth that in Paul 'the flesh' is not the
body as such, but the motion of rebellion against God.[3]

In considering the doctrine of Saving Faith in S. Irenaeus
we approach the crux of this most important section of the
present study. In emphasizing the importance of this, one
may make bold to claim that he, and only he, who shows
himself able aright to expound what is the nature of
Faith has proved himself to be adult in Christian stature.
Furthermore, here is the acid test of the fidelity of
S. Irenaeus to Biblical, and in particular to Pauline
Christianity. The name of S. Paul will for ever be
associated with the formula *'Justification by Faith'*. He, and
only he, who understands what Paul meant by Faith is an
essential Paulinist. We proceed therefore to subject the
works of S. Irenaeus to these tests. So typical is Irenaeus of

---

[1] e.g. Galatians 5₁₉₋₂₁.   [2] *Kyr.Ch.* p. 359.   [3] See p. 70 *supra.*

Catholicism at its best that the result of this inquiry will go far to determine the legitimacy of the historic Church's claim to be the guardian of the religion committed to her by our Lord. A number of charges brought against S. Irenaeus have already been examined and substantially rebutted. He had an adequate, and a Pauline, doctrine of the saving work of Christ and of the Atonement.[1] He taught a slightly confused but essentially reasonable doctrine of man, and one which accords with the Bible.[2] He took an adequate view of the gravity of sin, and laid due emphasis upon man's need of salvation.[3] S. Irenaeus was no Pelagian. His conception of sin was both reasonable and scientific, and also deeply ethical and spiritual.[4] Here too he did not depart from S. Paul. Essentially Pauline, also, was the conception of 'the Flesh'.[5] In contrast to all this we must now notice that some have held that Irenaeus was inclined to teach that the Christian life does not rest upon the ground of God's unmerited forgiveness received by humble and penitent faith, but is a process of earning merit in the sight of God by man's own efforts in obedience to the moral law.[6] No theme better merits attention than this, for there is no error that comes more easily than this upon well-meaning Christians who have failed to rise to the highest levels of spiritual experience. As antinomianism is the natural heresy of the morally careless, who are likely to be found without the fold, so this opposed failing of reducing Christianity to mere moralism is the natural heresy of the morally earnest, who more usually tend to gravitate into the Church. It is impossible to deny that historic Christianity has frequently been stained by this error.

[1] See pp. 186–94 *supra*.   [2] pp. 211–12, 217–21.   [3] pp. 214, 228–9.
[4] pp. 221–2.   [5] pp. 70, 231–2.
[6] This error has frequently been described as '*Legalism*'. This name is not inapt, as it points the obvious spiritual parallel to the standpoint of S. Paul's Judaizing opponents. However, both the terms '*Legalism*' and '*Moralism*' suffer from ambiguity. They have also often been given a higher connotation, and may be used not as names for a manifest error, but as words to emphasize that Christianity is an essentially ethical religion.

The most powerful attack upon this score has again come from Werner. He writes that the early Church, with its doctrine of the New Law, compromised the Pauline teaching that Christianity was not a system of moralism, but a new religion. That Irenaeus can quote Paul in a moralistic sense shows that he had not recognized the essential principle of Paul.[1] Irenaeus restored the fulfilling of the *natural law* as the way of Justification (IV.25.1, i.459). Though there is an obvious formal relationship of his position to S. Paul there is actually a deep difference, for Irenaeus made a distinction between the moral and the ceremonial law. Only the latter was merely pedagogic and relative. The former was soteriological and absolute.[2] The goal of legal education in Paul was freedom from the Law, in Irenaeus it was the Law of Freedom, *vivificatrix lex* (IV.34.4, Harvey, ii.271). Thus Werner claims that under what Irenaeus calls the law of 'free, not slavish obedience' a human action (and not divine grace, therefore) was still the first prerequisite of salvation.[3] Abraham's faith was that he freely obeyed the natural law, and looked for the promised Kingdom. Christians were in like position. '*Justification by Faith*' was therefore an alternative phrase for '*Justification by Natural Law*'. S. Paul used '*the justifying faith of Abraham*' to find the principle of Justification by Faith already in the old religion. S. Irenaeus, says Werner, used the same *theologoumenon* to find in Christianity the Old Testament idea of salvation by the fulfilling of the moral law.[4] Righteousness was not the consequence, but the requisite for salvation.[5] As the doctrine of salvation was the nerve of both Paul and Irenaeus there is no inner unity between them.[6] This is one of the points where Irenaeus showed a pseudo-Paulinism.[7] The Pauline thought of a new relation to God, resting on God alone and rejecting self-striving, was hidden from him. Thus the final verdict of Werner upon Irenaeus is: 'The hand is the hand of Esau, but the voice is the voice of Jacob.'[8] So also with

---

[1] *Paulinismus*, p. 93.   [2] ibid. p. 190.   [3] ibid. p. 191.   [4] ibid. pp. 194–5.
[5] ibid. p. 210.   [6] ibid. p. 213.   [7] ibid. p. 179.   [8] ibid. p. 202.

Ritschl, who maintains that the antithesis of the two Testaments of freedom and of slavery was expounded by Irenaeus in a sense very different from S. Paul. IV.**9**.2, i.400 puts the New Covenant in formal likeness to the Old as *legislation*. IV.**12**.3, i.410 unites both Law and Gospel in the conception of love, so as to eliminate a religious difference between them. Both Covenants contain the natural law by which the Patriarchs lived. When the Law renewed through Christ is described as life-giving and free (IV.**34**.4, ii.20–1), the freedom in mind is only a freedom from the additional ceremonial ordinances of the Law of Moses.[1] The distinction of fear and love is turned into one of degree (IV.**16**.5, i.425).[2] Contrary to all apostolic tradition Irenaeus maintained that within the divine Calling man must array himself in works of righteousness (IV.**36**.6, ii.32). The ground-relationship of man to God was therefore traced back to man's own control.[3]

A candid examination of the passages in question forces one to the conclusion that there is some show of right in these charges. In reading, however, one must be careful to bear in mind the underlying intention of S. Irenaeus. In general this appears to have been the desire to vindicate against the Marcionites the unity of the God of the Old and of the New Covenants. This was done by demonstrating the underlying unity of the two religions. To the men of the Old Covenant there was revealed true knowledge of the Supreme Being, the one Creator-God.[4] By revelation from Him the legal dispensation was instituted.[5] At first God revealed Himself by 'warning (the Jews) by means of natural precepts, which from the beginning He had implanted in mankind, that is, by means of the Decalogue'.[6] These 'natural precepts', which are the fundamental rules of moral life, including love of God and one's neighbour, are of eternal validity.[7] 'All natural precepts are common to us and to them (the Jews); ... but in us they have received growth and completion.'[8]

---

[1] *Entstehung d.a.K.* pp. 313–4.　[2] ibid. p. 315.　[3] ibid. p. 316.
[4] II.**11**.1, i.146; IV.**5**.1, i.386.　[5] III.**10**.2,5, i.282, 286.　[6] IV.**15**.1, i.419.
[7] See pp. 58–9 *supra*.　[8] IV.**13**.4, i.415; see also IV.**16**.4–5, i.424–5.

Because of the hardness of heart and idolatry of the Hebrews, however, God later subjected them to the bondage of the whole Mosaic Law. Those who 'had gone back in their minds to Egypt, desiring to be slaves instead of freemen', were 'placed for the future in a state of servitude suited to their wish'.[1] This discipline was an act of grace, in so far as the service of the Law was designed by God for the blessing of man and not for His own benefit.[2] These slavish precepts were the temporary and conditional self-revelation of God. Our Lord showed them up for what they were, and they are done away with in the Church.[3] There is now the 'new covenant which brings back peace, and the law which gives life'.[4] This is a covenant of liberty, in which circumcision is abolished.[5] The 'legislation . . . given in order to liberty' is comparable to, but better than, that once 'given in order to bondage'.[6] The bonds of slavery have been done away in order that God may receive not the obedience of servants but the better obedience of children.[7] All this forms the explanatory background for the more questionable statement: 'The Lord did not abrogate the natural (precepts) of the law, *naturalia Legis*,[8] by which man is justified.'[9] A happier statement of essentially the same sentiment is: God 'delivers a law suited both for slaves and those who are yet undisciplined; and gives fitting precepts to those that are free'.[10]

It will be seen that this 'moralism' of S. Irenaeus is essentially a lapse in expression, only to a minor degree a

---

[1] IV.**15**.1, i.419; see also IV.**15**.2, i.420; IV.**16**.3, i.423–4; IV.**16**.5, i.425; *Dem.* 8.

[2] IV.**14**.1, i.416–7; IV.**17**.1, i.426; IV.**32**.2, ii.5.

[3] IV.**15**.2, i.420; see also III.**2**.2, i.260; III.**12**.14, i.313; *Dem.* 35, 89, 95.

[4] IV.**34**.4, ii.20.

[5] III.**12**.14, i.313; see also IV.**16**.2, i.422–3; IV.**16**.5, i.425.

[6] IV.**9**.2, i.400.

[7] IV.**13**.2, i.414; see also IV.**4**.1, i.384; IV.**8**.2, i.397; IV.**11**.3, i.407; IV.**13**.4, i.415. Note: Irenaeus does not, however, appear anywhere to speak of the Gospel as '*the New Law*'.

[8] Harvey, ii.180.   [9] IV.**13**.1, i.412–3; cf. IV.**12**.5, i.411–2; IV.**15**.1, i.419.

[10] IV.**9**.1, i.399–400.

lapse in thought. His clear intention is to safeguard the
superiority of the Christian Gospel, but he is also under
strong controversial pressure to emphasize the unity of the
Old and New Covenants. He finds it difficult to do the latter
without suggesting that the difference between Old and
New is only one of degree. This tendency was powerfully
stimulated by two authentic New Testament motifs. The
Lord had spoken of the two great commandments of love to
God and to man as the essence of the old religion. S. Paul
had written of Abraham as justified by faith before receiving
the covenant of circumcision. In both these cases the nobler
side of Hebrew religion was quoted against the more external and conventional. This act of selection was entirely
legitimate as a prophetic summons to the people, but
inasmuch as there was a process of *selection* an idealized
picture was painted of the historic religion of the Old
Covenant. S. Irenaeus was naturally attracted by this
idealized picture, as it provided good ground for his polemic.
He therefore tended to dwell upon it in isolation from its
original background of thought. This helped to entrap him
into minimizing the element of novelty in the New Covenant.
The position is illuminated by the argument of such a passage as IV.12.2–3, i.409–10: 'But if He (Christ) had descended from another Father He never would have made
use of the first and greatest commandment of the law.' The
Christian life is a life of love. 'For we do never cease from
loving God, but in proportion as we continue to contem-
plate Him, so much we love Him the more.' This thoroughly
evangelical introduction should prevent one from being too
dismayed at the unhappy statement following: 'the precepts
of an absolutely perfect life . . . are the same in each Testament.' This is in reality only a method of saying that 'the
author of the law and the Gospel is shown to be one and
the same'.

We read, therefore, that the Law 'did beforehand teach
mankind the necessity of following Christ'.[1] All the doctrines

---

[1] IV.12.5, i.411; see also IV.2.4, i.380.

of Christ were predicted through the prophets, particular
mention being made of '*Justification by Faith*'.[1] 'For Christ is
the treasure which was hid in the field; . . . the treasure hid in
the Scriptures is Christ.'[2] So carried away is S. Irenaeus with
enthusiasm for the proposition that 'the patriarchs and
prophets sowed the word (concerning) Christ, but the
Church reaped',[3] that he takes liberties with history. 'Paul,
since he was the apostle of the Gentiles, says, "I laboured
more than they all". For the instruction of the former [i.e.
the Jews] was an easy task, because . . . they who were in the
habit of hearing Moses and the prophets did also readily
receive the First-begotten.'[4]

Beuzart is one who joins in the charge that Irenaeus made
the difference between the Law and the Gospel merely one
of degree, thus coming dangerously near to a denial of the
unique character of the Gospel. 'Irenaeus . . . does not see
anything in the second but the expansion of the first.
Christ has come to extend and complete the Law. The Old
Covenant is the embryonic Law, reduced to its rudiments;
the New Covenant is the Law unrolling all its consequences,
and come to its full expansion. . . . The difference which
exists between the Old and the New Testament is quantitative, not qualitative.'[5] Of the Ethiopian eunuch, who
found faith in Christ easy because he had been reading
Isaiah, it is said, 'nothing else (but Baptism) was wanting
to him who had already been instructed by the prophets'.[6]
This illustrates alike the charge and the answer to the charge.
Here is the closest kinship between the two Dispensations,
and equally a difference. The Ethiopian had been well
prepared for Baptism, but he had not been baptized.
Ready as he was to accept Christ, he was not yet a Christian.
Christ was not there to accept. The difference between a
promise, however binding and however descriptive of good
things to come, and the actual thing promised, cannot be

---

[1] IV.34.1–2, ii.18–19; *Dem.* 35.   [2] IV.26.1, i.461.   [3] IV.25.3, i.460.
[4] IV.24.1, i.457; see also IV.2.7, i.381–2.   [5] *Essai*, p. 137.
[6] IV.23.2, i.457.

dismissed as a difference of quantity. 'You will find that the whole conduct, and all the doctrine, and all the sufferings of our Lord, were predicted through (the prophets). . . . What then did the Lord bring to us by His advent?— know ye that He brought all novelty, by bringing Himself who had been announced.'[1] Here is a witness that in Christ there is infinitely more than a divine doctrine. There is a divine act.[2]

That the most essential significance of the life of Jesus to S. Irenaeus was that of an objective act of God in the world, and no mere teaching activity, is confirmed by the consideration that the *Recapitulation* is so adequate an exposition of that act. One whose mind was substantially satisfied to view the Lord as a prophet and martyr would have had no sufficient incentive to work out a profound doctrine of the Saving Work of Christ, and to repeat it constantly with persuasion and with emphasis. Rather one would find at most a perfunctory treatment. That S. Irenaeus quitted himself so well in treating of the *Recapitulation* is a sure token that to him this 'novelty' in the Lord's appearance was a matter of first-rate importance. It is not to be minimized to a matter of degree, despite isolated passages that can be quoted to support this position. We repudiate entirely Wendt's representation that men have only to obey the bidding of the Logos by the exercise of free-will, and they will receive perfection and heavenly immortality from God.[3] Rather we agree with Aall that S. Irenaeus sees Christ as a Redeemer and an historical personality, this being an interest distinct from the Greek Logos-thought.[4] Though some moralistic forms of expression may lie on the surface, at the profounder depths of thought and feeling there is a sure motion diametrically opposed to mere moralism. Whatever he may say in unguarded moments, one who so plainly teaches that man is saved not of himself, but by trust in something that God has done once and for all in Christ

---

[1] IV.**34**.1, ii.18; see also IV.**20**.10, i.446.   [2] See pp. 195–6 *supra*.
[3] *m.Vollkommenheit*, p. 24.   [4] *Logosidee*, p. 355.

is not to be labelled a 'legalist'. We cannot, however, forbear to regret some few of the expressions into which Irenaeus slips.

The result of the whole investigation is, then, to make it reasonable to expect in S. Irenaeus at least a fairly adequate conception of Faith. The first element in the Act of faith is assent to the truth. It is the firm and reasoned conviction that 'faithful is the saying, and worthy of all acceptation'. As is but natural in a work written to maintain a doctrinal tradition, this element is strongly represented in Irenaeus. 'So then we must believe God in all things, for in all things God is true.'[1] This 'believing in God' is acceptance of the Creed, and a 'full Faith' is a correct and complete Creed.[2] Once the 'Rule of Truth' is called the 'Rule of Faith'.[3]

The second element in the Act of faith is self-committal to the truth. It is to begin to live as if it *were* the truth. This element is also well represented in S. Irenaeus. One interesting passage appears to set out these two stages: 'We must needs hold the Rule of the Faith without deviation, and do the commandments of God, believing in God and fearing Him as Lord and loving Him as Father. Now this doing is produced by faith . . . and faith is produced by the truth; for faith rests on things that truly are. For in things that are, as they are, we believe; and believing in things that are . . . we keep firm our confidence in them.'[4] The sequence is fact, assent to fact, and committal of life, described as 'belief', 'fear', 'love', and 'confidence'. Of this faith Abraham is a great pattern. Having believed the promise, and on the strength of it taken up the life of a pilgrim,[5] 'Abraham, according to his faith, followed the command of the Word

---

[1] *Dem.* 43; see also I.3.6, i.15; I.**10**.2, i.43; II.**22**.2, i.198; II.**27**.2, i.218; III.**4**.2, i.264; IV.**24**.2, i.458; IV.**29**.2, i.475; V.**14**.4, ii.94; *Dem.* 98.

[2] IV.**33**.7, ii.10; see also I.**10**.2, i.43; I.**10**.3, i.44; II.**28**.3, i.222; III. **Pref.**, i.258; III.**1**.1, i.258; III.**3**.3, i.262; III.**4**.2, i.265; III.**21**.3, i.354; III.**24**.1, i.369; IV.**23**.1, i.455; IV.**26**.5, i.465; IV.**28**.2, i.472; IV.**30**.1, i.476; IV.**31**.3, ii.4; IV.**32**.2, ii.5; V. **Pref.**, ii.55; V.**1**.3, ii.57; V.**20**.1, ii.108; *Dem.* 86.

[3] *Dem.* 3.   [4] *Dem.* 3.   [5] IV.**5**.3, i.388; see also V.**32**.2, ii.142.

of God, and with a ready mind delivered up . . . his only-begotten and beloved son'.[1] In his pilgrimage he showed an 'undoubting and unwavering certainty of his spirit'.[2] The Christian has a faith like Abraham.[3] 'Our faith was also prefigured in Abraham . . . for he believed in things future, as if they were already accomplished, because of the promise of God; and in like manner do we also.'[4] Faith is trust in God.[5] It is seeing and accepting the light.[6] It is unswerving fidelity in following the light. 'For one is the way leading upwards for all who see, lightened with heavenly light: but many and dark and contrary are the ways of them that see not. . . . Wherefore it is needful for you, and for all who care for their own salvation, to make your course unswerving, firm and sure by means of faith.'[7] Faith is constancy in pursuit of the Christian calling.[8] It is submission to God, while unbelief is perverse resistance to His action.[9] Indeed, faith in S. Irenaeus is at times almost synonymous with obedience to the will of God. 'It is good to obey God, and to believe in Him, and to keep His commandment, and this is the life of man.'[10] In quoting 'Now, to believe in Him is to do His will',[11] Werner seems to have more justification than elsewhere in his argument that Irenaeus is inadequate and un-Pauline in his treatment of faith.[12] However, it will be noticed that this isolated phrase can be read as 'obedience is the same thing as faith', or with equal legitimacy, 'faith is the road to obedience'. The latter construction is supported to some extent by the consideration that the theme of the context is that man cannot come to know God unless He teach him. This is clearly contrary to the general notion that man is called to fit himself for God.

[1] IV.5.4, i.388.   [2] *Dem.* 24.   [3] IV.7.2, i.395.
[4] IV.21.1, i.451.   [5] IV.5.5, i.388; V.9.2, ii.76.
[6] IV.6.5, i.391; V.10.1, ii.78; V.28.1, ii.130.   [7] *Dem.* 1.
[8] IV.6.7, i.392; IV.16.1, i.422; V.6.1, ii.69; V.8.4, ii.74.
[9] IV.27.2, i.467; IV.28.2,3, i.472–4; IV.29.2, i.475; IV.37.3, ii.38; IV.39.3, ii.47; IV.41.3, ii.53.
[10] IV.39.1, ii.45; see also IV.13.1, i.413; IV.17.4, i.429; IV.15.2, i.421; IV.41.2, ii.51; V.9.3, ii.77; V.27.1, ii.129; *Dem.* 2, 3.
[11] IV.6.5, i.391.   [12] *Paulinismus*, p. 205; see also pp. 234–5 *supra*.

It will be seen that for S. Irenaeus faith is largely assent.
The voice of truth, speaking through the Church of the
authentic tradition, demands to be believed. God's sovereignty demands obedience. His good Fatherhood demands
childlike trust. Faith is the appropriate response to these
demands. Irenaeus lays himself open to criticism here. His
emphasis upon the first two stages of faith is such
that many would say that he teaches that faith is nothing
more than assent and submission. It must be confessed
that he is not entirely beyond suspicion of thus falling
short of the true principle of the Gospel.

The third element in the Act of Christian faith is
unquestioning and glad surrender of one's whole personality
in trustful friendship to the loving God seen in Jesus
Christ. The Incarnation, the life, and the Cross and Passion
of the Lord present the love of God with compelling appeal
to the heart. The response required is to give rein to the
impulse of the heart, and to allow the whole personality,
with all its affections, desires, powers, and will, to be
carried away by gratitude, admiration, trust, and love. This
is the vital element in Saving Faith, because self-committal
of life and thought to the truth as seen in Christ Jesus cannot
fully be made, and can never be sustained in strength without
an adequate emotional dynamic. The mind indeed gives direction to life, but the feelings provide the impetus. Both are
necessary. Thus nothing less than 'the faith that works by
love' will save to the uttermost. The invitation to *this* manner
of self-giving to God is surely the climax of the Gospel
message, and this experience it is that supplies new moral
strength to the convert. Whether or no S. Irenaeus gives an
adequate testimony to this element in faith is a crucial
question indeed, bearing as it does upon his grasp of the
Gospel.

The claim of S. Irenaeus to be in this important matter a
genuine Christian, alike Catholic and evangelical, largely
depends upon the following passages. 'Faith . . . endures un-
changeably, assuring us that there is but one true God, and

that we should truly love Him for ever, seeing that He alone is our Father.'[1] 'For to yield assent to God, and to follow His Word, and to love Him above all, and one's neighbour as one's self (now man is neighbour to man), and to abstain from every evil deed, and all other things of a like nature which are common to both (covenants), do reveal one and the same God.'[2] Here *assentire* and *abstinere* are parallels to *sequi* and *diligere*. The former are to some extent to be interpreted in terms of the latter. Furthermore, the humble, simple-minded man will 'believe in God, and continue in His love'.[3] Having a true opinion regarding God, he will continue in His love, and in subjection to Him.[4] 'We are saved, indeed, by means of faith and love.'[5] Faith can hardly be nothing more than bare intellectual assent for one who has this grasp upon 'the faith that works by love'. In all these passages it is a reasonable construction that *faith* is a personal attitude to a personal God with whom the believer holds communion. Other passages make faith a matter of personal attitude to Christ. This may be stated negatively: those who repulsed Jesus, who scorned and slew Him, showed thereby that they were unbelievers.[6] On the other hand, for the Church Christ is He *in quem et credimus, quem et diligimus*.[7] The context appears to justify rendering this as: 'in whom too we *trust*, and whom we love.' The immediate connexion is with a quotation from the lyrical and rapturous passage of Isaiah 25₉, together with 1 Peter 1₈, 'whom not having seen, ye love,' etc. The note of trust and glad surrender sounded in these texts may surely be found echoed in the sense given to *credimus*. There is also the noble evangelical invitation: 'Offer to (God) thy heart in a soft and tractable state . . . lest . . . thou lose the impressions of His fingers. . . . If thou, being obstinately hardened, dost reject the operation of His skill, and show thyself ungrateful toward Him, . . . thou hast at once lost both His workmanship and life.'[8]

[1] II.28.3, i.221–2. [2] IV.13.4, i.415. [3] II.26.1, i.215.
[4] III.20.2, i.349. [5] I.25.5, i.96. [6] IV.2.6, i.381.
[7] IV.9.2, Harvey, ii.170. [8] IV.39.2, ii.46–7; see also pp. 156–7 *supra*.

In the light of this reconstruction of the doctrine of
S. Irenaeus a criticism may usefully be attempted of the
many and various statements that have been made. Vernet is
content with the reduced estimate that faith was for Irenaeus the assent to revealed truth offered by the Church. Such
a passage as *Demonstration* 43, 'So then we must believe God
in all things, for in all things God is true', and *Dem.* 3 and 98,
are produced as evidence for this.[1] However, these do not
stand alone, and a judgement that would be damaging may
safely be rejected. The same applies to Beuzart's criticism
that of the Reformation conception of *notitia, assensus,* and
fiducia, as together constituting faith, S. Irenaeus had only
the first two, of which *notitia* predominates.[2] Plainly,
assent to the divinely-commissioned witness of the Church
regarding what God has done in Jesus Christ was for
Irenaeus an exceedingly important part of faith. It is the
indispensable foundation of ability to love and to obey God.
Yet Irenaeus certainly did not altogether neglect to build the
necessary structure upon that foundation. He is surely in
accord with Pauline doctrine. The Apostle does not anywhere carefully define Saving Faith, but he rejoices in the
Church's confession: 'Jesus is Lord.' This is indeed a pledge
of obedience, and even more, the raptured outburst of a
heart transformed by the love of God shed abroad, but it is
also by original principle the statement of a conviction that
had dawned upon the mind. S. Paul would have agreed that
it was the true work of an evangelist to spread that conviction,
as also to quicken it to its effectual fruit in a change of
affection and moral will.

Werner's criticism covers somewhat similar ground. He
maintains that faith is for Irenaeus not the sum of piety, but
its hypothesis, not trust in God, but its cause. Faith is the
confession of God as creator and ruler of the world, and
knowledge that He can and will do as He has promised. It
is the reason why men fulfil the demands of God.[3] In answer
we may observe as before that this is a part of what S. Irenaeus

---

[1] *Dictionnaire*, VII, col. 2492.   [2] *Essai*, p. 125.   [3] *Paulinismus*, p. 148.

says. It is a part he affirms with much emphasis, yet not more than a part. Werner continues that Irenaeus teaches that faith is the presupposition for the reception of the Spirit, not its effect. It is a performance of man, and not the power of God.[1] The passage cited is the moving one mentioned above, IV.**39**.2, ii.47. It is to be admitted that at first sight this is a legitimate construction to be placed upon such a phrase as: *Si igitur tradideris ei quod est tuum, id est, fidem in eum et subiectionem, recipies eius artem, et eris perfectum opus Dei.*[2] However, Vernet's comment upon this same text is preferable. While admitting that it appears to be Pelagian he points out that in the immediate context and in the preceding pages the interest of Irenaeus is simply to show that faith in man is free. In other places faith is plainly the gift of God, *Dei munus.*[3] Werner errs in pressing too hard the question whether good Reformation theology is to be found in S. Irenaeus. The fact is that it is not easy to describe faith as the appropriation by man of what God offers to do for him without speaking of it as 'the presupposition for the reception of the Spirit', thus falsely placing the initiative of the religious life with man and not with God. Only the careful language born of controversy can succeed in this. The controversy in question had not taken place, so it is hard on Irenaeus to blame him for not having expressed himself with the same scrupulous care as he doubtless would have done had he lived in the seventeenth century. He had, however, a sufficiently firm grasp of the fact that man cannot save himself, and is utterly dependent on God for all good things, to make it a not unreasonable supposition that had he been pressed with the question he would have agreed that faith itself is the gift of God. This point comes out more plainly in another of Werner's criticisms. We read that the conception of faith in S. Irenaeus was un-Pauline because, while more than mere intellectual assent, it was much less than the action of God

---

[1] *Paulinismus*, p. 149.   [2] Harvey, ii.299.
[3] *Dictionnaire*, VII, cols. 2492–3.

in man.[1] This criticism appears to be based on the quite
unfounded supposition that complete predestinarian doctrine is to be found in S. Paul, and should therefore be found
in S. Irenaeus. In the study of both it is surely as misleading
to describe faith bluntly as 'an action of God in man',
without regard to man's willing receptivity of that action, as
to speak of it simply as an action of the spirit of man, without
respect to the Divine Prevenient Grace enabling man to
believe.

Another criticism is advanced by Ritschl.[2] In pursuing
the theme that S. Irenaeus obscured S. Paul's fundamental
antithesis between the slavery of the Old Covenant and the
freedom of the New, Ritschl states that Irenaeus teaches
that Christ has increased the fear of God under the Gospel,
for sons should love and fear the Father more than slaves.
'But He has also increased fear; for sons should have more
fear than slaves, and greater love for their Father,'[3] *auxit autem
etiam timorem.*[4] This is claimed to convert the distinction
between fear and love into one of degree, which would
indeed be an unsound position were the love to be lost in the
fear. Ritschl is clearly in error here. In the first place there
are considerations arising from the context. Irenaeus first
eloquently proclaims that under the Gospel God calls men
to the principles of inward and spiritual morality based
upon love to God. Nevertheless, this order of freedom does
not lead to laxity. The moral standard for the Christian is
indeed stricter than for the Jew, because he is judged for
thoughts as well as deeds. The 'increase of fear' is a phrase
intended to express this sound position. Secondly, the New
Testament itself, following the Lord, constantly speaks of
'the fear of God' as a part of the experience of a Christian.
Thus there is Luke 12₅, 'But I will warn you whom ye shall
fear'; and also, Acts 9₃₁, Romans 11₂₀, 2 Corinthians 5₁₁,
Ephesians 5₂₁, Philippians 2₁₂, Hebrews 12₂₈, 1 Peter 1₁₇,
2₁₇, Revelation 11₁₈. There ought, therefore, to be a

---

[1] *Paulinismus,* p. 205.   [2] *Entstehung d.a.K.* p. 315.   [3] IV.**16**.5, i.425.
[4] Harvey, ii.192.

sacred awe in the intercourse with God of the soul: *'whom Thou dost bring up in Thy steadfast fear and love'* (*Second after Trinity*).

Werner makes the same criticism as Ritschl,[1] but the passages he quotes are only to the effect that those who have the fuller light of the Gospel and yet sin will have a severer punishment than others.[2] When the Word has set free the soul, so that man can follow God without fetters, 'subjection to the King' is increased, to the end that 'the piety and obedience due to the Master of the household should be equally rendered both by servants and children, while the children possess greater confidence'.[3] The distinction drawn here shows that S. Irenaeus rises above 'mere moralism'.

Hatch takes a broader view. Faith, one of the fundamental ideas of S. Irenaeus, is 'belief' or 'trust' according as the connotation is intellectual or religious. It starts with the response of the individual to the facts and arguments presented by the missionary. It is a voluntary act, and is nowhere spoken of as the gift of God.[4] We may allow a general measure of acceptance to the final verdict. 'In Irenaeus faith is sometimes belief and sometimes trust. Faith in Christ is based upon conviction, and it is the root from which all the spiritual blessings of Christians spring.'[5] However, Bonwetsch has a profounder judgement, which is that while 'faith' is often the content of the Christian Creed, and naturally also the acknowledgement of the truth preached by the Church, it is for S. Irenaeus according to its proper essence the surrender of the heart to God.[6] This issue must first be clarified by making a sharp distinction between 'faith' and 'The Faith'. It is unfortunate that in S. Irenaeus, as in the Church at large, a single term should have come to be used to denote two entirely different ideas. 'Faith' is the human response whereby God's gift of salvation is appropriated. 'The Faith' is the correct and whole-

---

[1] *Paulinismus*, p. 201.   [2] IV.**28**.2, i.472; IV.**36**.4, ii.30.
[3] IV.**13**.2, i.414.   [4] *Idea of Faith*, pp. 128–30.   [5] ibid. p. 140.
[6] *Theologie d.I.* p. 139.

some body of doctrine handed down in the authentic tradition. On the one hand, it is perhaps likely that the custom of calling a body of doctrine 'The Faith' would not have grown up among men who took scrupulous care always to make plain what is the nature of 'Saving Faith'. On the other, it is a usage that comes naturally to the lips of those who are conscious that inherent in their way of life is the profession of a Creed. Hence even so early as the later parts of the New Testament there are traces of 'The Faith' as distinct from 'faith'.[1] It is therefore dangerous to assume that the occurrence of this usage *of itself* necessarily indicates that 'faith by which salvation is appropriated' would be defined by a given writer as mere intellectual assent, though it carries with it a measure of suspicion. All the numerous references of S. Irenaeus to 'The Faith' in the definite sense of 'the Creed', or to 'our faith' where 'The Faith' is obviously meant, must be set aside as of less than immediate interest in the present discussion. One must take care to keep in mind mainly those contexts where Irenaeus is describing the way of salvation, and in particular, where he turns aside in his argument to offer that salvation to the reader. An examination of the passages collected above in the reconstruction of the concept of faith will then show that the surrender of the heart in love to God is not neglected as the crown of Saving Faith, and its vitalizing principle. We may safely set aside Ritschl's verdict that S. Irenaeus did not understand the conception of Justifying Faith, and herein echoes S. James rather than S. Paul.[2] Schmidt is correct in stating that from the side of man 'faith' is not an action, but humble reception from God.[3] The same applies to Seeberg's observation that in Irenaeus 'faith' is the reception of the activity of God.[4] Guarded yet positive assent may finally be given to Brunner's emphatic judgement that 'faith' in Irenaeus is evangelical, and even Pauline.[5] The assent is

---

[1] cf. 1 Timothy 1₁₉, 3₉, 4₁,₆, 6₁₀; 2 Timothy 3₈; James 2₁; Jude ₃.
[2] *Entstehung d.a.K.* p. 316.   [3] *Kirche b.I.* p. 150.
[4] *DG.* p. 349.   [5] *Der Mittler,* p. 226.

IRENAEUS CATHOLIC AND EVANGELICAL

positive, because Brunner is certainly on the right side. It must be guarded also, for the fact remains that 'faith' as intellectual assent overweighs 'the faith that works by love' more than some could wish to see. This is doubtless mainly due to the polemical rather than evangelical nature of *Adversus Haereses*. However, it is impossible entirely to banish the suspicion that it may to a minor degree be due to a lowering of evangelical tension in S. Irenaeus, as compared with S. Paul.

The judgement that in respect to his preaching of the Life of Faith S. Irenaeus was in all essentials a substantially sound Christian, at once truly Catholic and truly evangelical, is a conclusion of far-reaching consequence. If the immediate post-apostolic age is to be judged by its scanty remains one is forced to the conclusion that it was a time of impoverished religious experience. It is pleasing to think of the heroic Church of 'the early pure days' advancing with even steps from truth to truth. Unhappily this view is much too simple. The missionary overseas today finds that not all hearers of the Gospel fully appreciate the Faith they profess. The pagan background and presuppositions 'cling'. Outside the responsibly-organized Church there is commonly a medley of eccentric secession sects bearing the marks of the admixture of more or less of paganism with Christianity. Just as significant is the circumstance that among those who remain loyal to the Church there may be movements of thought and feeling regarding which the missionary may find it hard to decide whether here are inclinations toward heresy, or new apprehensions of Christian truth, the gift of yet other nations to the universal Church. The primitive Church was in the position of the younger Churches of today, save that it lacked the stabilizing influence of experienced counsel from Churches of tested tradition. Outside the Church were the eccentric and compromised, the definitely heretical, bodies. It is not to be forgotten that within the true Church were likewise some who walked with faltering steps. It would almost appear as if after the creative impulse of the Apostolic period the Church wavered, and then proved herself the subject of Christ's promise to S. Peter by 'pulling herself together'. In doctrine and Church discipline the marks of this were the providential emergence of the definitive Canon of Scripture, the interpretative Creed, and the authoritative Episcopate. The important part played by S. Irenaeus in this connexion is familiar, and hardly needs further emphasis. It would seem that a parallel movement took place in Christian piety and apprehension of the Gospel. There was an early tendency to interpret the Faith as no more than a new Law promulgated from a better Sinai, a Law which a man had to set himself to obey. However, the Spirit moved profounder minds within the Church to resist this tendency. There came in due season an equally providential reaffirmation that Christianity is actually a new religion of real Redemption, wrought out once for all by a divine Saviour and to be accepted by faith, and of an indwelling Spirit. It is not to be forgotten that the position of Irenaeus in this movement is no less important.

It would almost seem as if in the post-Apostolic period the impetus of conversion and the gift of the indwelling Spirit were being found less obviously sufficient than in the days of Paul to establish the sound moral life of the convert. To satisfy the claims of morality and Church order Christian leaders were coming to think more of the code of the New Law, and of the demand for loyalty to ecclesiastical organization. 1 *Clement* breathes this 'moralistic' atmosphere,[1] and S. Ignatius of Antioch somewhat more so. The '*Two Ways*' of the *Didache* verges on the Christianity of legislation[2] as does the *Epistle of Barnabas*.[3] '*The Shepherd*' of Hermas is definitely to be condemned as an impoverishment of the Gospel of grace.[4] Likewise, it is a tenable view that the writer of James 2₁₉ completely misunderstood what S. Paul had

---

[1] 1 *Clem.* 30.

[2] See also Chapter vi, which teaches the double moral standard.

[3] *Ep. Barn.* 2,4,19,21.

[4] *Vis.* II.2,3; *Mand.* I, IV.2, VI.2, XII.3 (a glaring example of Pelagianism), 4–6; *Simil.* V.3, VII.

meant by Justifying Faith. Faith is here represented as something merely intellectual, which may exist apart from the moral will and affections, in a satanic intelligence. From this error springs the writer's very natural objection to the formula '*Justification by Faith and not by Works*', which he found the Church to have inherited from Paul. The character of the work of S. Irenaeus is a welcome token that this deterioration of spirit was not universal in the primitive Church, or at least, that the Church speedily recovered from it. Irenaeus represents the survival or else the revival of a more truly Pauline, and more truly Christian strain. That this should be said of one of those figures who is a landmark in Catholic development is a pledge that the Church of his day was indeed the true People of God. Sometimes S. Irenaeus speaks in an accent strange to the ears of those instructed by the dogmatic definitions of the Councils, and in phrases which seem careless to the mind sharpened by the evangelical controversies of later centuries. This is true alike of his treatment of the Trinity, the Atonement, and of Saving Faith. Nevertheless, beneath the strange accent is the truth which the Church later enshrined as her heritage. None can take away his glory.

Chapter Thirteen

THE CHURCH

THE DOCTRINE of the Church in S. Irenaeus is distinctively Biblical and primitive Christian, and reproduces much of S. Paul's teaching. The Church to Irenaeus was the New Israel, and the True Israel, the prophetic and priestly People of God. A leading polemic interest of *Adversus Haereses* is the vindication against Marcion of the unity of the God of the Old and of the New Covenants, the continuity of the Jewish and Christian Faiths, and the authenticity of the Old Testament as Holy Scripture. The doctrine of the *New Israel* fitted in admirably with this polemic. It would be a mistake, however, to suppose that the doctrine of the Church in Irenaeus is superficial only, and a mere accident of the controversial issue. It is a profound part of his religious faith, and a valuable element in his constructive work.

In reconstructing the position of S. Irenaeus we first observe that, because the Jews, who had so often fallen into apostasy, had repudiated and crucified the Son of God, 'it pleased God to grant their inheritance to the foolish Gentiles, even to those who were not of the polity of God'.[1] The Church is the seed of Abraham, and has inherited the promise made to him.[2] It is the present 'synagogue of God, which God . . . has gathered by Himself'.[3] In history there have been, therefore, 'the two synagogues—that is, the two Churches', 'the elder and the younger Church'.[4] 'There were indeed two testaments among the two peoples.'[5] Christ 'does still fulfil in the Church the new covenant foretold by the law'.[6] The Church of Jerusalem, as 'the

---

[1] *Dem.* 95; see also IV.**21**.3, i.452.   [2] V.**32**.2, ii.142; see also V.**34**.1, ii.148.
[3] III.**6**.1, i.269.   [4] IV.**31**.2, ii.2–3; see also *Dem.* 94.
[5] IV.**32**.2, ii.5; see also IV.**21**.3, i.452.   [6] IV.**34**.2, ii.19.

Church from which every Church had its origin', is 'the metropolis of the citizens of the new covenant'.[1] In extending this idea, the writer to the Hebrews is followed in the doctrine that the religious institutions of Israel were 'a figure and a form of the Church'.[2] The Patriarchs, who were justified by faith, prefigured the Church.[3] The Exodus from Egypt was a 'typical exodus', but 'our true exodus . . . is the faith in which we have been established, and by which we have been brought forth from among the number of the Gentiles'.[4] God has taken out a Church which should be sanctified by fellowship with His Son.[5] The promise of the enlargement of Japeth was fulfilled in the calling of the Gentiles into the Church.[6]

In the Bible, the People of God is essentially a prophetic People. Furthermore, because the prophets were no mere accidental collection of individuals, but the embodiment of the truest aspirations of a nation, the prophetic People of God was also a priestly People. A religious community presupposes religious institutions. Hence the truest voice of Israel was neither the profound spiritual individualism of Jeremiah, nor the external institutionalism of the more primitive stages of the Law, or of later Phariseeism. It was the lofty religion of the 'Evangelical Prophet', the kernel of whose work is found in the four 'Servant Songs' of Deutero-Isaiah. Here is the perfect picture of the prophetic *nation*. God's way of speaking to the whole world is by preparing for Himself a Peculiar People. His way of vindicating Himself is by the miraculous restoration of His dispersed People to their own land and Temple. The world's true religion is therefore inseparably linked with the life of a particular holy nation, living in a certain Holy Land, and rejoicing in a purified cultus. Yet the purification and restoration of a community is not an end in itself. It is the means of preaching a universal Gospel. It is

---

[1] III.12.5, i.301.   [2] *Dem.* 26.   [3] IV.22.2, i.455.
[4] IV.31.1, i.476; see also IV.30.4, i.480.   [5] IV.20.12, i.449–50.
[6] *Dem.* 21, 41, 42.

a way for God to declare His truth. In the life of the People
the prophetic message is embodied. Not by any institution,
however pure and however venerable, does man live, but
by that truth. Ezekiel followed in this train, with more
practical application and practical effect, though with
perhaps less inspiration.

The outlook of S. Irenaeus was in essential conformity
with this Biblical tradition. Schmidt's observation is correct,
that it was specially the prophetic line in Israel on which he
fixed.[1] Full consideration has already been given to the
Church as the seat of religious authority.[2] It is most significant that this discussion covers almost everything of importance to be found on the topic of the Church. The case in
point is that S. Irenaeus laid great stress upon the Succession
of Bishops and Presbyters as the possessors of the gift of
truth, as the givers of the Creed, and as organs of doctrinal
authority. He had, however, little to say of them as channels
of sacramental grace. The power of Baptismal Regeneration
was indeed given by the Lord to the Apostles,[3] who, having
received the Holy Spirit, were granted the power to impart
Him in Baptism to those who believed.[4] Again, 'those upon
whom the Apostles laid hands received the Holy Spirit'.[5]
However, this goes little beyond simple New Testament
language, and Irenaeus does not discuss whether these functions were passed on in the Succession. Of the Eucharist he
writes, that Christ 'taught the new oblation of the New
Covenant, which the Church receiving from the Apostles
offers to God throughout the world'.[6] In this statement there
is no defined doctrine regarding the constitution of a regular
Sacrament. Furthermore, S. Irenaeus gives a hint that he held
a doctrine of the universal priesthood of all believers. This
does not, of course, in strict logic preclude the conception of
a special priesthood in addition, representatively exercising
the function which in principle belongs to the whole priestly
community, though if taken seriously it is bound to moder-

---

[1] *Kirche b.I.* p. 104.   [2] See pp. 24, 102–6 *supra*.   [3] III.17.1, i.334.
[4] *Dem.* 41.   [5] IV.38.2, ii.43.   [6] IV.17.5, i.430.

ate any *exclusive* claim regarding the function of that priest-hood. 'All the righteous possess the sacerdotal rank.'[1] Antonius Melissa and S. John of Damascus quote a Greek version of this to the effect that 'every righteous king possesses a priestly order'.[2] Later, referring back to this passage S. Irenaeus could write: 'I have shown that all the disciples of the Lord are Levites and Priests'.[3] Only a single passage speaks of the Succession as the guardian of admin-istrative discipline. The Apostles 'delivered up their own place of government to these men'.[4] The Church is in a position to produce the lists of past Bishops.[5] It is necessary that a good life accompany the possession of Orders if the Priest is to be a true servant of Christ,[6] and it is asserted that the Presbyters of the Church are actually of this character.[7]

The interest, then, for S. Irenaeus in the Church centres in the doctrine which she preaches and guarantees. The call he makes is never for submission to the Church on the ground that loyalty to the body is a salutary moral exercise. Always it is that men should accept the Apostolic doctrine from the Church, because this, and this alone, is God's saving truth. As Molvitz well observes: *Ecclesia autem fidem excitans homines ad id impulit ut Christo subiciantur. Itaque ecclesia utens Christus omnia recapitulat.*[8] Irenaeus was a Catholic Christian indeed. He was no individualist. He knew nothing of a faith which is purely interior and secret, or of a solitary walk of the soul with God. The institution-alism which is the inescapable concomitant of the life of an actual human community was accepted by him as a matter of course, being the natural background for personal piety. Indeed, he gloried in this institutionalism. Yet he did not love it for its own sake, but because the life of the Church set forth the Gospel by which the believer lives.

---

[1] IV.8.3, i.398.   [2] See Harvey, ii.167.   [3] V.34.3, ii.150.
[4] III.3.1, i.261.   [5] III.3.1, i.260; III.3.3, i.261-2.
[6] IV.26.3, i.463.   [7] IV.26.5, i.464-5.
[8] *De* Ἀνακεφαλαιώσεως *in Irenaei Theologia Potestate*, p. 41.

Schmidt reads a little too much into Irenaeus in stating that he teaches that the principle of the Church's unity is her one message, and that this unity is conditioned by inner spirit and not by outer organization.[1] The Catholicity of the Church is claimed to be determined by this message,[2] so that the *Kerygma* makes the Church what she is.[3] That the truth-giving and truth-guarding operation of the Holy Spirit is limited to the empirical Church of tradition is perhaps not strictly explicit in III.24.1, i.369–70, but the implication is undoubtedly there: 'Our faith, which, having been received from the Church, we do preserve, and which always, by the Spirit of God, renewing its youth, as if it were some precious deposit in an excellent vessel, causes the vessel itself containing it to renew its youth also. For this gift of God has been entrusted to the Church, as breath was to the first created man, for this purpose, that all the members receiving it may be vivified; and the communion with Christ has been distributed throughout it, that is, the Holy Spirit, the earnest of incorruption, the means of confirming our faith, and the ladder of ascent to God. "For in the Church", it is said, "God hath set apostles, prophets, teachers", and all the other means through which the Spirit works; of which all those are not partakers who do not join themselves to the Church, but defraud themselves of life through their perverse opinions and infamous behaviour. For where the Church is, there is the Spirit of God; and where the Spirit of God is, there is the Church, and every kind of grace; but the Spirit is truth. Those, therefore, who do not partake of Him, are neither nourished into life from the mother's breasts, nor do they enjoy that most limpid fountain which issues from the body of Christ.' Clearly the unity of organizational life and discipline in the Church is fundamental for S. Irenaeus. It is no less essential, natural, and axiomatic than is the unity of doctrine. Yet Irenaeus has hardly speculated upon the relation one to another of these marks

---

[1] *Kirche b.I.* pp. 96–7.   [2] ibid. pp. 107–9.
[3] ibid. p.170; see also Seeberg, *DG.* p. 310.

of the Church: the two qualities exist side by side. The actual argument of the passages cited by Schmidt in support of his first proposition is simpler than he claims, being more concerned with facts than with principles. Irenaeus simply asserts that the one universal Church is actually unanimous in all its members, and that this unanimity is a token that what she teaches is true.[1] For a similar reason one would express at least some hesitation in accepting Battifol's judgement upon the very difficult passage, IV.**33**.8 (Harvey, ii.262–3), namely, that the believer belongs to the Church spiritual by means of the Church visible, and to the Church visible by means of the precepts of the Apostles, and the Bishops who continue their office.[2]

A similar point arises regarding the place of the hierarchy. Bonwetsch states that S. Irenaeus nowhere teaches a priestly mediation of salvation, all believers having a priestly character. It is only in relation to doctrine that subordination to the Episcopate is necessary for salvation, seeing that the Bishops guarantee the saving truth.[3] We may say that Irenaeus knows nothing of the conception of 'infused grace' flowing to the believer from his Lord through the succession of Apostles, Bishops, and Presbyters, in a manner analogous to the electric current. He honours the Sacraments, and teaches their necessity, but is never found to speak as if faithful participation in sacramental rites duly observed were the pre-eminent way by which man is visited by the grace of God. Faith is first and foremost an attitude to God and His truth. It is not defined merely as the con-

---

[1] I.**10**.2, i.43; III.**12**.7, i.305; V.**Pref.**, ii.54; V.**20**.1, ii.108–9.

[2] *L'Église*, p. 246. The text in question runs as follows: Γνῶσις ἀληθὴς, ἡ τῶν ἀποστόλων διδαχή· καὶ τὸ ἀρχαῖον τῆς ἐκκλησίας σύστημα κατὰ παντὸς τοῦ κόσμου· *et character corporis Christi secundum successiones episcoporum, quibus illi eam quae in unoquoque loco est Ecclesiam tradiderunt, quae pervenit usque ad nos custodita sine fictione scripturarum tractatione plenissima, neque additamentum neque ablationem recipiens, et lectio sine falsatione, et secundum Scripturas expositio legitima et diligens, et sine periculo et sine blasphemia: et praecipuum dilectionis munus, quod est pretiosius quam agnitio, gloriosius autem quam prophetia, omnibus autem reliquis charismatibus supereminens.* (Trans. on p. 100 supra.)　　　[3] *Theologie d.I.* p. 124; see also Schmidt, *Kirche b.I.* p. 171.

dition for a means of grace to be efficacious to the individual.
So also the essential characteristic of the Bishops and
Presbyters is never described as an indelible mark implanted
by ordination.[1] The property of a Priest is much more that he
can impart sound doctrine than that he can duly perform
certain rites. All this may be accepted as most significant. It
is, however, presuming too much to say that subordination to
the Bishop is taught as necessary to salvation *only* in relation
to doctrine. This is certainly the figure that actually fills the
canvas, but Irenaeus does not appear to make this emphasis
a matter of theory or of theological principle. The Bishops
and Presbyters in all their offices are clearly accepted as
an inherent part of a Church outside which there is no
salvation. We cannot imagine S. Irenaeus formally placing
Baptism, for example, in a place secondary to right doctrine
as an essential for salvation, though the whole weight of
interest is actually in the doctrine.

In this matter Seeberg argues as follows. It is not the
Priesthood, but the common Faith, which gives the unity of
the Church. The Church is not merely the folk under the
Bishop, but the way is opened for this development, for
saving truth is in the hands of the Bishop. This idea of the
Episcopate was indeed brought in simply as a sanction for
the truth of what the Church said, but it could not stop there.[2]
Some parts of this statement have been criticized above, but
we may agree with the last dictum. It was difficult for the
position to remain as S. Irenaeus left it. We have seen that
he was on sound ground in making the voice of the Church
the basis of religious authority.[3] He was on natural ground
in defining the voice of the Church as the voice of her
leaders, the Bishops and Elders. He had, however, too much
confidence in the fact of *office*. He too readily assumed that
the official successor to the teacher of sound doctrine is the
one who must prove also the successor to the possession of
the truth.[4] The voice of the Church was consequently too

---

[1] See Schmidt, *Kirche b.I.* p. 73; Werner, *Paulinismus*, p. 60.
[2] *DG.* p. 311.   [3] See pp. 87–8, 107–11 *supra*.   [4] See p. 89 *supra*.

much the voice of those in the official succession, too little
the consensus of opinion of all those who, being good and
wise, have patiently conferred together. Institutions set up
in obedience to the voice of truth have a natural tendency
to remain through mere conservative instinct. Prophetic
inspiration commonly ebbs after it has flowed, thus
disturbing the healthful balance between the inward and
the outward. These two influences are sufficient to make it
impossible for the Episcopate to remain where it is found
in *Adversus Haereses*. Having been established in effect
as the exclusive mouthpiece of all the Faithful, it was but
a matter of time and natural causes for the Bishop to cease to
be dependent on the Church, and for the Church to become
dependent on the Bishop. This inevitability is, however, much
more the responsibility of the Christian world of later days
than of S. Irenaeus.

The connexion of this theology of the Church with the
teaching of the New Testament must now be determined.
The conception of the Church as the *New Israel* clearly took
its origin in the words of the Lord Himself. Twelve Apostles
were chosen, who were to sit upon twelve thrones on the
Judgement Day, the heads of the typical Twelve Tribes into
which the Christian Faithful were divided, like Israel of old.[1]
Like the Hebrews, Christ's disciples were God's flock, God's
sheep.[2] Isaiah's 'Vineyard of the Lord' is to be no longer the
Jewish nation, which is rejecting the Christ, but rather the
outsiders who are accepting Him.[3] In particular, the sacred
rite which the Lord appointed to mark the fellowship of His
own was a family meal in continuation of the Passover, the
venerable memorial of the Old Covenant, and the family
meal of the Old Israel.[4]

[1] Matthew 19₂₈, Luke 22₃₀.
[2] Luke 12₃₂: cf. Isaiah 40₁₁, Jeremiah 50₆, and Ezekiel 34. Matthew 25₃₂:
cf. Ezekiel 34₁₇. Matthew 26₃₁ and Mark 14₂₇: cf. Zechariah 13₇.
[3] Matthew 21₃₃-₄₁, Mark 12₁-₉, and Luke 20₉-₁₆: cf. Isaiah 5₁-₇ and Jeremiah
2₂₁.
[4] Matthew 26₂₆-₉, Mark 14₂₂-₅, Luke 22₁₅-₂₀.

As always when considering the development of Christian
thought and life during the first generation of the Church,
one next turns with especial interest to the work of S. Paul.
He uses three main conceptions in speaking of the Christian
Church. In the first place, he follows his Lord in teaching
the doctrine of the *New Israel*. Then also for him the Church
is the Body of Christ, and similarly, but less commonly, the
Bride of Christ. Finally, the Christian believer, and the
fellowship of Christians, are 'in Christ', and 'in the Spirit'.
It is to be observed that the two latter are based upon
practical and non-speculative considerations, while the
former is more properly theological.

The germ of the Pauline doctrine of the Body of Christ is
clearly 1 Corinthians 12₁₂-₃₁. The interest here is that of
practical moral exhortation. Each Christian brother is to
realize that he has a talent to employ in the service of his
Lord, and that this is true also of all his brethren. Therefore,
though some enjoy more apparent distinction and worldly
notice than others in this service, there is no place in the
Church for pride or odious comparisons, for envy or for
discouragement. Everyone is necessary, just as every organ
of the human body, great and small, is necessary. Brother is
gladly to co-operate with brother.

In *Le Corps Mystique du Christ* (Second Edition, Paris,
1936, Tome 1), Émile Mersch gives a very learned and
forceful exposition of S. Paul's doctrine of the Body of
Christ. To Mersch the very soul of Paulinism is the
'*Mystery*' of the union of all things in the Mystical Body of
Christ (pp. 94, 112, 152, 202, 204–5, etc.). The 'key-
passages' in the Apostle are such as Ephesians 3₁-₉ (p. 97),
and Ephesians 1₃,₇-₁₀ (p. 111). The method of exposition is
to show that scattered throughout the earlier Epistles there
are passing allusions to, and unformed statements of, that
'*Mystery*' of divine incorporation which comes to formal and
explicit expression in the key-passages. One of the most
important of such cases is the passage 1 Corinthians 12₁₂-₃₁
(pp. 146–7). Here is a description of the Mystical Body

(p. 148). However, as Mersch admits in opening, there is here only an 'occasional' or accidental mention of the Body, brought in through the need for demonstrating other points (i.e. the practical moral lesson referred to above) (p. 143). Thus, although Mersch labours so hard, and with some success, to vindicate a spacious doctrine of the union of all things in Christ as essential Paulinism, he is not far from admitting that the point from which this doctrine starts to develop is a simple practical need. (Mersch makes it a strong point that, though the essential doctrine of S. Paul is a unity throughout, the mode of expression shows development in the light of the Apostle's experience (pp. 99–100, etc.).)

With Mersch we look forward from the doctrine of the Body of Christ in 1 Corinthians, etc., to the doctrine found in Ephesians. Here is certainly much more than a simple doctrine of practical exhortation. In Ephesians the conception of the Mystical Body of Christ rises indeed to the stature of a profound and spacious philosophy. S. Paul does show how the raising up of the Church Catholic is the culmination of an eternal divine plan for the universe. However, the purpose of his demonstration is not so much to show this for its own sake, as to enforce the vast spiritual implications of the union of Jew and Gentile in the Christian fellowship. To bring out this interest is indeed the leading theme of Dr. J. Armitage Robinson's fine exposition of the Epistle to the Ephesians (Second Edition, London, 1909).[1] The union of Jew and Gentile in the Church is the same practical human problem as the reconciliation of brother with brother in the Church at Corinth. The latter case is the principle applied on a small scale, the former on the largest possible scale, inasmuch as to a Jew like S. Paul the yawning chasm between the Chosen People and the outer Gentile world was the fundamental division of the human race. The contrast between the practical simplicity of 1 Corinthians 12 and the profundity of Ephesians may be well expressed in mathe-

[1] See particularly pp. 9–10, 33–4, 55ff.

matical terms. In the later Epistle we have the same quantity, but raised to the highest power.

If one refers back to the construction already made of the doctrine of the Church as it is found in S. Irenaeus,[1] it will be observed that almost nothing is said by him of the element stressed by Mersch, the 'con-corporate' union of all believers in the Mystical Body of Christ.[2] It is to be admitted that here is a deviation from Pauline teaching, which is an important one in view of the prominence in S. Paul of the rich conception of the Body of Christ. It is a deviation that will almost certainly seem to be a serious lapse in the eyes of any theologian who is accustomed to look upon this particular exposition of the nature of the Church as a central and most precious part of Christian belief. In modification of the latter judgement it is to be urged that the failing of S. Irenaeus to reproduce the Apostle's doctrine at this point is not so radical as may seem at first sight. It is in part, at any rate, a divergence of manner of expression rather than of essential thought and intention, if what has been said above regarding the conception of the Body be allowed. It cannot be denied that the majestic unity of the Church Catholic, among every race, and in every time and place, is one of the dominant elements in the theology of Irenaeus. To preserve that unity is a paramount moral obligation resting upon every believer. Thus he does firmly hold to just those practical considerations which are the mainspring of S. Paul's doctrine of the Body of Christ. What is lacking in S. Irenaeus is the notion that all Christians, together with the Lord as their Head, form a 'Body' in the sense of a kind of mysterious supra-sensible substance. Christian theology has heard not a little of this conception, though whether it be truly Pauline is open to question. To Irenaeus the Church is a corporation conceived of throughout in 'common-sense' terms.

One may further observe that in his exposition of the life of the believer in the Church S. Irenaeus has little to say of

---

[1] See pp. 252–5 *supra*.
[2] σύνσωμος; Ephesians 3₆. See J. A. Robinson, *Ephesians* (2nd ed.), pp.78, 169.

the Christian as being 'in Christ', or 'in the Spirit', to use
alternative phrases roughly equivalent in the terminology of
S. Paul. Here is a more significant divergence from the
Apostle. That the believer is ἐν Χριστῷ is a conception reflecting the piety, the actual 'evangelical experience' of the
Christian. It is plain to the reader of the Acts of the Apostles
and the Pauline Epistles that the Churches for which S. Paul
speaks were supremely conscious of an immediate Divine
Presence in the midst. This Presence could be thought of
in terms of the Risen Christ, invisible but full of power and
glory, or in terms of Old Testament phraseology as 'the
Spirit of the Lord'. The Church and the individual felt that
in every action one was prompted and empowered by the
Divine Presence, so that every activity was the work of God.
One whose religious life was initiated, nourished, and
brought to practical expression by and in a religious society
thus indwelt by God in Christ could indeed say that Christ
was his spiritual atmosphere, his very breath of life. To use
the admirable phrase of Mersch : '*Le Christ devient donc
notre milieu et notre ambiance.*'[1] That Christ is the milieu of
the Church and her members is the thought behind S. Paul's
expression ἐν Χριστῷ. How fundamental is this conception
in the Apostle's thought and feeling may be appreciated
when it is realized that the momentous encounter with
Christ upon the road to Damascus, the event which Paul
regarded as constituting him equally with the Twelve a
witness to the Resurrection, and so an Apostle,[2] was nothing
other than the supreme example in his experience of the
mystical union 'in Christ'.[3] That all this should find so little
echo in S. Irenaeus is a lapse from New Testament piety
which cannot be entirely explained away.

The fact surely is that the unity of the Church around a
system of doctrine is an element that dominates the theology
of S. Irenaeus in a way that it does not the theology of S.
Paul. The Apostle was certainly deeply aware that the

---

[1] *Corps Mystique*, p. 137.   [2] 1 Corinthians 15₈₋₉; Galatians 1₁₁₋₁₇.
[3] cf. *Corps Mystique*, pp. 88–9.

Church exists to proclaim the Gospel of a crucified and risen Messiah. An important mark of the glorious unity of the Church was consequently 'one Faith'. However, the unity in which he chiefly gloried was the unity of love, the divine marvel that bond and free, man and woman, Jew and Gentile, were joined in one fellowship, and that the love of Christ could constrain the brethren to be gracious with one another despite all that displeases in human nature.[1] Thus the warfare of S. Paul was chiefly against a divisive spirit in the Church, in the Jew the spirit of exclusive privilege and self-righteousness, at Gentile Corinth the spirit of individualist disorder which marred the prophesying and the Eucharist. His polemic was only to a secondary degree against wrong opinions. On the other hand, S. Irenaeus was deeply interested in fighting a divisive doctrine. To him unity in doctrine and preaching is the very bond of Catholic unity.[2] Hence it is natural to find Irenaeus so frequently speaking of the Church as if it were merely a circle of disciples gathered around their faithful teacher, the Bishop. This undoubtedly reflects religion at a lower level than when Paul speaks of the Church as gathered into one in a fellowship 'in Christ'. However, we have some ground for supposing that S. Irenaeus would have redressed the balance had he

---

[1] Mersch perhaps goes too far in stressing this side of S. Paul. As some Protestants have erred through reading the Epistles as though Romans were the only one which really matters, so does Mersch with Ephesians. We may admit that judicial considerations are only of secondary and derived importance in the teaching of the Apostle (cf. *Corps Mystique*, pp. 112, 114), but in this sense only: that the doctrine of '*Justification by Faith and not by Works*' is a mode of expression adapted to those who instinctively and necessarily thought of man's relation to God in terms of legal justice. The *mode of expression* is indeed accidental, but the vital spiritual truth beneath is the utter bankruptcy of every system which encourages sinful man to hope, by his own efforts in obedience to externally imposed moral law, to attain to a good character, and to earn acceptance with God. Man's sole hope is that a loving and merciful God will freely forgive him when penitent, and will fill him with power divine if he will but entrust himself to Him. This vital truth is, together with the unity of all believers in the Mystical Body of Christ, the quintessence of Paulinism. It cannot, as with Mersch, be displaced to the status of something merely preparatory to the unity 'in Christ'.

[2] See pp. 255, 257–8 *supra*.

left us a work of piety in addition to his polemic writings. He is certainly not wholly blind to the glorious fact that a Christian is one united in love to a loving Father.[1]

There remains for consideration S. Paul's teaching concerning the Church under the aspect of the *New Israel*.[2] One may make bold to state that, despite all due weight rightly given to the Pauline teaching expounded above, the conception of the *New Israel* carries the best claim to be regarded as S. Paul's ideal philosophy of the Church. In Romans 9–11 the Apostle allows himself to be 'borne on contemplation's wing', and attempts to scan his new and wonderful religion from the viewpoint of God's eternal purpose in the government of the universe. When he does this he expounds the Church as the *New Israel*, the reconstituted People of God, the company of the faithful Remnant who are 'Israelites indeed', and the legitimate heir of every ancient promise. Nor are allusions to this conception wanting in other places.[3] The spacious and beautiful exposition in Ephesians of the Church as the Body of Christ rises indeed to the universal point of view, but with this never entirely ceases to be a practical moral exhortation addressed to a certain temporal situation. It is not so completely a pure theology of the Church as is the doctrine of the *New Israel*. If this be admitted of S. Paul's theology it will be seen that the Apostle spans the years that separate Our Lord from S. Irenaeus. The fundamentally Pauline character of the teaching of S. Irenaeus on the Church is established, for that which is central in Paul is central also in Irenaeus.

We may, in passing, briefly notice other New Testament strains echoed by Irenaeus. The writer to the Hebrews also sees the Church as 'the people of God'.[4] The Christians are one body with the heroes of Israel, and are their spiritual

---

[1] See pp. 242–3 *supra*.

[2] It is interesting that Mersch only mentions this side in passing (pp. 118–19), even though it comes to such clear expression in Ephesians 2₁₂.

[3] Romans 4₁₆; 1 Corinthians 10₁₈; 2 Corinthians 6₁₆; Galatians 3₇,₂₉, etc.; 4₂₆, 6₁₆.

[4] Hebrews 4₉.

heirs, though at a higher spiritual level.[1] So also the author
of 1 Peter writes to his brethren: 'But ye are an elect race, a
royal priesthood, a holy nation, a people for God's own
possession.'[2] Finally, the company of glorified Christians
is described in the Apocalypse as the Twelve Tribes of
Israel.[3] All this illustrates what unity there is in the New
Testament around that doctrine of the Church which lies at
the heart of S. Irenaeus.

The doctrine of the Sacraments in S. Irenaeus has already
been touched upon, but the matter is of such importance that
it merits more detailed consideration. Bousset argues that as
Irenaeus was a theologian, and no Mystery-preacher like
Ignatius, the Eucharist plays a proportionately minor role
in his scheme.[4] It is true that the dignity of the Holy Communion is treated of with much less emphasis in Irenaeus
than in Ignatius. This may to a large extent be due to the
general interest of his writings, which leads the author away
from the discipline and worship of the Church to questions
of doctrinal controversy. However, the Sacraments are by
no means relegated to a minor position. We may first reconstruct the position as it appears in S. Irenaeus.

It seems to be assumed that Baptism and the Eucharist
are to be administered by the Bishop and Presbyter alone,
but this is nowhere clearly stated.[5] Reception of Baptism is
a sign that a man has faith, and marks the beginning of a
full Christian life.[6] The 'Rule of Truth' is 'received by
means of Baptism'.[7] This appears to be an allusion to the
confession of Christian belief by custom made at Baptism.[8]
It is not clear whether Irenaeus regards the Creed-forms of
I.10.1, i.42, and *Dem.* 6 as Baptismal, but Baptism involves

---

[1] Hebrews 11. [2] 1 Peter 2₉.

[3] Revelation 7₄₋₁₀, 14₁,₃₋₄. It does not follow from the contrast between the
144,000 and the multitude 'out of every nation' (7₄,₉), that those sealed 'out
of every tribe of the children of Israel' are exclusively Jewish Christians, for
in 14₃₋₄ the 144,000 appear to have been purchased from the whole earth.

[4] *Kyr.Ch.* p. 341.   [5] See pp. 254–5 *supra*.   [6] IV.23.2, i.457.

[7] I.9.4, i.41.   [8] cf. Tertullian, *De Corona*, 3.

the confession of the Tri-une Name, and the Incarnation, Passion, and Resurrection.[1] Adult Baptism is pre-supposed. It is not clear whether Irenaeus speaks of infant Baptism, though it must have been coming into the Church about this time, as Tertullian objected to it a little later.[2] The argument that S. Irenaeus allows the Baptism of infants depends upon the assumption that the phrase 'being born again into God', which refers to Baptismal Regeneration in I.21.1, i.81 and III.17.1, i.334, has the same meaning in II.22.4, i.200. Against this is the fact that Regeneration is constantly spoken of without reference to Baptism. No further particulars are given as to the manner of baptizing, save that it is with water.[3] Baptism is 'for the remission of sins',[4] and brings the gift of the Holy Spirit, who abides only while the believer continues in a righteous life.[5] The most usual thought is that Baptism works Regeneration,[6] incorruption,[7] eternal life, and Adoption.[8] Irenaeus takes over from S. Justin Martyr the phrase 'Laver of Regeneration' as a name for Baptism.[9]

The Eucharist receives some considerable attention. In the consecration of the Eucharist the Logos unites Himself with the elements, and as it were becomes incarnate again. 'Therefore the mingled cup and the manufactured bread receive the Word of God, and the Eucharist becomes the body of Christ.'[10] If a fragment preserved in Oecumenius be accepted, the consecrated Eucharist is not actually flesh and blood.[11] Beuzart also claims that in the attack upon the claim of Marcus to transform wine into the blood of the Saviour Irenaeus disowns the idea of transubstantiation.[12] Nevertheless, the consecrated elements are 'no longer common bread',[13] 'but the Eucharist, consisting of two realities, earthly and

[1] *Dem.* 3. [2] *De Baptismo*, 18. [3] *Dem.* 41.
[4] III.12.7, i.305. [5] *Dem.* 41, 42.
[6] I.21.1, i.81; III.17.1, i.334; *Dem.* 3; *Frag.* XXXIV, ii.174.
[7] III.17.2, i.335; *Dem.* 7. [8] *Dem.* 3.
[9] Justin, *Apol.* I.61,66; V.15.3, ii.97. [10] V.2.3, ii.59.
[11] *Frag.* XIII, ii.165. [12] *Essai*, p. 165; I.13.2, i.51-2.
[13] cf. Justin, *Apol.* I.66, for this phrase.

heavenly'.[1] The elements may be described as the body and blood of the Lord,[2] and the communion of His body and blood.[3] To partake of this divinity-bearing Eucharist produces incorruption, that is, divinization.[4] It is possible that the phrase 'antidote of life', *antidotum vitae*,[5] is also intended as an epithet applied to the Eucharist.[6] This would represent φάρμακον ἀθανασίας in the Greek, which is reminiscent of the words of S. Ignatius of Antioch: ἕνα ἄρτον κλῶντες, ὅ ἐστιν φάρμακον ἀθανασίας, ἀντίδοτος τοῦ μὴ ἀποθανεῖν.[7]

Dualists, who deny such doctrines as Creation by a divine Logos, the Incarnation, and the salvation of the flesh, cannot logically offer the Eucharist, because it likewise involves the principle of the union of God and the world, and the use of the things of this world in the purpose of God. 'The Church alone offers this pure oblation to the Creator, offering to Him, with giving of thanks [the things taken] from His creation. . . . But how can they [the Gnostics] be consistent with themselves, [when they say] that the bread over which thanks have been given is the body of their Lord, and the cup His blood, if they do not call Him the Son of the Creator of the world, that is, His Word, through whom the wood fructifies and the fountains gush forth. . . . Then again, how can they say that the flesh, which is nourished with the body of the Lord and with His blood, goes to corruption, and does not partake of life? . . . For . . . the bread, which is produced from the earth, when it receives the invocation of God, is no longer common bread, but the Eucharist, consisting of two realities, earthly and heavenly.'[8] It is on account of this anti-dualist interest that, when S. Irenaeus is explaining that partaking of the Eucharist produces incorruption, it is the incorruption of the flesh that is spoken of.[9] It also accounts for the emphasis laid upon the fact that the offering of the Eucharist is an offering

---

[1] IV.18.5, i.435.   [2] IV.18.4, i.435.   [3] V.2.2, ii.59.
[4] IV.18.5, i.434; V.2.2–3, ii.59–60.   [5] Harvey, ii.102.
[6] III.19.1, i.344.   [7] *ad Eph.* XX.
[8] IV.18.4–5, i.434–5; see also V.2.2, ii.59.
[9] IV.18.5, i.434; V.2.2–3, ii.59–60.

made from God's own creation:[1] 'these thy *creatures* of bread and wine'.

The other main thought of S. Irenaeus regarding the Eucharist is that it is 'the new oblation of the New Covenant'.[2] The theology which maintained the continuity of the Christian religion with the religion of Israel was glad to claim the Church as the *New Israel*. It was naturally also glad to find in the Church that which corresponded to the sacrificial system of the Old Testament. This was clearly in accord with the mind of the Lord, for Christ Himself associated His Last Supper with the Passover ritual. Irenaeus therefore writes: 'And the class of oblations in general has not been set aside. . . . Sacrifices there were among the People (the Jews); sacrifices there are, too, in the Church: but the species alone has been changed, inasmuch as the offering is now made, not by slaves, but by freemen.'[3] The Lord, in 'giving directions to His disciples to offer to God the first-fruits of His own created things' (i.e. bread and wine), ful-filled the prophecy of Malachi that praise and a pure sacri-fice should be offered to God among all the Gentiles.[4] 'The oblation of the Church, therefore, which the Lord gave in-struction to be offered throughout all the world, is accounted with God a pure sacrifice.'[5]

The application of this Old Testament language to the Eucharist by no means necessitates the idea that Irenaeus taught that Christ is sacramentally offered to the Father. In considering the death of Christ we have already observed the obscurity which undoubtedly envelops the sacrificial thought of the Bible.[6] The notion of a sacrifice as '*a present offered to God*' was in circulation in the ancient world, and is found very occasionally in the Bible. There is, however, no certain evidence that to the Jew of our Lord's time '*sacrifice*' involved more than the simple sense of '*a divinely*

---

[1] IV.17.5, i.430; IV.18.1, i.431–2; IV.18.4, i.434.
[2] IV.17.5, i.430.   [3] IV.18.2, i.432.   [4] IV.17.5, i.430.
[5] IV.18.1, i.431; see also IV.17.6, i.431; IV.18.4, i.434.
[6] See pp. 178–83 *supra*.

ordained means of worship and of access to God'. There is
some ground for claiming that this simple sense is reflected
in the teaching of Jesus and the New Testament writers. It
would not do too readily to assume on this account that the
Gentile Irenaeus must have shared this mental background,
but, on the other hand, we are entitled to reject the assumption that his speaking of *'sacrifice'* necessarily presupposes the
notion of an offering made to God.[1] Certainly he nowhere
makes any explicit statement that Christ is sacramentally
offered to the Father in the Eucharist, and such a doctrine
would hardly harmonize with his non-substitutionary exposition of the death of Christ.[2] We find, rather, that the
Sacrifice of the Eucharist is one of praise, and of thanks-
giving for the good things of this world, as accords with the
name. 'Εὐχαριστεῖν is used once with the sense of 'to con-
secrate'.[3] The Sacrament was ordained by the Lord for the
disciples 'that they might be themselves neither unfruitful
nor ungrateful'.[4] 'It behoves us to make an oblation to God,
and in all things to be found grateful to God our Maker
. . . in fervent love, offering the first-fruits of His own
created things',[5] 'rendering thanks for His gift, and thus
sanctifying what has been created'.[6] The incense of the
offering is the prayer of the saints.[7] Consequently the
primary condition for making the offering aright is sin-
cerity of intention and righteousness of life. 'God is not
appeased by sacrifice.' A sacrifice offered in perfect order
by one who does not love his neighbour profits nothing.
'Sacrifices, therefore, do not sanctify a man, for God stands
in no need of sacrifice; but it is the conscience of the offerer
that sanctifies the sacrifice when it is pure, and thus moves
God to accept as from a friend.'[8] The reason that the Church
alone offers the Sacrifice is that she alone is pure. The hands

[1] Of the Eucharist we read, 'The Church alone offers this pure oblation
to the Creator' (IV.18.4, i.434), but the sense is that it is right to offer of the
material Creation to the *Creator*-God. This is not the sacramental offering
of *Christ.*   [2] See pp. 63, 193–4 *supra.*   [3] I.13.2, i.51; Harvey, i.115.
[4] IV.17.5, i.430.   [5] IV.18.4, i.434.   [6] IV.18.6, i.436; see also IV.18.1, i.431.
[7] IV.17.6, i.431.   [8] IV.18.3, i.432–4.

of the Jews are full of blood, while the conventicles of heretics sin against God by their insults to the Father.[1] The
sacramental cup is also *compendii poculum*, which Harvey
renders, 'the cup which recapitulates (the suffering of
Christ)'.[2] This may well mean that the Eucharist is symbolical of the recapitulating death of Christ.

It is worthy of note that, at least so far as the Eucharist
is concerned, the interest of S. Irenaeus centres in the
Sacrament as a prophetic act. The presence of the sacred
rite in the Church typifies, sets forth, and serves as a token
of the truth of certain doctrines. Thus, the Eucharist speaks
of the Creatorship of the Supreme God, the Incarnation of
the Lord, the Resurrection of the flesh, and the unity of the
religions of the Old and New Covenants. It would be a great
mistake, however, to suppose on this account that S.
Irenaeus would have described the Lord's Supper as 'merely
a symbol', in the sense that it could be supposed to have
been instituted by the Lord for the express purpose of
giving to the disciples a perpetual reminder of certain
doctrines. This would be a much-impoverished and quite
artificial view of the teaching of Irenaeus. The essential
significance of the whole life of the Church for Irenaeus is
that it sets forth and preaches God's saving truth. The
Eucharist is the focal point of the life of the Church. Em-
pirically, therefore, the Eucharist is the central act of worship, and of fellowship one with another and with the Lord,
while theologically it is a solemn and prophetic preaching.
This may be claimed as a New Testament position, for it is a
conception akin to the nearest approach that the New Testament makes to a theology of the Holy Communion, namely,
S. Paul's exposition: 'For as often as ye eat this bread, and
drink the cup, ye proclaim the Lord's death till He come.'[3]

*Ad hanc enim ecclesiam propter potentiorem principalitatem
necesse est omnem convenire Ecclesiam.* We can almost

---

[1] IV.18.4, i.434–5.   [2] III.16.7, i.330; Harvey, ii.88.
[3] 1 Corinthians 11₂₆.

say that S. Irenaeus did himself an ill service in penning
the lost Greek original of this momentous phrase.[1] It can
never be known with precision what he intended by it,
yet it is the first statement in Christian literature which on
a reasonable construction may be read as a foundation for
the claim of Roman primacy. Those controversialists to
whom on the one hand the establishment from the Fathers,
or on the other the overthrow, of the claims of the Papacy
is a matter of first importance have not unnaturally fixed
upon this passage. It has even been brought forward as the
most important single passage in *Adversus Haereses*. This
has undoubtedly distracted the attention of many investigators from the more important and valuable things that
Irenaeus had to say about the Catholic Church.

The background to this statement is that disputants
should 'have recourse to the most ancient Churches with
which the Apostles held constant intercourse, and learn
from these what is certain and clear with regard to the present question'.[2] Irenaeus gives several examples of such
honoured Churches. There is Asia, the Church of Polycarp.[3]
There is Jerusalem, 'the metropolis of the citizens of the new
covenant'.[4] Above all, there is 'the very great, the very ancient,
and universally known Church founded and organized
at Rome by the two most glorious apostles, Peter and
Paul'.[5]

Of the Church of Rome Irenaeus continues: *Ad hanc enim
ecclesiam propter potentiorem[6] principalitatem necesse est omnem
convenire Ecclesiam, hoc est, eos qui sunt undique fideles, in qua
semper ab his, qui sunt undique, conservata est ea quae est ab
Apostolis traditio.*[7]

---

[1] 'For it is a matter of necessity that every Church should agree with
(or 'resort to') this Church (Rome), on account of its pre-eminent authority.'
(III.**3**.2, i.261; Harvey ii.9.)

[2] III.4.1, i.264.   [3] III.**3**.4, i.263.

[4] III.**12**.5, i.301.   [5] III.**3**.2, i.261.

[6] Harvey's text reads *potentiorem*. *Potiorem*, a correction for the *pontiorem*
of the *Claromontanus* MS., is adopted by Massuet.

[7] Harvey, ii.9.

The details of the long controversy which has raged around this statement are very adequately summarized, from the Roman point of view, by Vernet. He observes the misfortune that the lost Greek original cannot be deduced with certainty at several important points. Added to this, the construction allows alternative combinations of various clauses and words. This leaves a measure of uncertainty which can never be cleared up. In general it is clear that *principalitas* refers to the status of the Roman Church, and not to the Imperial supremacy of the city. Irenaeus does not regard the importance of the Roman Church as a reflection of the civic importance of the capital. Rather does it spring from the dignity of her apostolic foundation. Again, *convenire* is definitely to be rendered '*agree*' and not '*resort to*' or '*assemble*'. S. Irenaeus is not merely saying that it is Rome's prerogative to call together the universal Church in Synod. These are seen as unfounded Protestant attempts to minimize the sense of the text.[1] There is furthermore some measure of agreement that *in qua* should be made to refer to *omnem Ecclesiam*, thus making *necesse est* indicate logical necessity, in preference to the usual ancient reference to *hanc ecclesiam* (i.e. Rome), with *necesse est* in consequence denoting moral obligation.[2] Harvey (ii.9) makes *in qua* the equivalent of an original ᾗ, '*inasmuch as*'. Manucci claims that the second *qui sunt undique* is a mistaken repetition of the first. One helpful suggestion is that *hoc est* introduces an explanatory periphrasis for '*Catholic*', a word which some would expect here.[3] This would make the perplexed last portion of the sentence run: 'in which the

[1] *Dictionnaire*, VII, cols. 2430–7.

[2] So also Battifol, *L'Église*, p. 250. Bonwetsch states that for the apostolic tradition to proceed from the Roman Church agrees better with the context, for the tradition to proceed from the whole Church agrees better with the grammar (*Theologie d.I.* p. 123). Schmidt, however, observes that the proposition is senseless if *in qua* does not refer to Rome, for otherwise all that is said is that those who are everywhere in the Church preserve the apostolic tradition (*Kirche b.I.* p. 83).

[3] Schmidt, *Kirche b.I.* p. 85; Battifol, *L'Église*, p. 250.

apostolic tradition has always been preserved by those who are Catholic.'

In comment upon all this it may first be observed that by primary connotation *principalitas* refers to primacy *in time*, and corresponds to *antiquitas* rather than *auctoritas*. However, the use of the adjective *potentior* answers rather to the derived meaning of primacy *in rank* and *influence*. Furthermore, the pre-eminent prestige of Rome does not rest upon sheer age. In this respect the Roman Church is excelled by that of Jerusalem, a Church which on this ground is also accorded a place of honour (III.12.5, i.301). The prestige of Rome is based upon the circumstance that her Church was founded by the two greatest Apostles, i.e. it is connected with the nature of the message she has to declare: with her authority, in fact. It is by no means so necessary to support the translation of *convenire* as 'agree'. One can certainly imagine S. Irenaeus saying such a thing, to judge from his general view of the Church. However, he only gives this solitary treatment of the position of the Roman Church, so there is no passage which may be adduced as positive evidence to support the giving to *convenire* other than its usual meaning of 'resort to', 'gather together to'. On the other hand, some support for 'resort to' may possibly be found in the argument of the succeeding chapter: 'Suppose there arise a dispute relative to some important question among us, should we not have recourse to the most ancient Churches with which the Apostles held constant intercourse, and learn from them?' (III.4.1, i.264). *Et si de aliqua modica quaestione disceptatio esset, nonne oporteret in antiquissimas recurrere ecclesias, in quibus Apostoli conversati sunt, et ab eis de praesenti quaestione sumere* (Harvey, ii.15–16). There is, then, a middle view. *Convenire ad* may quite well mean '*to gather together to*', but without the precise connotation of assembly in a Synod. It would then mean much the same as *recurrere in* of III.4.1, with the general sense that 'one must certainly go to Rome', i.e. 'one must take account of what is being thought at Rome'. We may probably accept

Vernet's view that *in qua* refers to *omnem Ecclesiam*, rejecting Schmidt, and also Harvey's restoration of the Greek original. It will be observed that no translation of this passage can be more than conjectural, though the following rendering would give the most likely variants.

'It is $\left\{\begin{array}{l}\text{logically}\\ \text{morally}\end{array}\right\}$ necessary that every Church should

$\left\{\begin{array}{l}\text{take account of}\\ \text{agree with}\\ \text{resort to}\end{array}\right\}$ this Church, on account of its

$\left\{\begin{array}{l}\text{more powerful}\\ \text{pre-eminent}\end{array}\right\}$ authority, that is the faithful everywhere,

in which $\left\{\begin{array}{l}\text{whole}\\ \text{Roman}\end{array}\right\}$ Church the apostolical tradition has been

preserved by those who are everywhere (Catholic).'

Whatever it is that S. Irenaeus regards Rome as possessing, it is something possessed pre-eminently, but not exclusively, for as Battifol observes, *potentior* is comparative.[1] This supports Hitchcock's judgement, who as an original for *principalitas* rejects αὐθεντία, 'sovereign authority', and ἀρχή, 'jurisdiction', for the softer πρωτεῖον, 'prestige'.[2] The *potentior principalitas* of the Roman Church is, then, the possession in a unique and supreme degree of that which is the possession of the whole Church. For S. Irenaeus the whole Church is the final religious authority. The sacred *kerygma* in which every part of the Church is agreed is nothing other than God's last and best word to man, the rule with which all religious teaching must square. The token that the heretics are not of that one and true Church is that the great Churches, which are the acknowledged leaders of that body to which Irenaeus points as *the* Church, are of superior antiquity, and can alone boast an apostolical foundation. Here and there he picks out a name for honourable mention, and in each case fixes attention upon the worth of the

---

[1] *L'Église*, p. 251.

[2] *Irenaeus*, p. 252. Battifol, however, prefers αὐθεντία to πρωτεία, as the latter does not permit of a comparative (*L'Église*, p. 252).

founder. Is it Jerusalem? Here is the original Church,
founded by the Apostles.[1] Is it Asia? He dwells upon the
greatness of Polycarp, himself a pupil of the Apostles.[2] But
what Church can compare with Rome? She is the life-work
of the two greatest of the Apostles. Known of all and knowing all, she is a supreme witness to the united voice of the
Church. If it is necessary for each and all to consent to the
voice of the whole Church, how necessary is it for all to
consent to Rome? To S. Irenaeus Rome was most certainly an authority none must question, as she cannot be
imagined as ever in error. The word 'infallible' to some extent
begs the question, for the use of it imports into the discussion
the results of later definition. It is nevertheless a word which
it is difficult to do without. With this proviso we may say
that Irenaeus regarded Rome as the very corner-stone and
typification of a whole structure of ecclesiastical infallibility.

It is, however, important to bear in mind that the whole
argument deals with the preservation of an original doctrinal tradition, and not at all with the discipline or government of the outward or practical life of the Church. This is
in accord with the general attitude of S. Irenaeus. Vernet
certainly stretches a point when he claims that here is a
judicial primacy looked at by Irenaeus from the point of
view of doctrine.[3] Irenaeus is thinking here in terms of
doctrine only. Furthermore, there is not present any conception of a jurisdiction which can impose new legislation
upon subject powers, for the authority of the Church in
general, and of Rome as the case in point, is purely a conservative force. For S. Irenaeus original tradition was the
complete religion. He had no conception of the possibility of
drawing out the implications of old and formless teaching
into a new and formal dogma. To him a newly-formulated
dogma would have been a contradiction in terms. Above
all, as Vernet has the insight to admit,[3] Irenaeus has never
considered the problem of another Church of apostolic
foundation coming in opposition to Rome. Such a painful

---

[1] III.12.5, i.301.   [2] III.3.4, i.263.   [3] *Dictionnaire*, VII, col. 2437.

thing would be to him inconceivable. It is axiomatic that all the Churches agree because they all alike follow the true tradition. To inquire of S. Irenaeus what side he would take in case of mutual anathematization is to ask a question to which he has no answer. He is stating the facts about Church unity as he knows it, rather than any theory in the light of which hypothetical problems may be answered. In this sense Seeberg is right in saying that the judgement upon Rome is historical, not dogmatic.[1] The pro- and anti-Roman controversy has obscured all these factors, and with it to some extent the vital doctrine of this Father of the Church. The most valuable element in the whole of Schmidt's interesting work on Irenaeus is undoubtedly that he goes behind these confusions. On essentially right lines is his exposition of the conception of the Church in Irenaeus as that of the *Kerygma*-bearer, even though he over-simplifies and over-states the case in good Lutheran zeal to centre everything in the preaching of 'the Word'.

We have, however, seen that the position taken by S. Irenaeus is one which had within it a tendency to drift into the specifically hierarchical system. Once the pre-eminent authority of Rome had been marked out, the course of this drift was sufficient to place the Bishop of Rome in a pre-eminent position among the hierarchy. It is inherent in any system of authority to find within itself a single supreme authority, once it is faced with the possibility of internal controversy. In consequence it is clear that the statements of S. Irenaeus regarding the Church of Rome have within them not the germ of Papal primacy, but more exactly the potentiality for that germ to be generated. Within this strict limitation we may agree with Vernet, that though Irenaeus does not say that the Roman Church is sovereign he yet leans toward this.[2]

In conclusion, S. Irenaeus is certainly a Catholic Christian, though not a Catholic as some have been. We cannot imagine

[1] *DG*. p. 308.　　　[2] *Dictionnaire*, VII, col. 2437.

him representing, as some 'Catholic' types appear to have done, that the most essential purpose of Christ's incarnation, life and teaching, cross and passion, and resurrection, was that the Eucharist might be established upon earth. Christ came to perform the work of Championship, and the Holy Communion is derived from this. Furthermore, Irenaeus would hardly have conceived of the mission of the Church in terms of early Jesuit zeal to carry the Sacrament of Baptism to the ends of the earth. Rather, the Church carries to the nations the preaching of the saving truth. Men are to be baptized into the Church so that they may be nourished in that Apostolic Gospel. S. Irenaeus is therefore definitely an institutional and sacramental Christian, but is no victim of the quasi-physical 'electric current' conception of the institutions and Sacraments of the Church. In short, he is a Catholic, and no Protestant, yet a Catholic whose Catholicism avoids just those tendencies against which Protestants have usually felt they were principally called to protest. S. Irenaeus is revealed as a Catholic who firmly grasps the principle which Protestants have generally regarded as set forth in their systems, namely, that the purpose of the Church is to proclaim the Word of God. His comprehensive genius is an excellent guide for that healthy Christianity which aspires to be at once truly catholic and truly evangelical.

Chapter Fourteen

THE CHRISTIAN HOPE

IT IS a simple task to reconstruct the millenarian scheme of S. Irenaeus. Millenarianism is one of the most robust elements in his thought and piety. The subject of the Christian Hope is treated fully and emphatically, with a wealth of quotation from the apocalyptical portions of the Old and New Testaments. No part of his theology is more plainly of directly Biblical and Hebraic inspiration than this. The sheet-anchor of all is the assertion, so utterly contrary to his general expository usage when other parts of the Bible are in review, that apocalyptical Scripture must not be interpreted in an allegorical or symbolical manner. It is fundamental that a literal interpretation is alone legitimate.[1] S. Irenaeus is thus firmly attached to the hope of a terrestrial Millennial Kingdom. He is more rigorous than S. Justin Martyr, whom he follows in this hope, for Justin can admit that some orthodox Christians reject the earthly Kingdom of the Saints. Only the resurrection of the flesh is insisted upon as an essential doctrine.[2] On the other hand, Irenaeus denounces the opinions of those who, 'ignorant of God's dispensations', deny 'the mystery of the resurrection of the just, and of the kingdom which is the beginning of incorruption', as 'derived from heretical discourses'.[3]

S. Irenaeus believed that he was living in 'the last times'.[4] 'The End' was not to be expected immediately, however, as the division of the kingdom of the earth into ten, one of the signs of 'the End', had not yet taken place.[5] The last of the six 'days of creation', each of one thousand years, is in progress, for the Lord suffered on the sixth day.[6] The world will come to an end after six thousand years.[7]

[1] V.35.1–2, ii.151, 153.   [2] *Dial.c.Tryph.* 80, 81.   [3] V.32.1, ii.141.
[4] IV.Pref.4, i.376.   [5] V.30.2, ii.136–7.   [6] V.23.2, ii.118.   [7] V.28.3, ii.132.

279

As 'the End' approaches Antichrist will come to set up his kingdom. The present spread of apostasy and heresy is indeed part of this.[1] The Roman Empire will be dissolved into ten kingdoms, the ten horns of Daniel 7₂₄.[2] Satan will then supplant these, and rule at Jerusalem for his three and a half years,[3] in which days the Church will be persecuted.[4] Antichrist will aspire to displace all idols as objects of worship, 'concentrating in himself all Satanic apostasy'.[5] Thus will 2 Thessalonians 2₄ be fulfilled. 'And there is, therefore, in this beast, when he comes, recapitulation made of all sorts of iniquity and of every deceit, in order that all apostate power, flowing into and being shut up in him, may be sent into the furnace of fire.' In him 'is concentrated the whole apostasy of six thousand years'.[6] It is most interesting to observe that in this recapitulation there is something exactly parallel to the *Recapitulation* worked by Christ. Satan, the representative head of the wicked, will constitute himself the champion of evil, and on his being defeated all the power of evil will come to an end.[7]

When Satan's allotted span is complete the Lord will come to earth in power and glory. He will 'come in the same flesh in which He suffered, revealing the glory of the Father'.[8] He will destroy the kingdom of the Beast,[9] and cast him into the lake of fire.[10] The righteous, whose spirits have been waiting in Paradise,[11] 'shall rise again, having their own bodies, and having also their own souls, and their own spirits'.[12] This will take place at the sound of the Last Trumpet.[13] The body, rising and partaking of incorruption, will be a glorious body.[14] S. Irenaeus attached great importance to the General Resurrection, and in particular to the resurrec-

[1] IV.**Pref**.4, i.376.   [2] V.**25**.3, ii.123; V.**26**.1, ii.125–6; V.**30**.2, ii.136.
[3] V.**25**.3, ii.123; V.**30**.4, ii.138.
[4] V.**26**.1, ii.126; see also V.**29**.1–2, ii.134.
[5] V.**25**.1, ii.122; see also V.**28**.2, ii.131.
[6] V.**29**.2, ii.134–5.   [7] cf. Molwitz, pp. 46–7.
[8] III.**16**.8, i.332.   [9] V.**26**.1, ii.126.
[10] V.**30**.4, ii.138; see also IV.**33**.1, ii.6–7; V.**26**.2, ii.127.
[11] V.**5**.1, ii.66; see also II.**34**.1, i.251; V.**31**.2, ii.140.
[12] II.**33**.5, i.250.   [13] V.**13**.1, ii.87.   [14] V.**7**.2, ii.71.

tion of the flesh, which was denied by the Gnostics.[1] The bodily resurrection of believers is generally in view, with much less said concerning the resurrection of the wicked to judgement. 'Yet, reluctant as they may be, these men shall one day rise again in the flesh; . . . but they shall not be numbered among the righteous, on account of their un-belief.'[2] These will come in the condition in which they lived and died.[3] Presumably the wicked will have only a body and animal soul, as they have not received the Spirit.[4]

The wicked, both fallen angels and men, will then be finally judged. Irenaeus was indeed familiar with the idea of judgement as continuous and present. 'The death of the Lord is the condemnation of those who fastened Him to the Cross . . . but the salvation of those who believe in Him.'[5] Therefore there is a division of the souls of the good and evil in the unseen world, so 'that each class receives a habitation such as it has deserved, even before the judgement'.[6] However, at the Second Coming of the Lord there will be the Great Judgement, 'the day of retribution on which the Lord will render to everyone according to his works'.[7] Christ will then 'apply the rule of just judgement to all'.[8] This Judgement is final. The Lord 'judges for eternity those whom He doth judge, and lets free for eternity those whom He does let go free'.[9] Upon unbelievers 'there is a vengeance without pardon in the judgement'.[10] Most commonly judgement is the function of the Lord

---

[1] I.22.1, i.85; II.29.2, i.229–30; III.16.6, i.329; IV.22.2, i.455; V.2.3, ii.60; V.3.2, ii.62; V.5.2, ii.67; V.6.1–2, ii.68–70; V.7.1, ii.70–1; V.13.1,3,4, ii.87–90; V.15.1, ii.95–6; V.33.1, ii.144; V.34.1–2, ii.148–9; V.35.2, ii.155; V.36.3, ii.157; *Frag.* XII, ii.164; *Frag.* L, ii.181.

[2] I.22.1, i.85; see also II.33.5, i.250.

[3] *Frag.* XII, ii.164.   [4] See pp. 206–7 *supra*.

[5] IV.28.3, i.473; see also IV.27.4, i.469; IV.37.1–2, ii.36–7; V.26.2, ii.128; V.27.1–2, ii.128–30; V.28.1, ii.130; *Dem.* 69, 97.

[6] II.34.1, i.251.   [7] II.22.2, i.197.

[8] V.16.6, i.329; see also I.10.1, i.42; III.5.3, i.268; III.18.5, i.341; IV.20.2, i.440; IV.33.13, ii.16; IV.36.3, ii.29; V.32.1, ii.141; *Dem.* 8, 41, 56, 85.

[9] IV.28.3, i.473.   [10] *Dem.* 56.

Jesus at the appointment of the Father, but sometimes the Judge is described simply as 'God'.[1] S. Irenaeus, however, also held the doctrine that men judge themselves. 'On as many as, according to their own choice, depart from God, He inflicts that separation from Himself which they have chosen of their own accord. But separation from God is death . . . and the loss of all the benefits which He has in store. Those, therefore, who cast away by apostasy these forementioned things, being in fact destitute of all good, do experience every kind of punishment. God, however, does not punish them immediately of Himself.'[2] It is to be noticed that in this scheme the good and evil rise together, and the Judgement takes place before the Millennial Reign of the Saints upon earth. S. Irenaeus thus had a simpler arrangement than Justin, who on the basis of Revelation 20₅ taught that the Saints rose first, and that the resurrection of unbelievers to judgement took place at the end of the thousand years.[3] The only hint that Irenaeus was a Post-millenarian appears to be: 'It behoves the righteous first to receive the promise of the inheritance . . . and to reign in it, when they rise again to behold God in this creation which is renovated, and that the judgement should take place after-wards.'[4] In the absence of other evidence this rather vague passage need mean no more than that the Resurrection takes place before the Judgement.

The fate of the Devil and the other fallen angels, and of wicked men and heretics, is punishment in a hell of ever-lasting fire.[5] The Saints, restored to their now glorified bodies, will live upon a renovated earth with Christ as King. The Creation will then be 'freed from the bondage of cor-ruption', and restored to its primaeval condition.[6] 'The Creation, having been renovated and set free, shall fructify

[1] III.25.4, i.372; IV.27.4, i.469; *Dem.* 8.
[2] V.27.2, ii.129; see also IV.39.4, ii.48; V.28.1, ii.130.
[3] *Dial.c.Tryph.* 81.   [4] V.32.1, ii.141.
[5] I.10.1, i.42; III.4.2, i.265; III.23.3, i.365; IV.27.4, i.470-1; IV.28.1-2, i.471-2; V.26.2, ii.127; V.28.1, ii.130; V.35.2, ii.154.
[6] V.36.3, ii.157; see also V.32.1, ii.141-2.

with an abundance of all kinds of food.'[1] This fruitfulness Irenaeus described in his celebrated and curious quotations from Papias. 'The days will come in which vines shall grow, each having ten thousand branches, and in each branch ten thousand twigs, and in each twig ten thousand shoots, and in each one of the shoots ten thousand clusters, and on every one of the clusters ten thousand grapes, and every grape when pressed will give five and twenty metretae of wine. And when any one of the saints shall lay hold of a cluster another shall cry out "I am a better cluster, take me".'[2] It is with some surprise that one reads that Papias claimed these and other curious sentiments as words of the Lord Himself.[3] We may rather agree with Eusebius that 'he appears to have been of a very limited understanding, as one can see from his discourses'.[4] Upon Isaiah 11₇: 'the lion shall eat straw like the ox', Irenaeus quaintly remarks: 'And this indicates the large size and rich quality of the fruits. For if that animal, the lion, feeds upon straw, of what quality must the wheat itself be whose straw shall serve as suitable food for lions?'[5]

Irenaeus preserves the idea of the Messianic Banquet[6] which will then take place. The righteous 'shall have a table at hand prepared for them by God'.[7] It is emphasized against the Gnostics that the Millennial Kingdom is to be bodily and terrestrial. Christ 'cannot by any means be understood as drinking of the fruit of the vine . . . above in a super-celestial place; nor, again, are they who drink of it devoid of flesh'.[8] 'Neither is the substance nor the essence of the creation annihilated . . . but "the *fashion* of the world passeth away".'[9] The Millennial Age is the seventh of the thousand-year 'days of creation'. Irenaeus writes of 'the times of the Kingdom, that is, upon the seventh day . . . in which God rested from all the works which He created,

[1] V.33.3, ii.145.   [2] V.33.3–4, ii.146–7.   [3] ibid.   [4] *H.E.* III.xxxix.13.
[5] V.33.4, ii.147; see also V.34.1, ii.148; V.34.4, ii.150–1.
[6] cf. Mark 14₂₅.
[7] V.33.2, ii.145; see also V.34.3, ii.150; V.36.2,3, ii.156–7.
[8] V.33.1, ii.144.   [9] V.36.1, ii.155.

which is the true Sabbath of the righteous, in which they shall not be engaged in any earthly occupation'.[1] S. Irenaeus frequently mentions the Kingdom of God, and shows that he thinks of it as both present and future. The coming Millennial Kingdom is the climax of that which is already at work in the world since the coming of Christ. Irenaeus here clearly reproduces an important element in the teaching of our Lord, in writing that the true preaching of the Gospel consists of 'declaring His dispensations with regard to man, and forming the Kingdom of God beforehand, and preaching by anticipation the inheritance of the holy Jerusalem';[2] *et Christi regnum praeformans, et haereditatem sanctae Hierusalem praeevangelisans.*[3] The 'times of His Kingdom, in which the Spirit does, in the most gentle manner, vivify and increase mankind',[4] appears to refer to the present. Other passages are less plain.[5] More commonly the Kingdom is the future Kingdom.[6]

The earthly Millennial Kingdom is not, however, an end in itself. It is the final stage of preparation for the ultimate destiny of man. It is the 'commencement of incorruption, by means of which Kingdom those who shall be worthy are accustomed gradually to partake of the divine nature'.[7] 'The righteous shall reign in the earth, waxing stronger by the sight of the Lord; and through Him they shall become accustomed to partake in the glory of God the Father, and shall enjoy . . . communion with the holy angels, and union with spiritual beings.'[8] It will also be a time of progress. Those who receive the Kingdom 'make constant advance in it for ever'.[9] As is natural under conditions of progress, there are grades of spiritual exaltation in paradise, but

---

[1] V.33.2, i.144; see also V.30.4, ii.138.   [2] IV.26.1, i.461.
[3] Harvey, ii.235.   [4] IV.20.10, i.446–7.
[5] IV.24.2, i.458; IV.27.1, i.466; *Dem.* 1, 28.
[6] IV.22.2, i.455; IV.25.3, i.460; IV.28.2, i.472; IV.33.11, ii.13–4; V.26.2, ii.127; V.30.4, ii.138–9; V.32.1, ii.141; V.33.2–3, ii.144–5; V.35.1–2, ii.152–5; *Dem.* 41, 42.
[7] V.32.1, ii.141.   [8] V.35.1, ii.152; see also V.35.2, ii.155.
[9] IV.28.2, i.472.

'everywhere the Saviour shall be seen according as they who see Him shall be worthy'.[1] The Son and the Spirit will still be Mediators of God to man. 'They ascend through the Spirit to the Son, and through the Son to the Father, and . . . in due time the Son will yield up His work to the Father.'[2]

The ultimate perfection and final blessedness of the Saints is to behold and rejoice in the Vision of God. 'Our face shall see the face of the Lord, and shall rejoice with joy unspeakable.'[3] The vision of the glorified Lord will in time work the open vision of God as He is in Himself. 'God . . . having been seen at that time indeed (on earth), prophetically through the Spirit, and seen, too, adoptively through the Son . . . shall also be seen paternally in the Kingdom of heaven; the Spirit truly preparing man, . . . and the Son leading him to the Father, while the Father, too, confers incorruption for eternal life, which comes to every-one from the fact of his seeing God.'[4] S. Irenaeus cries out: 'What shall it be when, on rising again, we behold Him face to face; when all the members shall burst into a continuous hymn of triumph, glorifying Him? . . . It will render us like unto Him, and accomplish the will of the Father.'[5] 'The man who loves God shall arrive at such excellency as even to see God, and hear His word, and from the hearing of His dis-course be glorified to such an extent, that others cannot behold the glory of his countenance. . . . And the disciple will be perfected.'[6] To search into the perfect Father will produce perfection,[7] and life and immortality.[8]

The main interest in the Millenarianism of S. Irenaeus is that it illustrates one of the leading obscurities of historic Christian theology. The Gentile Church has never been very happy in its understanding of Eschatology, this most distinctively Hebrew element which is so clearly a part of

---

[1] V.36.1–2, ii.155–6.   [2] V.36.2, ii.156; see also V.35.1, ii.152.
[3] V.7.2, ii.72.   [4] IV.20.5, i.442.   [5] V.8.1, ii.73; see also V.13.3, ii.89.
[6] IV.26.1, i.461–2; see also V.36.3, ii.157.   [7] II.18.6, i.183.
[8] IV.20.6, i.443.

Biblical religion, and which had at least some place in the message of our Lord Himself. We may say that the trouble is that the Greek or Greek-tutored mind has had to choose either to be much more or else much less materialistic in conception than the Hebrew. When, for example, a Hebrew eschatological writer spoke of an angel, and then of the voice of the Lord, he was using alternative modes of expression for what was to him fundamentally the same thing. To his mind a 'word' of God was not purely abstract, the temporary expression of a thought. It was a concrete entity proceeding from God, and existing apart from Him. On the other hand, an 'angel' was simply a divine messenger. The Hebrew mind had not normally sufficient pictorial imagination to visualize an angel as a person, whether actual or mythological, or to find it a natural occupation to clothe him with a *form*, painting a portrait in white robe and wings after the manner of western artists. An 'angel' which was nearer an embodied message than a messenger was not very different from a 'word' which was more an embodied message than a figurative sound. This psychology, at once concrete and non-pictorial, lies behind the fantastic imagery of Hebrew apocalyptic literature.

The typical Gentile mind has always felt that this imagery must be either purely symbolical or else completely realist and descriptive. Thus the more intellectual and cultured type of Greek-tutored mind has tended to make Biblical Eschatology too abstract. The visions have been interpreted as allegories, or the embodiment of a set of abstract spiritual ideas in graphic (but frequently repellent) symbolism. The essential spirit of Eschatology has in consequence evaporated, with the loss of the authentic Christian witness to the urgent expectation of God's *real victory* in this world. On the other hand, many types of Gentile Christian of a robust piety, but of less intellectual or æsthetic taste, have refused to let slip the triumphant certainty of expectation which eschatological religion brings. These have perforce felt constrained to interpret the Hebrew Apocalypses in a manner much more

purely material than their original intention warrants. As
they are not 'mere symbolism' they must be pictorially and
materially descriptive. Thus it has at times been almost forgotten that the kernel of the Revelation of S. John, for
example, is a word of assurance to the persecuted, and a
pledge to the subjects of Nero that it is God who rules on
high. This Gospel has been seen as a mere by-product to the
supposed *real* interest of the book in providing mysterious
data for the calculation of the supposed historical 'end of the
world'. Those who are not content to spiritualize the Apocalypse commonly treat it with excess of literalism as a book
of celestial blue-prints.

S. Irenaeus is found at the mercy of these strange currents
of the mind. Though he is a Gentile with a Greek-tutored
mind, who can use with conviction much of the traditional
language of the Apologists, he is also firmly grounded in
primitive and Biblical Christianity. He is eminently one
who conceives of the Gospel as first and foremost the message of an actual and historical saving work of God in Christ,
for the redemption of sinful and helpless man. Such a one is
likely to have an underlying instinctive feeling for Eschatology. He proves himself undeterred by the element of the
bizarre and uncanny. He exults in the sense of crisis brought
home to every believer in his every act, and of hope un-
dismayed, that is bred of the confident anticipation of God's
speedy cosmic victory. Yet in this his thinking is conditioned
by current ignorance of Hebrew psychology. His piety
dictated adherence to the literalist and material tradition of
Millenarianism, and to a studied departure at this point
from his customary usage of Scripture allegorism. This departure, and his revelling in the childish fancies of Papias,
was no perverse freak of genius. It was not something unconnected with the true spirit and valuable work of the man,
as some have maintained. It was a circumstance that illustrates the position of S. Irenaeus as a Biblical theologian.
In him is illuminated a problem which has ever vexed the
Church, and which remains to this day.

Vernet appears a little disconcerted that the opinions of Irenaeus do not coincide at every point with the doctrines of later Catholicism. In particular, the view was later pronounced heretical that the righteous enter upon the beatific vision of God not immediately, but only at the coming of the Millennial Kingdom. It is consequently stated by Vernet that the Millenarianism is the weakest part of the whole work, being a medley of the Church's witness and of doubtful or erroneous theories.[1] This part of the theology can be taken away without destroying the rest of the system. It is merely something developed against the Gnostic denial of the Second Coming.[2] This judgement is not altogether just, as it misses the vital point that Millenarianism is essentially not one link in a theological chain, but an emotional tension throughout the chain. It is quite correct to claim that the grand system of Creation by the Hand of God, the Fall, the Incarnation, the Recapitulation by the Champion, and of Salvation by Faith in His Saving Work, advancing to ultimate Perfection, can be held in its entirety apart from any consideration of whether or no there is to be a terrestrial Millennial Kingdom, either immediately or in the dim future. Most emphatically, however, must it be asserted that this in no way involves any kind of admission that the Millenarianism of S. Irenaeus is an element unconnected with the vital spring of his religion. His Chiliasm is a witness, a somewhat distorted witness indeed, yet a witness for all that, to the intensity of primitive Christian faith.

S. Irenaeus views the history of the world as a development from present imperfection to ultimate perfection. In his eschatological expectation is the token that he is not content to view this evolution dispassionately, as an historian. He is passionate as a prophet who hungers and thirsts to see that evolution speedily consummated in a heaven and earth utterly transformed, with God's sheer majesty gloriously displayed to every creature. Apocalyptic religion is the faith of the man who burns against the sin of the world, and who

---

[1] *Dictionnaire*, VII, col. 2507.   [2] ibid. col. 2505.

knows that the sinful world may quite possibly burn him. By contrast, systematic philosophical and evolutionary religion is typical of quiet men in a world that has grown polite to Christ. In Irenaeus is seen an essay in evolutionary religion. Nevertheless it is the evolution of a man who knows what it is to see his fathers and brethren in the Faith nerve themselves to face a martyr's death, at the hands of a pagan world which is the very embodiment of Satan. The Church is strong to endure this only when fortified by the expectation of God's shattering world-victory. When the politer age dawns the final chapters of *Adversus Haereses* are deleted as superfluous or offensive, in token that men can value the System, yet be repulsed by the Vision. This does not cause a loss of balance in the theology, but speaks of a decline of emotional tension in the theologian. Certainly the Millenarianism of S. Irenaeus was not drawn in by mere polemic interest. It is one essential manifestation of his spirit as a primitive and Biblical Christian, to whom the Gospel spelt not contemplation only, but actual and glorious redemption from real and grievous bondage.

Of real value at this point is the work of Robert Frick in *Die Geschichte des Reich-Gottes-Gedankens in der alten Kirche bis zu Origenes und Augustin* (Giessen, 1928). He points out that the conception of the Kingdom of God plays an important part in the eschatology of S. Irenaeus, and that this is a Biblical interest. The word βασιλεία occurs more than thirty times in Biblical quotations. At times it is used otherwise than in an eschatological sense, but in general the Kingdom is the Divine Rule, or the heavenly Kingdom in opposition to the world.[1] However, this robust eschatology is nevertheless a spiritualized one. (This is claimed as a Johannine element in Irenaeus.)[2] The coming of the earthly Kingdom of Glory is not imagined as a catastrophe, but as the perfection of a development.[3] The popular eschatological picture has for Irenaeus its deepest meaning as the last stage of human education for communion with God. A

[1] *Reich-Gottes*, p. 60.   [2] ibid. p. 59.   [3] ibid. p. 60.

spiritual content has thus been introduced.[1] Bousset also
observes that S. Irenaeus puts the thought of development
into eschatology, because he explains the necessity for the
earthly intermediate Kingdom as a further opportunity for
men gradually to accustom themselves to the glory of God.
Thus the idea of Chiliasm is expounded in an evolutionary
manner.[2] One would, however, say that this double position
is not the construction of Irenaeus, as though he himself were
attempting a synthesis of contrasting elements. He is rather
to be seen as one who, remaining within the primitive
tradition of the Church, is yet seeking to give a rationale of
the SavingWork of Christ, and to exhibit it against the background of a doctrine of Creation. It is always the theology
that is developed within the eschatology. However, the two
elements of evolution and of crisis are admirably blended.
Finally, Seeberg is right in stating that the eschatology of
S. Irenaeus springs from the central point of his religion, but
incorrect in making this connexion consist in the circumstance that the Word descended into the creature to lift him
above the angels.[3] The eschatology does not spring out of
the redemption system. It is the emotional background to
the system, yet a background that is an inherent part of the
picture.

Vernet makes the interesting observation that, though
S. Irenaeus does not mention Purgatory by name, all that is
good in his doctrine of maturation in the Millennial Kingdom is embodied in the later doctrine of Purgatory.[4] In
criticism we may say that the conception of Purgatory
admits into theology a principle that much eases the exposition of the Christian Hope as completely rational. It is
manifest that very few Christians are mature in faith and
experience at the time of their death. Most have a measure
of grace, and many blemishes. Many others have been held
back on the path of life by hard circumstance of heredity or
environment. To damn all who are not in *this* life 'soundly

[1] *Reich-Gottes*, p. 64.   [2] *Kyr.Ch.* p. 354.   [3] *DG.* p. 377.
[4] *Dictionnaire*, VII, col. 2507.

converted' is to consign to hell the bulk of the human race, notwithstanding the rich possibilities of good to be found in all but the minority of hardened and abandoned ones. This would be to impugn God's goodness. On the other hand, to admit to heaven all 'decent fellows', whether or no they have had any conscious experience of Christ, is in effect to deny the relevance of Christian salvation to human life. The *via media* demanded by ethics and reason is thus to teach that the destiny for most is a further chance of spiritual discipline and development beyond the grave. S. Irenaeus admirably fulfils this need. We may therefore say that he foreshadows all that is good and necessary in the doctrine of Purgatory, without the superstitions which have at times hung around it.

SUMMARY

IN CONCLUSION it may be said that S. Irenaeus was a Biblical theologian. He was indeed *homo unius libri*. Driven by lack of scientific and historical knowledge of the Old Testament he was forced to share with his Gnostic adversaries a subjective method of exegesis. In consequence he was compelled to appeal to the '*Living Voice*' of the Church as a means of bearing down heretical cavils by institutional solidarity and weight of numbers. Thus was to be determined the true teaching of Scripture and Tradition. The '*Living Voice*' of the Church was therefore the essential and determinative factor in whatever he actually taught. However, the strain of Christian life for which he spoke was a profoundly Biblical, Hebraic, and primitive one. His constant quotation of Biblical texts was arbitrary and forced, but it was much more than an outward form. It was a true token of his inward spirit.

In '*The Two Hands of God*' is found an exposition of the nature of God which is of direct Biblical inspiration. It is an exposition in which are safeguarded in all fullness the religious interests of the worship of a Personal God, at once utterly transcendent and in immediate contact with His worshippers, and of the Christian religion as a life of trust in a Divine and Incarnate Lord. Speculative and cosmological interests are firmly relegated to a secondary place. In this S. Irenaeus was a forerunner of the Christian doctrine of the Trinity. The *Recapitulation* by Christ the Champion is an adequate theology of the Saving Work of Christ, viewed as an actual and historic resolution of man's real moral bondage. This theology was a true development of New Testament thought. In his preaching of the Gospel the clarity of witness to the conception of evangelical Saving Faith is unfortunately a little obscured. The pressing needs of the time were doubtless mainly responsible for this, for the defence of orthodoxy fixed the mind too exclusively upon faith as assent to the Creed. However, we cannot entirely exclude the suggestion that there had been a certain decline of spiritual exaltation as compared with S. Paul. Nevertheless, S. Irenaeus was essentially a genuine Christian, a Pauline Christian, a Christian at once evangelical and catholic. The New Testament is followed by him also in the doctrine that the Church is the *New Israel*, the prophetic and priestly People of God. Here is an essentially corporate Christianity that is not purely institutional, for the emphasis is upon the Christian message, not simply upon the ecclesiastical office. Allegiance is demanded not so much to the Apostolic Successors, who are the means to an end, as to the Apostolic Creed. In final token that the religious experience of Irenaeus was robust and prophetic rather than quiet and speculative is his Millenarianism. This too is a Biblical and primitive element.

That all this may be claimed for S. Irenaeus of Lugdunum is a matter of profound significance in the evaluation of the historic development of the Christian religion. Irenaeus is eminently a representative type. He belongs to no mere section of the Church. He speaks for no extreme wing of opinion. The circumstances of his birth and residence and active work betoken his place in Christian tradition. He is a milestone in the development alike of that which has become regarded as typically Eastern and Greek, and of that which is called Western and Latin. Furthermore, Irenaeus was not a simple believer who, untroubled by the questions which agitate the mind of the thinking world, could live and move within the sphere of non-dogmatic Christian experience. He would play his part in transplanting the Faith out of the rich but narrow seed-bed of Jewish Christianity into the spacious but unsheltered expanses of the pagan world. Thus he had to face heresy. He essayed the problems of Christian philosophy and cosmology, and to such good effect that he left behind him what is perhaps the most satisfying attempt at a systematic Christian theology that has been preserved to us from the great formative period which lies between the close of the New Testament and the opening of the Arian controversy. From the secular culture of his Age and the Apologistic tradition the Greek wind blew strongly through his work. Nevertheless, the Faith has not sunk to a bare moralism, nor been refined away into a philosophy. Nor has Christianity hardened into mere institutionalism. There remains a robust religion of real moral Redemption by the miraculous visitation of this world by an Almighty and Living God, in the Person of His Incarnate Son. All this is involved in the claim that S. Irenaeus was a Biblical Christian, fundamentally faithful to the mind of his Lord, substantially following the tradition of the Apostle to the Gentiles.

Some who have compared the life and thought of the actual historic Church with the Figure of her Divine Founder have been filled with misgiving and regret. They have been quick to detect and to lament evidences of legal 'entanglement in the yoke of bondage,' and of contamination with pagan thought. The Bride of Christ has been portrayed as anything but 'a glorious Church, not having spot or wrinkle or any such thing'. This is only natural, for whoever makes the contrast between the Lord and His servants, and between the ideal and the actual, is bound to condemn his fellows, and himself to feel condemned. Certainly the Church has often been found in Babylonish Captivity, and is often so found today. Nevertheless, that one who is so typical of historic ecclesiastical and dogmatic Christianity, and who was himself so formative in its development, should on examination be found so authentic and Apostolic a Christian is most significant. The critical study of S. Irenaeus should serve to calm some misgivings. It should serve to silence some of the less happy charges that have been hurled at our Holy Mother the Church.

Indexes

I. INDEX TO SUBJECTS

II. INDEX TO EXTRA-BIBLICAL PROPER NAMES

III. INDEX TO TEXTS OF S. IRENAEUS

N.B. 1.—*This list includes not only passages of Irenaeus quoted or expressly commented upon, but also parallels to such passages, and supporting references, as listed in the footnotes at many points.*

2.—*As the present work does not cover every subject treated of by Irenaeus it is not claimed that every significant passage in his works is listed below, but it is comprehensive for the ground covered.*

· 3.—*The system of capitation used in reference to 'Adversus Haereses' is that of Massuet and Migne.*

4.—**3.**4, *51n. represents Chapter **3**, paragraph 4, page 51 of this volume (footnote).*